Richard B. Day was born in Canada in 1942. He was educated at the University of Toronto and subsequently did postgraduate work there and at the University of London, where he received his doctorate in 1970. Since then he has taught in the Department of Political Economy in the University of Toronto. In addition to numerous articles on Marxist and Soviet economics and related topics, Professor Day has written *Leon Trotsky and the Politics of Economic Isolation* (Cambridge, 1973) and is the editor and translator of N.I. Bukharin, *Selected Writings on the State and the Transition to Socialism*.

Richard B. Day

NLB

The 'Crisis' and the 'Crash'

Soviet Studies of the West
(1917–1939)

British Library
Cataloguing in Publication Data
Day, Richard B.
    The Crisis and the Crash
    1. Economic history – 1918–1945 – Historiography
    2. Marxian economics
    1. Title
    330.9181'2   HC57

ISBN 978–1–78873–005–1

Verso
UK: 6 Meard Street, London W1F 0EG
US: 20 Jay Street, Suite 1010, Brooklyn, NY 11201

Verso is the imprint of New Left Books

Filmset in 10 on 12pt Plantin by
Servis Filmsetting Ltd, Manchester

Printed in the United States

Contents

For Tara, Geoffrey, and Christine

Preface

This book represents the first of a two-part study. The second part will cover the period from 1939 to the early 1970s, from war through Cold War to the interlude of détente. Research for the present volume required rather more time than originally expected. Almost nothing had been written on the subject, and the sources were scattered and difficult to locate. Without the assistance of several librarians the project could not have been completed. In particular I am indebted to those librarians who operated the inter-library loan service on my behalf—Elizabeth Thompson, Dallas Lowe, Sandra McCaskill, Margaret Byrne, and Jeanne Keller, all of Erindale College, University of Toronto. For granting me access to their holdings by way of this service I am indebted to the universities of Alberta, Chicago, California, Illinois, Washington (Seattle), and Wisconsin; also to Brown, Columbia, Cornell, Duke, Harvard, Indiana, Stanford, Princeton, Yale, and York universities; and to the Department of National Defence (Kingston), the Harvard Law School, the Hoover Institute, the National Library (Canada), the New York Public Library, and above all the Library of Congress.

For providing me with support and encouragement at critical junctures I am grateful to Robert W. Davies (University of Birmingham), Robert H. McNeal (University of Massachusetts), and H. Gordon Skilling (University of Toronto). For financing the leave time needed to transform the research material into a manuscript I wish to thank the Canada Council, more specifically the Killam Programme, which generously supported the project with a Senior Research Scholarship. To my children, who were too young to be fully aware of their sacrifice, I offer both my thanks and my apologies. And to my wife, whose critical editorial assistance was, as usual, both brutal and kind, I acknowledge a very real debt for transforming the original manuscript into something more coherent. All responsibility for errors of fact or interpretation remains my own.

10 October 1980

I
From 'Capital' to Marxist Theories of Imperialism

Liberal economists are not in the habit of praising the economic works of Karl Marx. In particular they take issue with the concepts of 'value' and 'surplus-value', which Marx used to explain his theory of industrial exploitation. Apart from these conceptual disagreements, however, many liberals do acknowledge that Marx's *Capital* broke new ground in the theory of business cycles. Joseph Schumpeter, one of the great economists of the twentieth century, wrote of *Capital*: 'We find practically all the elements that ever entered into any serious analysis of business cycles, and on the whole with very little error. Moreover, it must not be forgotten that the mere perception of the existence of cyclical movements was a great achievement at the time. Many economists who went before [Marx] had an inkling of it. In the main, however, they focused their attention on the spectacular breakdowns that came to be referred to as "crises". And those crises they failed to see in their true light, that is to say, in the light of the cyclical process of which they are mere incidents. They considered them . . . as isolated misfortunes that will happen in consequence of errors, excesses, misconduct or of the faulty working of the credit mechanism. Marx was, I believe, the first economist to rise above that tradition. . . . This is enough to ensure him high rank among the fathers of modern cycle research.'[1] Himself profoundly aware of the relation between politics and economics, Schumpeter added that Marx's contribution went beyond a technical analysis of the cycle: Marx was also 'the first economist of top rank to see and to teach systematically how

[1] Joseph A. Schumpeter, *Capitalism, Socialism and Democracy*, third edition, New York and Evanston 1962, pp. 40–41.

economic theory might be turned into historical analysis and how the historical narrative may be turned into *histoire raisonnée*.[2]

For Marx's followers, one of the difficulties created by *Capital* was that of distinguishing between *periodic* industrial crises and the *terminal* crisis, or 'crash', of the capitalist system as a whole. Marx and Engels frequently expressed the hope that the coming cyclical crisis would signal the collapse of capitalism as a historically conditioned mode of production. But Marx also spoke of the cycle as if it were a permanent phenomenon. In *Capital* Volume 1 he compared it to the movement of the heavenly bodies: 'Just as the heavenly bodies always repeat a certain movement, once they have been flung into it, so also does social production, once it has been flung into this movement of alternate expansion and contraction. Effects become causes in their turn, and the various vicissitudes of the whole process, which always reproduces its own conditions, take on the form of periodicity.'[3] In *Capital* Volume 3 Marx observed, 'The industrial cycle is of such a nature that the same circuit must periodically reproduce itself, once the first impulse has been given.'[4] The logic of *Capital* suggested that the pattern of the cycle must change as capitalism passed through successive historical stages, but the text itself gave few indications of the kinds of changes that might occur. As Schumpeter remarked, Marx used the term 'crisis' to characterize both a specific moment of the cycle and an entire period of capitalism's gradual decay: 'Believing that capitalist evolution would some day disrupt the institutional framework of capitalist society, he thought that before the actual breakdown occurred, capitalism would begin to work with increasing friction and display the symptoms of fatal illness. To this stage, to be visualized . . . as a more or less prolonged historical period, he applied the same term.'[5]

Nearly every Marxist has been tempted to detect harbingers of systematic collapse in successive crises. Engels was the first to argue that 'normal' crises had had their day and that a change of system

---

[2] Ibid., p. 44.

[3] Karl Marx, *Capital* Volume 1, translated by Ben Fowkes, Penguin Books in association with New Left Review, Harmondsworth 1976, p. 786.

[4] Marx, *Capital* Volume 3, Moscow 1961–2, p. 477.

[5] Schumpeter, p. 41.

was at hand. Soviet Marxists paraphrased Engels's conclusion, referring to the 'general crisis' of capitalism. In their view, periodic crises had given way to a *period of crisis*: classical capitalism had been replaced by the stage of imperialism, and the consequent intensification of contradictions made the final collapse merely a matter of time. Implicitly, the 'general crisis' of capitalism repudiated the theory of the cycle given in *Capital*. Modern capitalism was said to be characterized by a *chronic* crisis, *chronic* unemployment, and *chronic* excess industrial capacity, all of which stood in the way of new investments. Thus applied, the theory of imperialism helped to clarify the problem of historical stages at the expense of theoretical sophistication. Soviet economists, as Schumpeter said of pre-Marxist writers, 'failed to see [periodic crises] in their true light, that is to say, in the light of the cyclical process of which they are mere incidents'. The theory of imperialism was thereby detached from the Marxist theory of the cycle and was used to 'prove' the impossibility of capitalism's recovery from the First World War.

To say that the theory of the 'general crisis' of capitalism repudiated the Marxist theory of the business cycle is to criticize not the concept of imperialism but its application by Soviet economists. The fact is that *Capital* inspired several theories of imperialism, all of which claimed to be Marxist in origin and character. For analytical purposes this study will divide the rival theories into two broad schools of thought, one associated with Rudolf Hilferding, the other with Rosa Luxemburg. In *Finance Capital*, a forerunner of Lenin's *Imperialism*, Hilferding argued that rapid capital accumulation created the threat of overinvestment in key industries and a declining rate of profit. Faced with this danger, capitalists organized trusts and cartels, barring entry to new competitors and diverting new capital into colonial ventures. Luxemburg attached an entirely different significance to colonies: in her judgement the problem of inadequate markets constituted a chronic flaw in the capitalist system; the realization of 'surplus-value', or profit, depended upon opportunities to export surplus commodities that could not otherwise be sold. Luxemburg's major economic work, *The Accumulation of Capital*, exerted a less direct but ultimately more important influence upon Societ economic theory than the writings of Hilferding or Lenin. This chapter will explore the theoretical background of Soviet Marxism by surveying Marx's theory of cyclical fluctuations and its relation to subsequent disagreements about the imperialist stage of capitalist development.

1. Marx on the Cyclical Pattern of Capitalist Development

With the concepts of 'value' and 'surplus-value' Karl Marx endeavoured to explain the laws of motion of capitalist society. Industrial workers, he maintained, sold their labour-power to capitalists, receiving in exchange a wage sufficient to reproduce labour-power in accordance with the prevailing level of subsistence. When the capitalist sold the commodities produced by the workers, he realized not only his costs of production, but profit as well. The secret of profit, or surplus-value, was unpaid labour. If the working day were twelve hours, the worker might create sufficient value to cover the costs of wages, materials, and wear of equipment in eight hours. During the remaining four hours he would create surplus-value. His position in the productive process was analogous to that of the medieval serf: just as the serf performed unpaid labour in return for access to the land, so the industrial worker performed unpaid labour in return for access to the means of industrial production. The attempt by capitalists to increase profit by raising the rate of exploitation (or the ratio of unpaid to paid labour) represented the dynamic force of change in capitalist society.

In competitive conditions every capitalist hoped to raise labour productivity and lower costs of production through labour-saving technology. 'The battle of competition', Marx wrote, 'is fought by the cheapening of commodities.'[6] Some capitalists would respond successfully to the competitive challenge, while others would fail to do so and be absorbed by their rivals. Existing capital would thus be centralized, and the accumulation of new capital would be concentrated in fewer but larger firms. The *law of the centralization and concentration of industrial capital* followed inevitably from competition.

[6] *Capital* Volume I, p. 777.

Periodic waves of bankruptcy were normal in capitalist conditions, because the goal of production was profit and not the use of the products. The rationality of investment was measured by neither social utility nor the use-value of the commodities produced, but by its profitability, which depended upon exchange-value and the price to be had in the market. The *law of value* compelled capitalists to maximize individual profits, but had the paradoxical effect of tending to lower the social average rate of profit, for only living labour could be exploited and made to yield surplus-value. The *law of the falling rate of profit* operated through the progressive replacement of labour by machines.

Because living labour was the sole source of surplus-value, changes in the wage rate critically influenced production and investment decisions. A wave of investment presupposed an abundance of cheap labour, a reserve army of unemployed workers, who could be absorbed into production without disturbing the operation of existing firms. In *Capital* Marx described this reserve army as the result of a *law of population* peculiar to the capitalist mode of production, which caused labour periodically to become 'relatively superfluous'.[7] Subsequently, when speaking of the 'general crisis' of capitalism, Soviet economists referred to chronic and 'absolute' unemployment. It may thus be salutary to quote Marx directly. In *Capital* he argued that the law of population acted in and through the business cycle: 'The path characteristically described by modern industry, which takes the form of a decennial cycle (interrupted by smaller oscillations) of periods of average activity, production at high pressure, crisis, and stagnation, depends on the constant formation, the greater or less absorption, and the re-formation of the industrial reserve army or surplus population. In their turn, the varying phases of the industrial cycle [first]recruit the surplus population, and [then] become . . . the most energetic agencies for its reproduction.'[8] In the case of the law of the falling rate of profit Marx likewise saw cyclical fluctuations superimposed on an underlying trend. This law, he commented, 'acts only as a tendency. And it is only under certain circumstances

[7] Ibid., p. 783.
[8] Ibid., p. 785.

and only after long periods that its effects become strikingly pronounced.'[9]

Marx's consistent emphasis on the cyclical pattern of capitalist development proved incompatible with the thinking of many later Marxists, who linked the rise of imperialism to an allegedly chronic 'problem of markets'. Marx believed that the absorptive capacity of markets varied over time: the capitalists created a market when they re-employed workers and expanded production, eroded the market when they did the reverse. The alternating process of market creation and destruction came to be misunderstood partly because of an apparent contradiction between Volumes 2 and 3 of *Capital*. In Volume 3 Marx commented that the 'final cause of all real crises always remains the poverty and restricted consumption of the masses'.[10] But in Volume 2 he dismissed underconsumptionist theories this way:

'It is a pure tautology to say that crises are provoked by a lack of effective consumption. . . . The capitalist system does not recognize any forms of consumer other than those who can pay, if we exclude the consumption of paupers and swindlers. The fact that commodities are unsaleable means no more than that no effective buyers have been found for them, i.e., no consumers (no matter whether the commodities are ultimately sold to meet the needs of productive or individual consumption). If the attempt is made to give this tautology the semblance of greater profundity, by the statement that the working class receives too small a portion of its own product, and that the evil would be remedied if it received a bigger share, i.e. if its wages rose, we need only note that crises are always prepared by a period in which wages generally rise, and the working class actually does receive a greater share in the part of the annual product destined for consumption. From the standpoint of these advocates of sound and "simple"(!) common sense, such periods should rather avert the crisis. It thus appears that capitalist production involves certain conditions . . . which permit the relative prosperity of the working class only temporarily, and moreover always as a harbinger of crisis.'[11]

[9] *Capital* Volume 3, p. 233.
[10] Ibid., p. 472; cf. p. 239.
[11] *Capital* Volume 2, pp. 486–7.

How could Marx argue that a shortage of markets was the 'final cause' of crises and simultaneously claim that underconsumptionist theories were tautological? The apparent inconsistency is resolved by the fact that the 'final cause'—or the contradiction between production and consumption—was but one expression of the more general problem of 'disproportionalities'. Absorption of the reserve army into production (full employment) contributed to labour shortages, exerted upward pressure on wages, and thereby weakened the incentive to expand the market through new investments. The result, according to *Capital*, was a 'disproportion between capital and exploitable labour-power'.[12] From this particular disproportion Marx turned to the need to maintain a 'proportional relation of the various branches of production'.[13] In Volume 2 he developed this theme through schematic illustrations of the process whereby capital was reproduced. The schemes were not designed to show that a stable equilibrium, or even a 'dynamic equilibrium' (a phrase often used by his followers to describe smooth economic growth) could ever become a normal feature of capitalist society. On the contrary, Marx held that periods of genuine equilibrium occurred only immediately after crises: 'The crises are always but momentary and forcible solutions of the existing contradictions. They are violent eruptions which for a time restore the disturbed equilibrium.'[14] More important than these fleeting moments were the phases of expansion and contraction. Thus Marx used the schemes of proportionate reproduction to demonstrate that 'the proportionality of the individual branches of production springs as a continual process from disproportionality'.[15]

To do so he divided the whole of social production into two Departments. Department I produced means of production and materials, Department II consumer goods. Capitalists and workers in Department I bought consumer goods from Department II, and capitalists in Department II bought machinery (fixed capital) and materials (circulating capital) from Department I. The flow of

[12] *Capital* Volume 1, p. 770.
[13] *Capital* Volume 3, p. 239.
[14] Ibid., p. 244.
[15] Ibid., p. 251.

values between the two Departments had to be balanced if simple reproduction of existing capital was to be guaranteed: 'Such a balance accordingly appears as a law of reproduction on the same scale.'[16] If Department II spent more on machinery and materials than it currently received from Department I in payment for consumer goods, several effects would follow: there would be a net addition to the flow of social purchasing power; prices would rise in Department I; further investments would be encouraged; and growth would occur. 'We do not need here to go any further into the opposite case. . . . There would be a crisis—a crisis of production—despite reproduction on a constant scale.'[17]

Variations in the flow of social purchasing power were unavoidable in capitalist society, since fixed-capital replacements occurred unevenly. From the standpoint of accounting practices, the depreciation of industrial plant and equipment unfolded smoothly. If a machine were slated to last twelve years, it would nominally wear out by one-twelfth annually, the cost of depreciation being included in the selling price of the product. But as Marx pointed out, 'Reality . . . is in fact quite different from that method of average accounting. In the second year the machine may run better than in the first. And yet after twelve years it is no longer usable. It is the same as with a cow, whose average life is ten years, but which does not for that reason die by a tenth each year, although at the end of the ten years it must be replaced.'[18] At any time prior to physical replacement the capitalist could spend all or part of his depreciation account, or what Marx called the 'accumulation fund', on additional equipment. An unexpected demand for new fixed capital would generate a 'boom'; a sudden decline in the rate of capital expenditures would precipitate a crisis. The unpredictability of fixed-capital expenditures required that a policy of 'continuous relative overproduction' be applied in anticipation of any contingency. In a planned economy a cushion against demand fluctuations would be a first priority. 'Overproduction of this kind is equivalent to control by the society over the objective means of its

---

[16] *Capital* Volume 2, p. 540.

[17] Ibid., p. 543.

[18] Marx, *Theories of Surplus Value*, translated by G.A. Bonner and Emile Burns, London 1954, p. 354.

own reproduction. Within capitalist society, however, it is an anarchic element.'[19]

The movement of capitalist production was anarchic, but not random. Although Marx never presented a complete theory of the cycle, he did, as Schumpeter remarked, provide 'all the elements' out of which a theory could be constructed. Reassembling comments from various sections of *Capital*, one might argue that a comprehensive theory would run something like this. Crises would typically begin in Department I with a falling demand for means of production. The loss of employment in this sector would then curtail demand for consumer goods, causing overproduction to become general. As wages fell and purchasing power shrank, capitalists in Department II would be forced to reduce their costs of production in response to a contraction of the market. Renovation of plant and equipment would become necessary in the interest of survival, even if a portion of their fixed capital might yet be physically usable: 'Catastrophes, crises, etc. are the principal causes that compel such premature renewals of equipment on a broad social scale.'[20] The compulsive replacement of fixed capital is the 'material basis for the next turnover cycle' and 'one of the material foundations for the periodic cycle'.[21]

Before industry could be re-equipped it would first be necessary to renovate and replace the machines that produce machines. Initially, the capacity of Department I would lag behind the recovery of demand, and enterprises in Department II would bid up the price of equipment and materials. The profit rate in Department I would rise above that in II, and new capital would flow into the industries supplying means of production. 'Hence labour-power, means of subsistence for this labour-power, fixed capital in the form of the means of labour . . . and productive materials, are all withdrawn from the market, and an equivalent in money is cast into the market. . . . In capitalist society, . . . where any kind of social rationality asserts itself only *post festum*, major disturbances can and must occur constantly. . . . Since elements of productive capital are . . . being withdrawn from the market [or

[19] *Capital* Volume 2, pp. 544–5.
[20] Ibid., p. 250.
[21] Ibid., p. 264.

quickly bought up] and all that is put into the market is an equivalent in money, the effective demand rises, without . . . providing any element of supply. Hence prices rise, both for the means of subsistence, and for the material elements of production.'[22]

Competition and the incentive of a rising profit rate would prompt capitalists in Department I to invest as heavily as possible. But by the time this new productive capacity became fully operative, the original wave of investment demand from Department II would be declining. The reserve army would have returned to production; the approach of full employment would drive wage rates up and pose a threat to the rate of profit. Nevertheless, the expansion of production would not typically stop at this point. Instead would come the period of speculation, fuelled by the expansion of credit due to the slowing of productive investment and the accumulation of idle money-capital. Purchasing commodities in the hope of further price increases, speculators would accumulate stocks. As speculative began to prevail over real investment, the final turning point of the cycle would draw near. Marx described this phase in *Capital*:

'One stream of commodities now follows another [into the market], and it finally emerges that the earlier stream had only seemed to be swallowed up by consumption. Commodity capitals now vie with each other for a space on the market. The late-comers sell below the price in order to sell at all. The earlier streams have not yet been converted into ready money, while payment for them is falling due. Their owners must declare themselves bankrupt, or sell at any price in order to pay. This sale, however, has absolutely nothing to do with the real state of demand. It has only to do with the *demand for payment*, with the absolute necessity of transforming commodities into money. At this point the crisis breaks out. It first becomes evident not in the direct reduction of consumer demand, the demand for individual consumption, but rather in . . . the reproductive process of capital.'[23]

The role of credit in the final stage of the cycle was to accelerate 'the violent eruptions of this contradiction—crises—and thereby

[22] Ibid., p. 389–90.
[23] Ibid., pp. 156–7.

the elements of disintegration of the old mode of production'.[24] The extension of credit amplified the crisis; it was not the cause, and a more temperate monetary policy would moderàte but not eliminate the business cycle. The root of the crisis lay in the slower rate of real capital investment. From the standpoint of individual capitalists, especially in Department II, the decision not to invest might be of no immediate consequence. The value of the currently used-up fixed capital, plus any newly accumulated money-capital, need only be preserved through deposit in a bank account. The bank might then use the deposit to finance inventory growth and speculation elsewhere. The demand for Department II's output might even grow. But in Department I the crisis would result; final demand for consumer goods would shrink, and the crisis would then spread to Department II. The 'final cause' of the crisis would be an inadequate consumer market; its 'material basis' would be the uneven reproduction of fixed capital.

The historical tendency of the capitalist mode of production was therefore to pass repeatedly through the successive stages of the business cycle. The system was anarchic, but the anarchy was regulated by ascertainable laws. The problem was that these laws of capitalism asserted themselves, as Marx said, *post festum*. There was no foresight or planning on a social scale. Although created by the workers through the embodiment of their own labour-power, capital commanded that same labour-power mercilessly. Even the capitalist became the unwitting victim of the process, for each cycle enhanced the centralization of capital. 'One capitalist always strikes down many others', and 'along with the constant decrease in the number of capitalist magnates, . . . the mass of misery, oppression, slavery, degradation, and exploitation grows'.[25] The relations of production were becoming a fetter on the developing forces of production. Capitalist private property, Marx declared, 'in fact already rests on the carrying on of production by society', through huge concentrated enterprises.[26] He concluded: 'The centralization of the means of production and the socialization of labour reach a point at which they become incompatible with their capitalist

---

[24] *Capital* Volume 3, p. 432.
[25] *Capital* Volume 1, p. 929.
[26] Ibid., p. 930.

integument. This integument is burst asunder. The knell of capitalist private property sounds. The expropriators are expropriated.'[27]

2. 'Third Parties' and Imperialism: Engels, Kautsky, Luxemburg

When Marx died in 1883 *Capital* was still incomplete. Volume 1 had appeared in 1867; the manuscripts of Volumes 2 and 3 were left to Friedrich Engels to edit and publish. The years during which Engels worked on the manuscripts were known as the 'Great Depression', until they were divested of that title by the catastrophe that began in 1929. During the third quarter of the nineteenth century large investments had been made in railways, steamships, engineering industries, and mining. After 1873 this demand fell away, causing a secular decline in prices and rates of profit that lasted until 1896. In Germany the years of stagnation prompted a new era of industrial concentration in the form of trusts and cartels. Protective tariffs were raised to exclude foreign competition and permit industry-wide pricing agreements, enforced by restrictions on output. The German pattern of industrial development confirmed Marx's insight into the concentration and centralization of capital, but it also suggested that the traditional business cycle might be brought under control. These changes made a sharp impression on Engels.

In his introduction to the 1884 edition of Marx's *Poverty of Philosophy* Engels considered the notion that 'chronic stagnation would necessarily become the normal condition of modern industry, with only insignificant fluctuations'[28]—a remark Soviet authors would often cite when writing of capitalism's 'general crisis'. When he published Volume 3 of *Capital* in 1894 Engels footnoted the work with much more definite comments. The productive forces of capitalism, he claimed, were beginning to 'outgrow the control of the laws of the capitalist mode of commodity exchange'. Two factors were held responsible for this trend: 'the new and general mania for a protective tariff' and the related growth of trusts 'which

[27] Ibid., p. 929.
[28] Marx, *The Poverty of Philosophy*, New York n.d., p. 18.

regulate production, and thus prices and profits'.[29] Erecting obstacles to new domestic competition, trusts and cartels encouraged the export of redundant capital and minimized the threat of 'local over-speculation'.[30] It now appeared that 'most of the old breeding grounds of crises and opportunities for their development have been eliminated or strongly reduced'.[31] As Engels summarized: 'The acute form of the periodic process, with its former ten-year cycle, appears to have given way to a more chronic, long drawn out alternation between a relatively short and slight business improvement and a relatively long, indecisive depression—taking place in the various industrial countries at different times.'[32]

By discounting the probability of recurrent cycles of the old style Engels initiated a fundamental reorientation of Marxist thought, which was now to be inflected towards the new theory of imperialism. With modern transportation and communications, the arena of capitalist instability was no longer the nation-state but appeared to have become the world economy as a whole. Other countries, having industrialized, were challenging British control of the export trade and creating the conditions for 'the ultimate general industrial war, which shall decide who has supremacy on the world market. Thus every factor which works against a repetition of the old crises carries within itself the germ of a far more powerful future crisis.'[33] Where Engels spoke of an 'industrial war', other Marxists were to substitute 'imperialist war'.

Marx had discussed the role of foreign markets when explaining the law of the falling rate of profit. This tendency, he maintained, might be offset if capital were invested in more lucrative ventures overseas and if low-cost food and materials were imported.[34] But Marx had ascribed subordinate importance to these factors. His analysis of the cycle concentrated on the 'material basis' of economic fluctuations, and when he developed his reproduction schemes he explicitly abstracted from foreign trade and investment and explored the internal contradictions of capitalism. For Marx

[29] *Capital* Volume 3, p. 118.
[30] Ibid., p. 478.
[31] Ibid.
[32] Ibid., pp. 477–8.
[33] Ibid., p. 478.
[34] Ibid., pp. 232–3.

there was no doubt of the theoretical—as opposed to practical—possibility of realizing the entire value of the social product within a self-contained capitalist economy. In expanded as in simple reproduction it was necessary only that proportionality be maintained between the two Departments. Engels departed from this approach for a reason Marx would have considered theoretically erroneous. According to Engels, the expansion of capitalism into new lands resulted from *chronic overproduction*. A clear portent of underconsumptionist theories of imperialism can be seen in this comment by Engels: 'The daily growing speed with which production may be enlarged in all fields of large-scale industry today is offset by the ever-greater slowness with which the market for these increased products expands. What the former turns out in months can scarcely be absorbed by the latter in years. Add to this the protective tariff policy. . . . The results are a general chronic overproduction, depressed prices, falling and even wholly disappearing profits.'[35]

Sanctioned by the authority of Engels, the idea of chronic overproduction soon became a prevalent theme in later Marxist writings, culminating in the work of Rosa Luxemburg. The intermediate position between Engels and Luxemburg was assumed by Karl Kautsky, 'official' theorist of the German Social Democratic Party. In Kautsky's view, effective demand on the part of workers and capitalists could never absorb the output of capitalist industry: 'Demand from the side of the capitalists and the workers whom they exploit is insufficient to absorb the means of consumption created by large-scale capitalist industry. The latter must search for an additional market beyond the limits of capitalism—in regions that do not yet produce in a capitalist manner.'[36] Understanding that *chronic* underconsumption could not logically yield an explanation of *cyclical* crises, Kautsky revised Marx's analysis of business cycles. He replaced the uneven reproduction of capital with the fortuitous discovery and subsequent exhaustion of new markets. Prosperity, he asserted, depended upon fresh sources of demand, but 'every epoch of prosperity, which accompanies every

[35] Ibid., p. 428.
[36] Quoted in E. Leikin, 'Kautskyanstvo v Teorii Imperializma', *Pod Znamenem Marksizma*, XI (November 1926), p. 184.

important expansion of the market, is condemned in advance to be short-lived, and a crisis is its natural culmination'.[37] Impending exhaustion of the world market pointed to the inevitability of chronic industrial depression. In 1902 Kautsky wrote this:

'According to our theory this development is a necessity. . . . There must come a time, and it may be very soon, when it will be impossible for the world market even temporarily to expand more rapidly than society's productive forces, a time when overproduction is chronic for *all* industrial nations. . . . The continued existence of capitalist production remains possible, of course, even in such a state of chronic depression, but it becomes completely intolerable for the masses of the population; the latter are forced to seek a way out of the general misery, and they can find it only in socialism.'[38]

Following the example of Engels, Kautsky related the movement towards combination in industry to the threat of chronic depression. The capitalists had first formed cartels, then they had raised tariffs so as to extract a surplus-profit from the domestic market. With this surplus-profit they were able to lower export prices, thereby expanding the scale and reducing the unit costs of production. But these methods would succeed only until other capitalists adopted the same strategy. Then the struggle to acquire markets by force would commence: 'Colonial and expansionist policies arrive on the scene. These policies in turn either cause or threaten to cause conflicts among the competing imperialist powers. . . . The further preparations required for war likewise benefit the cartel economy; and the result is ever-multiplying colonial adventures and risks of war.'[39]

Modern capitalism required foreign outlets both to dispose of surplus production and to invest the surplus-profits acquired in the metropolitan countries. High cartel prices caused a restriction of domestic demand and forced redundant capital to find investment opportunities abroad. To the extent that capital exports speeded the industrialization of agrarian countries the capitalists merely has-

[37] Ibid.
[38] Quoted in Paul M. Sweezy, *The Theory of Capitalist Development*, New York and London 1970, p. 198.
[39] Quoted in Leikin, pp. 173–4.

tened the inevitable collapse. In 1907 Kautsky enlarged upon the views he had expressed in 1902:

'Production is increasingly finding its limit in the market. If the capitalist mode of production exceptionally raises productivity with regard to mass products, it simultaneously reduces to a minimum the mass consumption of the workers who produce these products; that is, it produces an increasing surplus of mass consumption goods that must be sold outside the working class. A market for this surplus is created primarily by the destruction of primitive rural domestic industry and handicrafts—first in the home country and then in other countries. But this kind of market expansion takes place much more slowly than the expansion of industry. The latter, from time to time, encounters ever-newer obstacles.'[40]

Fearful that the outbreak of imperialist wars would jeopardize the Social Democratic programme of a peaceful transition to socialism through electoral victory, Kautsky insisted that although imperialism had economic causes it was not an economic necessity: 'From the standpoint of economic development it is completely unnecessary and even harmful.'[41] Capitalism required foreign trade, but there was no necessary connection between trade, protectionism, and the use of force. In 1912 Kautsky declared that imperialism 'is not the equivalent of the natural and necessary attempt of capital to expand and open up new markets and spheres for investment; it is only a special method of pursuing this effort, the method of force. . . . The use of force is in no way a necessary condition of economic progress.'[42] If the expansion of world trade were rationally pursued, the capitalists would promptly dismantle protective barriers. International cartel agreements would allow the advanced countries to 'penetrate much more energetically and with fewer obstacles . . . into all the countries of the eastern part of the world'.[43] On these grounds Kautsky urged German capital to abandon the naval arms race with Britain and to forge an alliance to curtail the expansion of Russia. 'From a purely economic viewpoint', he reasoned, 'it cannot be ruled out that capitalism will

[40] Ibid., p. 183.
[41] Ibid., p. 177.
[42] Ibid., p. 197.
[43] Ibid., p. 199.

survive yet another phase, outgrowing [national] cartel policies and in foreign affairs reaching the stage of ultra-imperialism.'[44]

In the writings of Engels and Kautsky one finds the antecedents of Luxemburg's famous thesis that the accumulation of capital is impossible without 'third-party' markets. Luxemburg was a curious figure in this respect, stressing the role of consciousness in the proletarian revolution but simultaneously expounding a theory of the automatic and systemic collapse (or *Zusammenbruch*: breakdown) of capitalism through imperialist wars. In *The Mass Strike, the Political Party and the Trade Unions* (1906) she argued that the strike would awaken class consciousness like 'an electric shock'.[45] The fighting organizations of the proletariat could not be structured from above but would arise spontaneously 'from the whirlwind and the storm'.[46] During the German revolution of 1918 Luxemburg underlined the importance of spontaneity by adopting the anarchist slogan of Bakunin, 'In the beginning was the deed.'[47] How was the emphasis upon proletarian subjectivity to be reconciled with a mechanistic theory of economic breakdown? For Luxemburg there was no contradiction: the subjective transformation of proletarian consciousness followed logically from the objective impossibility of the worker's continuing to function as proletarian. In *The Accumulation of Capital* (1913) she argued that Marx's reproduction schemes had misrepresented the process of market creation. The decisive flaw of *Capital* was that it 'cannot explain the actual and historical process of accumulation'.[48] Only in non-capitalist markets was it possible to realize the surplus-value that the capitalists must accumulate for purposes of expanded reproduction.

'Realization of the surplus-value', she wrote, '. . . requires as its prime condition . . . that there should be strata of buyers outside capitalist society. Buyers, it should be noted, not consumers, since the material form of the surplus-value is quite irrelevant to its

[44] Leikin, *Pod Znamenem Marksizma*, XII (December 1926), p. 153.

[45] Rosa Luxemburg, *The Mass Strike, the Political Party and the Trade Unions*, translated by Patrick Lavin, Colombo, Ceylon 1964, p. 27.

[46] Ibid., p. 31.

[47] Luxemburg, *Spartacus*, translated by Eden and Cedar Paul, Colombo, Ceylon 1966, p. 21.

[48] Luxemburg, *The Accumulation of Capital*, translated by Agnes Schwarzschild, London 1963, p. 348.

realization. The decisive fact is that the surplus-value cannot be realized by sale either to workers or to capitalists, but only if it is sold to such social organizations or strata whose own mode of production is not capitalistic.'[49] In *Capital* Marx had ignored the role of 'third parties', dealing instead with an abstract reproduction scheme in which all incomes were understood to derive, directly or indirectly, from the capitalist production of commodities. In other words, all exchanges were assumed to be financed by purchasing power initially put into circulation by the capitalist class. Marx had then divided the social product into three categories: the portion representing expenditures on plant, materials, and machinery; that representing wage payments; surplus-value. The first two parts of the social product were automatically realized in order that production could continue from one year to the next. Even a portion of the surplus-value constituted no problem, since it provided for capitalist consumption and was purchased by the capitalists from one another. The problem, in Luxemburg's view, concerned the remaining portion of the surplus-value, that intended for accumulation and reinvestment. Her question was elegantly simple: who could buy the commodities that embodied this surplus-value within the context of Marx's assumptions?

Clearly, the workers could not do so; their wages were already accounted for. Yet if the capitalists were to buy these commodities they would have no incentive to embark upon expanded reproduction. The exchanges would all be financed, *ex hypothesi*, from the capitalists' own pockets. The total money-capital commanded by the collective capitalist would therefore remain constant. While production might expand in such circumstances, it would be not capitalist production (production for profit), but merely production for its own sake. Even if the capitalists did realize the balance of the surplus-value themselves, they would at best temporarily ward off an ultimately insurmountable contradiction:

'. . . such a solution only pushes the problem from this moment to the next. After we have assumed that accumulation has started and that the increased production throws an even bigger amount of commodities on to the market the following year, the same question arises again: where do we then find the consumers for this even

[49] Ibid., pp. 351–2.

greater amount of commodities? Will we answer: well, this growing amount of goods will again be exchanged among the capitalists to extend production again, and so forth, year after year? Then we have the roundabout that revolves around itself in empty space. That is not capitalist accumulation, i.e., the amassing of money-capital, but its contrary: producing commodities for the sake of it; from the standpoint of capital an utter absurdity. If the capitalists as a class are the only customers for the total amount of commodities, apart from the share they have to part with to maintain the workers—if they must always buy the commodities with their own money, and realize the surplus-value, then amassing profit, accumulation for the capitalist class, cannot possibly take place.'[50]

Capital's 'aim and goal in life' was said to be 'profit in the form of money and the accumulation of money-capital'. The reproduction schemes did not explain—so Luxemburg believed—the source of a net addition to purchasing power, without which economic growth was inconceivable. 'So there must develop right from the start an exchange relationship between capitalist production and the non-capitalist *milieu*, where capital . . . finds the possibility of realizing surplus-value in hard cash for further capitalization.'[51] In view of the attractiveness of Luxemburg's reasoning to Soviet economists, it must now be stated quite clearly how she misinterpreted *Capital*.

In *Capital* Volume 2 Marx explained that some capitalists were always buying without selling; others were selling without buying.[52] The same point may be expressed differently: some capitalists were investing their money-capital, while others were accumulating. This was true because the lifetimes of various elements of fixed capital differed and because investment opportunities were never uniform throughout the economy. Luxemburg posited an impossible situation when she assumed that expanded reproduction meant that *all* capitalists were accumulating a cash hoard simultaneously. What expanded reproduction actually required was a net addition to purchasing power (or demand),

[50] Luxemburg, 'The Accumulation of Capital—An Anti-Critique', in Rosa Luxemburg and Nikolai Bukharin, *Imperialism and the Accumulation of Capital*, translated by Rudolf Wichmann, Kenneth J. Tarbuck ed., London 1972, p. 57; cf. *The Accumulation of Capital*, pp. 334–5.

[51] Luxemburg, 'Anti-Critique', p. 59.

[52] *Capital* Volume 2, pp. 536–9.

which could be achieved through a net expenditure from accumulation funds. Luxemburg denied that these funds could be the source of new demand, since they were already committed to the replacement of currently functioning fixed capital. She overlooked the fact that, as Marx said, fixed capital is like a cow: its average life may be ten years, but it 'does not for that reason die by a tenth each year'. To be more precise, Luxemburg did not consider the possibility that accumulated money-capital could be reinvested before the original fixed capital was physically worn out. She did not see that (leaving aside the matter of monetary expansion) economic growth depended upon the simple condition that dishoarding (investment) exceed hoarding (saving). If a net depletion of accumulation funds caused an increment to effective demand, then a wave of expansion would necessarily result without any recourse to 'third-party' markets. Should any individual capitalist contemplate an expenditure that exceeded his available resources, he would, as Marx observed, borrow the difference. Those capitalists who were not yet prepared to spend their accumulation fund would not permit it to lie idle. Surplus-value, wrote Marx, was 'absolutely unproductive in its monetary metamorphosis. . . . It is a "dead weight" on capitalist production.'[53] Funds would therefore move from those capitalists with no immediate need to those desirous of expanding their operations, the relation between the two groups being mediated by the interest rate.

Marx abstracted from 'third parties' because he saw that they were not essential to understanding reproduction. There could be no doubt that it was theoretically possible to realize the surplus-value, provided inter-industrial relations of proportionality were maintained. Should it happen that the distribution of production did not match the prevailing demand, then foreign trade might enter to redress the disproportion. Alternatively, trade might arise from considerations of comparative cost or from the export of capital in search of a higher return. A full explanation of the penetration of capital into the non-capitalist environment required only the law of the falling rate of profit and a proper understanding of the business cycle. By reinterpreting *Capital* in terms of a theory of chronic market inadequacy, or a chronic 'realization crisis',

[53] Ibid., p. 574.

Luxemburg and Kautsky obscured what Marx took to be the real pattern of capitalist development. Ironically, their shared economic analysis led them to diametrically opposed political positions. Kautsky proposed to resolve the market problem through the co-ordinated ultra-imperialist exploitation of backward countries (thus defending them from Russia). Luxemburg gave her life for the revolution that, by her own logic, should have come about spontaneously in the aftermath of a more or less automatic capitalist collapse.

3. 'Finance Capital' and Imperialism: Hilferding, Lenin, Bukharin

In German Marxist literature the work on imperialism that adhered most faithfully to Marx's methodology was Rudolf Hilferding's *Finance Capital* (1910). More than any other text (apart from *Capital* itself), Hilferding's book evoked a positive response from Russian Marxists prior to the revolution. On the first page of *Imperialism, The Highest Stage of Capitalism* (1915), Lenin acknowledged his debt to *Finance Capital*. 'This work', he wrote, 'gives a very valuable theoretical analysis of "the latest phase of capitalist development".' If Lenin had doubts about Hilferding's work, they had to do not with its interpretation of Marx but with Hilferding did not go so far, although he did cause Lenin to remark that the author of *Finance Capital* exhibited a tendency to 'reconcile Marxism with opportunism'. In the 1920s Hilferding substantiated Lenin's presentiment by twice serving as Social Democratic finance minister of the Weimar Republic. Nevertheless, that the author of *Finance Capital* exhibited a tendency to 'reconcile Marxism with opportunism'. In the 1920s Hilferding substantiated Lenin's presentiment by twice serving as Social Democratic Finance Minister of the Weimar Republic. Nevertheless, Hilferding's impact on Soviet economists could be seen as late as 1931, two years after Stalin had denounced Bukharin for the theory of 'organized capitalism'. Throughout the 1920s Soviet Marxism moved towards an eventual confrontation between the views of imperialism set forth by Luxemburg and Hilferding.

Seeing no evidence of a chronic problem of markets, Hilferding concentrated on institutional change and on Marx's theme that the socialization of production was inherent in the growth of gigantic capitalist firms. The displacement of living labour-power by machinery, or the rise of what Marx called the 'organic composition of capital', was shown to lengthen the time required for the transformation of money-capital through the stage of fixed capital and back into money-capital. The prolongation of the turnover period lessened the adaptability of industry to short-run changes and encouraged dependence on the banks and recourse to credit. A second characteristic of modern capitalism provided additional impetus towards the integration of the banks and industry. When capital became tied up for long periods, the operation of the law of value and the tendency towards equalization of the rate of profit across enterprises was impaired. An abnormally high rate of profit might still be offset in any particular industry through an inflow of new capital; an outflow of established capital in response to a declining rate of profit was more problematic. Once involved in the financing of industrial operations, the banks passed the point of no return and found themselves obliged to protect their interest by collaborating in the formation of trusts and cartels. The larger the trusts and cartels became, the greater were their credit requirements. Industrial combination thus tended to stimulate a parallel centralization of banking capital. The two forms of combination were mutually reinforcing, and the result of their interaction was the eventual merger of the banks with industry. 'I call banking capital', wrote Hilferding, 'or money-capital that in this way is really transformed into industrial capital, finance capital. . . . An ever-larger share of the capital employed in industry is finance capital, or capital at the disposal of the banks and used by the industrialists.'[54]

Developing this alternative explanation of the origins of imperialism, Hilferding integrated his analysis with the Marxist theory of the business cycle. He showed both that the new institutions of modern capitalism were rooted in the 'material basis' of the cycle and that cyclical variations in the rate of profit enhanced the trend towards trustification and cartelization. During a period of cyclical expansion prices and profits rose most quickly in Department I,

[54] Rudolf Hilferding, *Das Finanzkapital*, Frankfurt am Main 1968, p. 309.

among industries producing the means of production. A rise in the price of machinery and materials would tend to depress the rate of profit in the lighter industries of Department II. Conversely, during an economic contraction the rate of profit would fall most abruptly in Department I, as heavy industrial producers found themselves forced either to produce for inventory or to slash prices in face of excess productive capacity. Industrial combination offered a way to stabilize the profit rate for both groups. During a contraction the extractive and metallurgical industries had a natural interest in combining with enterprises that used their products; during an expansion the reverse would be true, and light industries would be more anxious to acquire means of production relatively cheaply by amalgamating with supplier firms. Thus the pressure in the direction of organization was continuous throughout all phases of the business cycle: 'the difference in the rate of profit . . . pushes towards combination. For a combined enterprise the fluctuations in the rate of profit are eliminated.'[55]

Finance capital strove to surmount the law of value and the price mechanism of capitalist society by means of centralized control over production. Gearing output to changes in the market, organized capital attempted artificially to raise the profits of cartel members by siphoning off a share of the surplus-value created in enterprises that normally bought their products. Industrial combinations sought to suppress competition; and 'cartel profit', according to Hilferding, represented 'the appropriation of profit from other branches of industry'.[56] The only defensive action open to unorganized capitalists was to form combinations of their own. Every formation of a cartel or trust thus had the consequence of promoting further industrial organization. In those firms that for one reason or another were not suited to combination, the average rate of profit would decline to a level such that it covered production costs and yielded no more than the rate of interest prevailing in the market, in other words, the rate of return the unorganized capitalist might earn if he ceased operations altogether and lent his capital or invested in shares. The fact that every capitalist had to earn at least the current rate of interest imposed an objective limit on cartel pricing.

[55] Ibid., p. 263.
[56] Ibid., p. 316.

Nevertheless, the limit allowed sufficient latitude to creat a powerful disincentive to investment in unorganized industries, with their comparatively low rate of return. The cartels themselves, despite their accumulation of surplus profit, were similarly reluctant to expand their collective productive capacity, lest they produce too much and bring prices back down. It followed that one of the inevitable consequences of capitalism's new institutional framework was to stimulate the export of capital from metropolitan countries to the colonial periphery. The principal factor behind imperialist aggression was the quest for a higher rate of profit, not a chronically inadequate market.

Disagreeing with Luxemburg and Kautsky on the origins of the imperialist stage, Hilferding also repudiated the argument of Eduard Bernstein and other 'revisionists' to the effect that organized capital might emancipate itself from the classical business cycle. 'This opinion', he declared, 'takes absolutely no account of the internal nature of crises. It is only by seeing the cause of the crisis solely in the overproduction of commodities, due to ignorance of the situation on the market, that one can believe that cartels are able to suppress crises through restricting production.'[57] In reality, crises arose from inter-industrial disproportionalities, and in spite of their express purpose of regulating production relative to demand, the new organizational forms invariably broke down in the struggle over surplus-value.

For all their rational organization, the individual members of a cartel faced an irresistible temptation to thwart the collective interest by overinvesting in response to upwardly distorted prices in the rising phase of the business cycle.[58] Normally, the central office of a cartel allocated production quotas based upon the productive capacity of the members, an increase in capacity being the obvious way the individual firm might enlarge its market share. Competition within the organization thereby contributed to the onset of relative overproduction. The greater the redundancy of productive potential, the more stubbornly would the cartel attempt to maintain prices once the crisis arrived, and the more aggravated would its effects be on the unorganized capitalists. By contributing

[57] Ibid., p. 400.
[58] Ibid., pp. 354–5.

to bankruptcies elsewhere, the cartels in effect undermined their own prices and were forced to restrict output still further. At this stage the technological superiority of large combined enterprises revealed its own internal contradiction. A drop in output would significantly raise unit costs of production in firms with high fixed costs; smaller 'outsiders' would then intervene with less sophisticated equipment to compete with and dissolve the cartel; and the cyclical anarchy of the system would be restored. Cartels neither prevented crises nor reduced their severity; they could only 'modify' them to the extent that they temporarily transferred the negative effects to non-organized industries.[59] Social Democrats who believed that the traditional pattern of the business cycle had been surmounted were making the logical error of confusing quantity with quality:

'Partial regulation, that is to say, the grouping of one branch of industry into a single enterprise, has precisely no effect upon the relationships of proportionality within industry as a whole. The anarchy of production is not suppressed by a quantitative diminution of its different elements together with the simultaneous reinforcement of their effectiveness and intensity; it cannot be suppressed gradually or for limited periods. Regulated production and anarchic production are not quantitative opposites, and by forever adding a little more "regulation" anarchy cannot be transformed into conscious organization. . . . The question of who controls production, and to whom it belongs, is a question of power. A universal cartel, which would direct the whole of production and thereby suppress crises, is economically conceivable, although it is a social and political impossibility because it would collide with an antagonism of interests pushed to the extreme. To expect individual cartels to suppress crises is to demonstrate an incomprehension of the causes of crises and of the mechanism of the capitalist system.'[60]

In all its essentials, Hilferding's account of imperialism conformed to Marx's methodology. But Hilferding did diverge from Marx with respect to monetary phenomena. Whereas *Capital* held that monetary crises arose from and interacted with industrial

[59] Ibid., p. 404.
[60] Ibid., pp. 402–3.

crises, Hilferding believed that the concentration of bank capital and its union with industry would make major financial disturbances most improbable. With their far-flung domestic and international affiliations, modern financial institutions were simply too large and diversified to be drawn into the abyss even by the cyclical difficulties of the great industrial enterprises in which they invested. Previous monetary and credit crises had been due to excesses of speculation. Controlling virtually the whole of society's money-capital, the banks were now in a position to throttle speculation at will. The role of speculators was further curtailed by the tendency on the part of cartels and trusts to bypass commercial capital and deal directly with one another, and even with retailers. In addition to these organizational changes, Hilferding professed to see a basic change in capitalist psychology: 'Those mass psychoses that speculation provoked at the beginning of the capitalist era, those happy times when every speculator believed himself God the Father, creating a world out of nothing, appear to have passed forever.'[61]

It was arguments such as these that led Lenin to comment that the author of *Finance Capital* tended to combine Marxism with opportunism. Hilferding was intrigued by the question of just how far the process of capitalist organization might go. At one point he allowed his imagination to wander:

'The question arises as to where the limit to cartelization lies. The answer is that there is no absolute limit, but rather a continuous tendency towards expanded cartelization. . . . Hence the result of the process would be a universal cartel, the whole of capitalist production consciously regulated by an organ fixing the dimension of production in every sphere. The fixing of prices is therefore purely nominal and signifies nothing more than the division of the global product among the magnates of capital on the one hand and the mass of the remaining members of society on the other. . . . Money no longer plays any role. It can disappear completely because what is involved is a division of things and not a division of values. With the disappearance of the anarchy of production there also disappears the material expression, or the objectivity of value on the part of the commodity, and therefore money as well. . . .

[61] Ibid., p. 399.

This is a society consciously regulated within an antagonistic form. . . . Finance capital, in its final form, detaches itself from the fertile soil that gave it birth. The circulation of money ceases to be of any use.'[62]

In a fully organized society the law of value would no longer determine the allocation of the forces of production. The 'social division of labour', mediated by money and the market, would be replaced by a 'technical division of labour', mediated by a central office that would prevail over the whole of production as if over the members of a single cartel or the divisions of a single enterprise. For the first time in history capital would overcome its internal contradictions and appear as a 'unified force'. In intellectual wanderings of this type Hilferding's attitude to finance capital became almost worshipful. Yet in contrast to Kautsky, who expected the phase of 'ultra-imperialism' to become reality, Hilferding invariably retreated from such fantasies to emphasize that the practical limit to organized capitalism lay in the class struggle. An organized variant of capitalism would pose the question of property relations in its 'clearest, most precise and pointed expression at the same time as the question of organizing the social economy is itself resolved by the development of finance capital'.[63] Production would be objectively socialized within the integument of capitalist society, but as Marx predicted, the final stage of a planned economy could not be reached until the expropriators were expropriated. Such was Hilferding's position in 1910. In the final chapter of *Finance Capital* he made this declaration:

'The tendency of finance capital is towards the establishment of social control over production. But it is socialization within an antagonistic form: the control of social production remains in the hands of an oligarchy. The struggle for the expropriation of this oligarchy constitutes the last phase of the class struggle between the bourgeoisie and the proletariat.

'The socializing function of finance capital considerably facilitates the elimination of capitalism. Because finance capital has brought the principal branches of production under its control, it is enough for society, through its conscious executive organ, the State,

[62] Ibid., pp. 321–2.
[63] Ibid., p. 323.

once conquered by the proletariat, to seize finance capital in order immediately to command the principal branches of production. . . . The seizure of six big Berlin banks would at once signify control over the principal branches of large-scale industry.'[64]

The fallacy in Hilferding's reasoning lay in his belief that the working class might seize power peacefully, that the capitalist state, 'conquered' through an electoral victory, might serve the class interests of the workers just as it had served the bourgeoisie. During his second period of office in the Finance Ministry Hilferding came into conflict with Hjalmar Schacht, president of the Reichsbank, and was forced to resign. When Adolf Hitler came to power in 1933 an embittered but still optimistic Hilferding predicted that the Nazis would not last more than six or eight weeks: as soon as Hitler laid hands on the Reichsbank he would be driven from the chancellorship.[65] Had Hitler taken seriously the official Nazi programme and its demand for the end of 'interest slavery', the prediction would probably have proven sound. But Hitler was more realistic than the economic cranks in the Nazi movement. To soothe the anxiety of finance capitalists he reappointed Schacht to the Reichsbank. Eight years later the Nazis dominated most of Europe and Rudolf Hilferding died in the hands of the Gestapo.

Among Russian Marxists Lenin alone understood the second volume of *Capital* with subtlety equal to Hilferding's. To many historians Lenin's *Imperialism* has seemed to be little more than a popularized version of *Finance Capital*, written by a political tactician basically disinterested in real theory. This casual appraisal of Lenin as a theorist results from a tendency to overlook the significance of some of his earliest writings. The link between *Capital* and Lenin's mature view of imperialism may be seen in his debates with the Russian Narodniks during the 1890s.

As agrarian socialists and populists, the Narodniks believed that the full-scale development of capitalism in Russia was impossible: Russian industry was a historical latecomer and could never compete successfully with more advanced countries in the struggle for markets. The emergence of mechanized enterprises, they held, would destroy cottage industry and impoverish the peasants,

[64] Ibid., pp. 503–4.
[65] See Yvon Bourdet's Introduction to *Le Capital Financier*, Paris 1970, p. 31.

thereby contracting the internal market, preventing the growth of a Russian proletariat, and proving that Marxism, a uniquely Western doctrine, had no relevance to Russian conditions. The Russian road to socialism, these writers argued, lay through self-organized peasant communes. Lenin first responded to the Narodniks in 1893 with a paper entitled 'On the So-Called Market Question'. He argued that the dissolution of self-sufficient peasant households and handicraft production could have no other effect than to *expand* the domestic market by creating a rural proletariat and bourgeoisie. Impoverished peasants would be forced to sell their labour-power so as to acquire the means of subsistence they once drew from the land; and the rural bourgeoisie, by undertaking commercial agriculture, would create a market for farm implements and manufactured consumer goods. Peasant impoverishment, far from impeding the rise of capitalism, was 'a condition of capitalism and strengthens it'.[66] The growth of capitalism in the countryside would erase the traditional village commune and provide the rural allies of the proletariat upon whom Lenin would later rely in formulating the concept of the *smychka*, or alliance between industrial workers and the poor and middle peasants for the construction of socialism.

Lenin's early essays are important for their anticipation of the questions later raised by Rosa Luxemburg. She inquired how surplus-value might be realized in a country where pre-capitalist producers had already been eliminated, and answered: the capitalists would have to find new 'third-party', or non-capitalist, producers to exploit. When the Narodniks raised the same issue Lenin replied that displacement of pre-capitalist economic forms was merely the first step in an endlessly progressing division of labour: 'the limits of the development of the market, in capitalist society, are set by the limits of the specialization of labour. But this specialization, by its very nature, is as infinite as technical developments.'[67] Once commodity production took root, each article would be broken into its component parts and made the object of specialized manufacturing and new investments. Each wave of investment would end in a crisis because of disproportionalities, or what Lenin termed 'the unevenness of development inherent in

---

[66] V.I. Lenin, *Collected Works*, 45 volumes, Moscow 1972–4, Volume 1, p. 102.
[67] Ibid., p. 100.

capitalism'.[68] 'The ruin of small producers is tremendously accelerated by this spasmodic growth of the factory; the workers are drawn into the factory in masses during a boom period, and are then thrown out. The formation of a vast reserve army of unemployed, ready to undertake any kind of work, becomes a condition for the existence and development of large-scale industry.'[69] Understanding the business cycle in Marx's terms, Lenin was perfectly satisfied that 'Marx proved in Volume II [of *Capital*] that capitalist production is quite conceivable without foreign markets, with the growing accumulation of wealth and without any "third parties".'[70]

To say that capitalism created its own market was clearly not to claim that the social product could be realized without difficulties: 'if one speaks of the "difficulties" of realization, of the crises etc. arising therefrom, one must admit that these "difficulties" are not only possible but are necessary as regards all parts of the capitalist product, and not as regards surplus-value alone. Difficulties of this kind, due to disproportion in the distribution of the various branches of production, constantly arise. . . . Without "difficulties" of this kind and crises, there cannot, in general, be any capitalist production.'[71] It was from these cyclical interruptions rather than from a chronic inadequacy of markets that capitalism received its impetus to geographic expansion:

'The various branches of industry, which serve as "markets" for one another, do not develop evenly, but outstrip one another, and the more developed industry seeks a foreign market. This does not mean at all "the impossibility of the capitalist nation realizing surplus-value". . . . It merely indicates the lack of proportion in the development of the different industries. If the national capital were distributed *differently*, the same quantity of products could be realized within the country. But for capital to abandon one sphere of industry and pass into another, there must be a crisis in that sphere; and what can restrain the capitalists threatened by such a crisis from seeking a foreign market, from seeking subsidies and bonuses to facilitate exports, etc.?'[72]

[68] Ibid., Volume 3, p. 591.
[69] Ibid., p. 545.
[70] Ibid., Volume 1, pp. 498–9.
[71] Ibid., Volume 3, p. 47.
[72] Ibid., p. 66.

A 'scientific', as opposed to 'romantic', analysis of capitalism indicated that an underconsumptionist account of capital's penetration of foreign lands distorted the real pattern of development. Echoing Marx's reference to the underconsumptionist tautology, Lenin declared that 'it is precisely in the periods which precede crises that the workers' consumption rises'.[73] The Marxist theory of the cycle grew out of the contradiction 'between the social character of production (socialized by capitalism) and the private, individual mode of appropriation', which resulted in unco-ordinated investments, unevenness, and crises.[74] 'To put it more briefly, the [romantic] theory explains crises by underconsumption (*Unterkonsumption*), the [scientific] by the anarchy of production. . . . But the question is: does the second theory deny the fact of a contradiction between production and consumption? *Of course not.* It fully recognizes this fact, but puts it in its proper, subordinate place. . . . It teaches us that this fact cannot explain crises.'[75] Nothing could be more senseless, Lenin concluded, than to say 'that Marx did not admit the possibility of surplus-value being realized in capitalist society, that he attributed crises to underconsumption'.[76] Lenin's fidelity to Marx on the matter of the business cycle is worth recalling, for by the early 1930s, with neo-Luxemburgism triumphant in Soviet economic discussions, the theory of disproportionalities would be relegated to the status of a bourgeois 'prejudice'. By denouncing Rudolf Hilferding Soviet Marxists would in fact cut their final ties with Lenin himself, and mechanically reiterate the law of unevenness without any awareness of its origins and meaning.

The anti-Narodnik essays explain the enthusiasm with which Lenin endorsed all but the most speculative sections of *Finance Capital*. His own *Imperialism* did popularize *Finance Capital* in the sense of summarizing the new relationship between banks and industry with a lawyer's brevity and accompanying data. However, Lenin's work also differed from Hilferding's in its greater emphasis upon the contradictions of modern capitalism, contradictions that

[73] Ibid., Volume 2, p. 167.
[74] Ibid.
[75] Ibid., p. 168.
[76] Ibid., Volume 3, p. 58.

were now formulated more explicitly in terms of the *law of uneven development*: 'The uneven and spasmodic development of individual enterprises, of individual branches of industry and of individual countries is inevitable under the capitalist system.'[77] For the first time, *Imperialism* consistently applied the concept of disproportionate growth to the relations between nation-states. Showing how different countries passed through different stages of development at different times, Lenin held that by establishing their own hegemony over colonial territories the more advanced countries compelled newcomers, like Germany, to find an outlet for commodity and capital exports through militarism.

The fact that entire countries developed unevenly meant that the shifting balance of military and economic power would inevitably lead to imperialist wars aimed at the redivision of colonial possessions. With reference to Kautsky Lenin commented: 'Certain bourgeois writers (whom K. Kautsky . . . has now joined) have expressed the opinion that international cartels . . . give the hope of peace among nations under capitalism. Theoretically this opinion is absolutely absurd, while in practice it is sophistry and a dishonest defence of the worst opportunism.'[78] Kautsky's 'silly little fable about "peaceful" ultra-imperialism' was nothing but 'the reactionary attempt of a frightened philistine to hide from stern reality'—from imperialist war and its revolutionary implications.[79] The events of 1914 had made a mockery of the Social Democratic hope for a peaceful transition to socialism. Arguing that monopoly capital would peacefully complete the process of socialization, Kautsky and others had failed to see that the emergence of monopoly capital was itself dialectical, that monopolies were inherently unstable and periodically disintegrated in the struggle to appropriate surplus-value. In this respect, Lenin might have cited a comment by Marx in *The Poverty of Philosophy*:

'In practical life we find not only competition, monopoly and the antagonism between them, but also the synthesis of the two, which is not a formula, but a movement. Monopoly produces competition, competition produces monopoly. Monopolies are made from

[77] Lenin, *Selected Works* 3 vols., Moscow 1960–61, I, p. 759.
[78] Ibid., p. 770.
[79] Ibid., p. 788.

competition; competitors become monopolists. If the monopolists restrict their mutual competition by means of partial associations . . . competition becomes [more desperate] between the monopolists of different nations. The synthesis is of such a character that monopoly can only maintain itself by continually entering into the struggle of competition.'[80]

Without quoting Marx directly, Lenin made the same point: 'the monopolies, which have grown out of free competition, do not eliminate the latter, but exist over and alongside of it, and thereby give rise to a number of very acute, intense antagonisms, frictions and conflicts'.[81] Preoccupied with the advance of organizational perfection, Kautsky had ignored 'the very profound and fundamental contradictions of imperialism: the contradiction between monopoly and free competition which exists side by side with it, between the gigantic "operations" (and gigantic profits) of finance capital and "honest" trade in the free market, the contradiction between cartels and trusts on the one hand, and non-cartelized industry on the other, etc.'[82] The statement that cartels could abolish the business cycle was 'a fable spread by bourgeois economists'.[83]

Lenin and Hilferding agreed that large-scale capital had become temporarily more organized at the expense of more violent fluctuations in prices and profits elsewhere. Thus partial organization and partial state intervention on behalf of finance capital made cyclical crises all the more inevitable: 'The privileged position of the most highly cartelized, so-called *heavy* industry, especially coal and iron, causes "a still greater lack of co-ordination" in other branches of industry.'[84] The 'privileged sectors' of industry might try to avert the political consequences of the business cycle by creating 'privileged sections among the workers' or a 'labour aristocracy', but this fact did nothing more than explain the political basis of opportunism: it did not justify the theory of a peaceful transition to socialism. Marx had foreseen the 'aristocracy of the working class'

[80] Marx, *The Poverty of Philosophy*, p. 128.
[81] Lenin, *Selected Works*, I, p. 781.
[82] Ibid., p. 806.
[83] Ibid., p. 731.
[84] Ibid.

as early as *Capital* Volume I[85]; he had not for that reason become a parliamentary cretin.

Through persistent emphasis on the internal contradictions of imperialism, Lenin avoided what he considered to be the greatest weakness of *Finance Capital*, Hilferding's uncontrolled urge to extend the concept of 'organized capitalism' to the logical extreme such that capital's appearance as a 'unified force' could be imagined. He admitted that monopoly prices might be sufficiently effective to dull the forces of competition and forestall technological progress in the short run, but these were the achievements of 'parasitic, decaying capitalism'.[86] A 'pure' variant of capitalism, an integral unity between implacable rivals, was as much a fiction of an overactive imagination as Kautsky's 'ultra-imperialism' or Luxemburg's chronic inadequacy of markets. 'The very concept of purity', Lenin declared, 'indicates a certain narrowness, a one-sidedness of human cognition, which cannot embrace an object in all its totality and complexity'.[87]

When reviewing the literature of this period, the historian is struck by the contrast between Lenin's perception of the shortcomings of the Narodnik and Social Democratic theorists and his indulgence towards his own youthful associate, Bukharin. Several years later (in 1922) Lenin noted in his political testament that although Bukharin was 'the most valuable and biggest theoretician of the party', it was also true that 'his theoretical views can only with the very greatest doubt be regarded as fully Marxist, for there is something scholastic in him (he has never learned, and I think never has fully understood, dialectics)'.[88] From an early date Lenin and Bukharin differed on the most basic questions of methodology. Lenin always stressed the internal contradictions that resulted in uneven development; Bukharin just as consistently thought in terms of social systems moving from one phase of equilibrium to another under the conscious guidance of the state.[89] Bukharin's

[85] Marx, *Capital* Volume I, p. 822.
[86] Lenin, *Selected Works*, Volume I, p. 793.
[87] Lenin, *Collected Works*, XXI, p. 236.
[88] 'The Suppressed Testament of Lenin', in *Leon Trotsky on the Suppressed Testament of Lenin*, New York 1946, p. 7.
[89] See Richard B. Day, 'Dialectical Method in the Political Writings of Lenin and Bukharin', *Canadian Journal of Political Science*, IX, no. 2 (June 1976), 244–60.

tendency to exaggerate the organizational potential of modern capitalism, even to go beyond Hilferding in this regard, first became apparent in 1915 with his article 'Towards a Theory of the Imperialist State'.

In the years of the First World War every European government, that of Germany in particular, intervened in production and distribution on an unprecedented scale. In this trend Bukharin found confirmation of the hypothesis first sketched by Hilferding: the role of the state was changing in accordance with capitalism's inherent laws, and the change could not be reversed. By integrating the productive organizations of modern capitalism with an overarching political structure, the ruling class of capitalist society had achieved a greater degree of internal coherence than ever before. Marx had studied the epoch of competitive capitalism, when political pluralism and rival parties had been needed to represent the divergent interests of various groups within the ruling class. But with the advent of imperialism 'all the former political organizations of the ruling classes gradually lose their *differentia specifica*, being converted into a single imperialist party; all-embracing blocs containing all the bourgeois parties, . . . complete unity on questions of foreign policy, and the disappearance of all remnants of democratism and the former liberalism—all of these factors visibly illustrate this process'.[90] Carried away by Hilferding's ideas, Bukharin exclaimed that the integration of industrial and banking capital had eliminated 'the different subgroups of the ruling classes, uniting them in a single finance-capitalist clique'.[91] A new form of 'collective capitalism' had arisen; the imperialist state was now functioning as 'a collective, joint capitalist'.[92]

The need to concentrate economic authority had converted 'each developed "national system" of capitalism into a "state-capitalist" trust', or what Bukharin described as a 'new Leviathan beside which the fantasy of Thomas Hobbes appears as a child's toy'.[93] Not only had the state taken over some forms of enterprises and entered

[90] N.I. Bukharin, 'K Teorii Imperialisticheskovo Gosudarstva', in *Revolyutsiya Prava: Sbornik Pervyi*, Moscow 1925, p. 28.
[91] Ibid., p. 25.
[92] Ibid., p. 21.
[93] Ibid., p. 30.

into partnership with separate capitalists in others, but other forms of controls had also proliferated, governing the types of commodities produced, the materials employed, and the prices charged. The flow of commodities across national boundaries was regulated by import and export controls; within national frontiers rationing performed a similar function. 'As a result, the anarchic commodity market has been replaced to a large degree by the organized distribution of the product, in which the supreme authority is . . . the state power.'[94] Implementing 'the collective will of the consolidated bourgeoisie as a whole', the triumphant state at last made it possible to overcome the struggle over the distribution of surplus-value, which for Marx had been the source of all change in capitalist society. The whole of society's money-capital had been mobilized by the state bank through the issue of diverse forms of securities, and the capitalists had been converted into 'shareholders', receiving 'dividends' from the all-embracing state-capitalist trust.[95] In Bukharin's mind Hilferding's dream of 'organized capitalism' became a grotesque nightmare. *The Economics of the Transition Period* (1920) carried this argument to its logical conclusion: capitalism was experiencing a transition 'from an irrational system into a rational organization, from an economy without a subject into an economic subject'.[96]

'In sum', Bukharin concluded, 'the reorganization of finance-capitalist relations of production has followed a path towards universal state-capitalist organization, involving the elimination of the commodity market, the conversion of money into a unit of account, the organization of production on a state-wide scale, and the subordination of the entire "national-economic" mechanism to the goals of international competition; in other words, mainly to war.'[97]

Had either Hilferding or Kautsky indulged in such exuberance, Lenin would have unleashed a storm of angry rhetoric. But he restrained himself during the early war years and congratulated Bukharin for his attacks on Kautsky and for his insistence that

[94] Ibid., p. 23.
[95] N.I. Bukharin, *Ekonomika Perekhodnovo Perioda*, Moscow 1920, pp. 32–3.
[96] Ibid., p. 14.
[97] Ibid., p. 34.

imperialist wars were inevitable.[98] Sharing Engels's view that capitalism had outgrown the classical laws of commodity exchange, Bukharin came to the parallel conclusion that the focus of contradictions had shifted to the international arena: the 'nationalization' of domestic industry had intensified the 'internationalization' of the economic struggle. 'History', Bukharin asserted in *The Economics of the Transition Period*, 'has now placed on the agenda the objective demand that the world economy become more organized. Today the world economic system has *no subject*; instead the system must become the *subject*. It must be transformed into an economic organization that behaves in accordance with a plan. It must become a "teleological unity" and an *organized* system. . . . Imperialism has proven itself incapable of solving this problem, and the military crisis has led to a crisis of the entire system.'[99] Bukharin prided himself on resolving the last difficulty bequeathed by Marx, that of transforming the theory of cyclical crises into one of crisis of the system.

But far from answering the question of how the systemic crisis would alter the classical business cycle, Bukharin simply counterposed an 'organized' domestic economy to the disorganized world economy. His conviction that contradictions could be confined almost exclusively to the international arena led to an ultimate clash with Lenin. In the anti-Narodnik essays Lenin had shown that the rivalry over markets resulted from *internal disproportionalities*. Were the domestic economy to be planned there would be no internal unevenness and therefore no need for wars. Bukharin's arguments were too ambitious. Commenting upon *The Economics of the Transition Period*, Lenin worried that Bukharin had abandoned Marxist dialectics in favour of idealism: 'often, too often, the author falls into a scholasticism of terms . . . and into idealism. . . . This scholasticism and idealism is in contradiction with dialectical materialism (that is, Marxism).'[100]

[98] See Lenin's Introduction to Nikolai Bukharin, *Imperialism and World Economy*, London 1972, pp. 9–14. For a complete survey of Lenin's relations with Bukharin during these years, see Stephen E. Cohen, *Bukharin and the Bolshevik Revolution*, New York 1973, pp. 25–43.

[99] Bukharin, *Ekonomika Perekhodnovo Perioda*, pp. 27–8.

[100] *Leninskii Sbornik*, Moscow 1929, XI, 400.

In the spring of 1919 Bukharin urged Lenin to include in the party's new programme an integral picture of imperialism fashioned after his own writings. Referring to the proposed revision as 'a bookish description of finance capitalism', Lenin retorted that no integral picture was possible, for imperialism was not a 'pure' phenomenon: 'Pure imperialism, without the fundamental basis of [competitive] capitalism, has never existed, does not exist anywhere, and never will exist. This is an incorrect generalization of everything that was said of the syndicates, cartels, trusts and finance capitalism, when finance capitalism was depicted as though it had none of the foundations of the old capitalism underlying it.'[101] From Lenin's point of view, the most essential feature of imperialism was 'not pure monopolies, but monopolies together with exchange, the market, competition and crises'.[102]

Although Lenin and Bukharin disagreed over fundamental issues, both were representatives of what this study will refer to as the 'Hilferding tradition'. This classification will be taken to include all theorists who began their analysis with the concept of finance capital and focused on the changing institutional structure of modern capitalism. Marx had foreseen the socialization of production within the capitalist integument. A perfect monopoly was a 'social' enterprise by definition, in the sense that it controlled the whole of society's means of production within a given branch of industry. For the theorists of the Hilferding tradition, the critical question was whether internal 'socialization' might eventually eliminate the rivalry over surplus-value that Marx viewed as the source of the cyclical dynamic of capitalist society. Bukharin thought 'organized capitalism' might mitigate cyclical movements and create the possibility of capitalist 'stabilization'. Other theorists of the same tradition, most notably Evgeny Preobrazhensky, attempted to build upon the lessons of 1929–33, using Marx's methodology to devise a new theory of monopolistic crises.

The polar antithesis of the Hilferding tradition in Soviet political economy was neo-Luxemburgism. Whereas Hilferding's approach incorporated Marx's theory of the *business cycle*, Luxemburg held that the capitalist system was driven to imperialist expansion by a

---

[101] Lenin, *Collected Works*, XXIX p. 165.
[102] V.I. Lenin, *O Programme Partii*, Moscow 1959, p. 286.

chronic contradiction between production and sales. The Stalinist theory of capitalism's 'general crisis', caused by an allegedly chronic 'problem of markets', broadly corresponded to Luxemburg's viewpoint. Thus by the end of the 1920s Soviet economic discussions polarized along what can be thought of as a Luxemburg-Hilferding divide. Eugen Varga, the leading Soviet authority on the world economy, revived Luxemburg's arguments in order to refute Bukharin's theory of 'organized capitalism'.

The denunciation of Bukharin might have facilitated a recovery of Marxist studies of the business cycle, particularly since the crisis of 1929–33 provided the historical context for a theoretical renaissance. By this time, however, the Stalinist bureaucracy was concerned to justify the Five-Year Plan and forced industrialization. The theory of the 'general crisis' held that no cyclical recovery was possible in the West; the chronic 'problem of markets' must give way to a new period of wars and revolutions, for which the Soviet Union had to be militarily prepared. When a recovery did begin, coinciding with the rise to power of Hitler and Roosevelt, the Stalinists spoke first of a depression 'of a special kind' and later of an expansion 'of a special kind'. By the end of the 1930s the 'special' cycle required a special explanation.

Unable to accept the Bukharinist version of 'organized capitalism', the Stalinists produced their own. Following the Luxemburgist tradition to its necessary conclusion, Varga affirmed that the capitalist state could indeed 'influence and modify the cyclical development of reproduction' by manipulating aggregate demand. For Luxemburg, armament expenditures had served as an artificial instrument of market creation. By tailoring monetary and fiscal policy to peaceful purposes, Varga suggested, the capitalist state could both reduce the likelihood of cyclical crises and alleviate the contradictions giving rise to imperialist wars. Ignoring the question of the internal structure of demand, or the need to preclude interindustrial disproportionalities through a comprehensive plan, Lenin's 'official' successors laid the groundwork for Khrushchev's policy of 'peaceful co-existence'.

2
Early Soviet Assessments of Capitalism

For Russian Marxists the years prior to 1917 were a time of political inactivity, personal frustration, and theoretical ferment. Enforced idleness aggravated personal animosities and splintered the revolutionary movement. With the collapse of the Tsarist autocracy, revolutionary perspectives were radically transformed.Overnight, the 'crash' of capitalism ceased to be a theoretical hypothesis and appeared to become a practical possibility. Once-bitter political rivals—Lenin and Trotsky the foremost among them—were reconciled in the struggle for the proletarian dictatorship. The last issue to concern the Bolsheviks at this juncture was whether capitalism might survive the war to renew its cyclical pattern. Time horizons had shortened, creating a more immediate uncertainty: which would collapse first, the Soviet Republic or the 'capitalist encirclement'?

To every leader of the Bolshevik Party it was clear that survival of the Russian revolution would depend on the triumph of the working class in Europe. For two years the euphoria prevailed, until it finally became obvious that Soviet Russia might be politically and economically isolated for a time. The prospect of isolation imposed the need for a critical reassessment. By 1919 the revolutionary tide had started to recede and capitalism began to give the appearance of flourishing. Hopes for a European revolution now gave way to an effort to extend the 'breathing space', which would ultimately result in the doctrine of socialism in one country. The transition from the revolutionary internationalism of 1917 to Stalin's defiant nationalism of 1925 can be traced and explained in terms of changing Soviet estimates of the fate of capitalism.

From time to time the prospect of a European revolution appeared likely. Late in 1918 the defeat of Germany brought workers out of the trenches and into the streets. Soviet hopes swelled, only to be cruelly deflated by the murder of Rosa Luxemburg and repression of the Communist Party of Germany in January 1919. In the same month Lenin called upon the working class of all countries to join in the formation of a Third (Communist) International. Meeting in March 1919, the Comintern adopted a resounding manifesto written by Trotsky. Ridiculing parliamentary compromises, the manifesto declared that all the achievements of Social Democratic opportunism had been buried in 'blood and muck'.[1] The task of the new International was 'to purge the [working class] movement . . . of opportunism . . . to unify the efforts of all genuinely revolutionary parties . . . and thereby [to] facilitate and hasten the victory of the Communist revolution throughout the world'.[2] If the German workers throw out the capitalists and their Social Democratic allies, Trotsky promised, 'All that is ours will be theirs. Our resources and our grain will be their resources and their grain for the common proletarian revolution.'[3]

A new possibility of a breach in the encirclement appeared with the Bavarian and Hungarian Soviet Republics. When the Bavarian Soviet fell in May 1919, Lenin wrote to Hungarian workers urging them to stand firm in their war against the Entente: 'All honest members of the working class all over the world are on your side. Every month brings the world proletarian revolution nearer. Be firm! Victory will be yours!'[4] But by August the Hungarian Soviet was crushed. Trotsky summoned Russian workers and peasants to accept labour 'mobilization' and 'militarization' in rebuilding the shattered economy. Trotsky's resignation to the likelihood of a period of Soviet isolation came at the very moment that the international horizon began to clear. In January 1920 the Allied Council formally lifted the blockade of Soviet Russia, and in the

[1] Leon Trotsky, *The First Five Years of the Communist International*, Volume 1: New York 1945, Volume 2: London 1953; Volume 1, p. 22.
[2] Ibid., p. 19.
[3] Trotsky, *Kak Vooruzhalas' Revolyutsiya*, 3 volumes, Moscow 1923–5, Volume 1, pp. 372–3.
[4] Lenin, *Selected Works*, III, p. 234.

following month diplomatic relations were established with Estonia. By November Lenin recognized that the period of revolutionary tumult must end; the hope for survival lay in the renewal of normal commercial ties with the capitalist countries. Britain was showing interest in a commercial agreement, causing Lenin to believe that the familiar mechanisms of imperialism were once more at work. The capitalists needed the restoration of Soviet grain exports and access to cheap materials; the Soviet government would therefore lease its resources to whatever brigands would pay the highest price. In the hope that the 'breathing space' would become 'a new and lengthy period of development', Lenin proclaimed that the revolution had 'won the right to . . . international existence in the network of capitalist states'.[5]

In March 1921, as the German Communist Party made another unsuccessful bid for power, the Soviet party met to introduce the New Economic Policy (NEP). The Kronstadt rebellion convinced Lenin of the need to curtail government impositions upon the peasantry and replace grain requisitioning with deliveries of consumer goods, some of which would be imported from the West. Pending a resurgence of the European revolution he urged Western Communists to forget 'the theory of the revolutionary offensive', regroup class forces, and win over workers from Social Democratic influences by leading the daily struggle over wages and taxes.[6] When the Comintern Third Congress assembled in the spring of 1921, Lenin spoke of 'a certain equilibrium, which, although extremely unstable, has nevertheless given rise to a peculiar state of affairs in world politics'.[7] The international revolution had not progressed 'along as straight a line as we had expected'.[8] The implication was obvious: 'We exist in a system of capitalist states.'[9]

1. Divergent Perspectives Among Party Leaders

The fading prospect of a world revolution reawakened earlier

[5] Lenin, *Collected Works*, XXXI, p. 412.
[6] Ibid., XXXII, p. 473.
[7] Ibid., p. 453.
[8] Ibid., p. 480.
[9] Ibid., p. 491.

disagreements within the Bolshevik leadership. For Lenin, accommodation to the new realities of the international situation came relatively easily. The law of uneven development had always implied the possibility of setbacks. The logic of *Imperialism* suggested that the 'weak links'—countries such as Tsarist Russia—would be the first to fall out of the capitalist world economy, just as weak firms had been driven into bankruptcy by classical crises. The complementary implication was that the stronger countries might benefit from an armed redistribution of markets, elimination of their competitors, and the centralization of economic power internationally. Imperialist wars could not be separated from the disproportionalities first analysed in *Capital*. Marx had said that crises 'are violent eruptions which for a time restore the disturbed equilibrium'.[10] In the same sense, Lenin referred to the unstable 'equilibrium' that had arisen by 1921.

Trotsky, on the other hand, had clashed with Lenin over the significance of unevenness even before the revolution. Whereas Lenin granted the possibility that the victory of socialism might occur first in several countries, 'or even in one country alone',[11] Trotsky was convinced that the Russian revolution would inaugurate capitalism's systemic collapse. A more or less simultaneous revolution in all of the leading countries would culminate in a United States of Europe. The disagreement grew out of Trotsky's belief that imperialism had created a *world economy* greater than the sum of its parts, a highly integrated system functioning in accordance with a *world division of labour*. Trotsky's imagery came directly from *The Communist Manifesto*, where Marx had described the historical mission of the bourgeoisie as the breaking down of 'national seclusion and self-sufficiency' and the establishment of 'intercourse in every direction, the universal interdependence of nations'.[12] As a world system, imperialism could not be dismembered piece by piece: a revolution in one country would be felt by all countries. The forces of production had transcended the nation-state; the revolution would complete the process by overcoming the final barriers to trade and capital movements. 'The place

[10] Marx, *Capital* Volume 3, p. 244.
[11] Lenin, *Selected Works*, I, p. 705.
[12] Marx and Engels, *Selected Works* 2 vols., Moscow 1962, I, p. 38.

of the cloistered national state must inevitably be taken by a broad democratic federation of the leading states, with the abolition of all tariff divisions.'[13] When Lenin expressed misgivings about the United States of Europe and pointed to the law of uneven development, Trotsky answered that 'this unevenness is itself extremely uneven. The capitalist levels of England, Austria, Germany, or France are not the same. But as compared with Africa and Asia all these countries represent capitalist "Europe", which has matured for the socialist revolution.'[14]

Were the advent of socialism delayed for one reason or another, Trotsky saw no possibility of a partial, cyclical recovery. On the contrary, imperialist struggles to enlarge 'national' markets would culminate in a state of 'permanent war': European civilization would suffer degeneration and a new barbarism. Either the workers would destroy the old order or imperialism would precariously restore itself 'on the bones of several generations'.[15] Disruption of the integrated imperialist world could have no other consequence than cumulative collapse of the system. The wartime inflation of currencies had already deprived capitalism of its regulating mechanism, leaving warfare as the prevailing mode of economic intercourse. Sharing some aspects of Bukharin's view of finance capital, Trotsky judged that capitalism had become irreversibly militarized:

'The debasement of paper money reflects the general mortal crisis of capitalist commodity circulation. During the decades preceding the war, free competition, as the regulator of production and distribution, had already been thrust aside in the main fields of economic life by the system of trusts and monopolies; during the course of the war the regulating-directing role was torn from the hands of these economic groups and transferred directly into the hands of military-state power . . . all [the] fundamental questions of the world's economic life are not being regulated by free competition, nor by associations of national and international trusts and consortiums, but by the direct application of military force . . .

[13] Trotsky, 'Natsiya i Khozyaistvo', *Nashe Slovo*, no. 135 (9 July 1915).
[14] Trotsky, *Sochineniya*, Moscow 1925–7, III, part 1, pp. 89–90.
[15] Trotsky, *The First Five Years*, I, p. 22.

through this slaughter finance capital has succeeded in completely militarizing not only the state but also itself.'[16]

Whereas Trotsky believed the wartime disintegration of currencies had destroyed the world market and the international division of labour, Bukharin emphasized the internal obstacles to capitalist recovery. In each of the imperialist countries finance capital had mastered the problem of domestic organization to a suicidal degree. According to Bukharin, the war had shattered capitalism's 'dynamic equilibrium'[17]—or the traditional pattern of normal business cycles—replacing it with 'military and semi-military production cycles'.[18] The full resources of each state-capitalist trust had been committed to the war effort with such single-mindedness as to convert the dynamic equilibrium of expanded reproduction into its opposite: *expanded negative reproduction*. Real values had not increased but were merely being displaced by fictitious values in the form of paper currency. By consuming fixed capital and neglecting the replacement of equipment, the imperialists had embarked upon economic development in reverse. 'Thus war is accompanied by a "distorted", regressive, *negative* character in the reproduction process. In each successive production cycle real production becomes narrower instead of expanding. "Development" follows a downward, steadily contracting spiral.'[19] Instead of building on Marx's analysis of the business cycle, Bukharin turned it inside out.

If the war had ended quickly, he conceded, its effects would have been similar to those of a classical crisis, clearing markets, eliminating redundant capital, and creating the conditions for fresh expansion. By destroying the means of production, however, the war had also destroyed the means of exploitation and therewith of further capital accumulation. The 'crash' of capitalism was no longer a matter for dispute, but had become a *questio facti*: 'The concrete state of Europe's economic affairs in 1918–20 clearly demonstrates that the period of disintegration has set in and that there are no symptoms of recovery in the *old* system of productive

<hr />

[16] Ibid.
[17] Bukharin, *Ekonomika Perekhodnovo Perioda*, p. 51.
[18] Ibid., p. 40.
[19] Ibid., p. 39.

relations . . . all the hard evidence points to the fact that the elements of dissolution and revolutionary breakdown are advancing with each month.'[20] On these grounds Bukharin announced that 'a restoration of the old capitalist system is definitely not possible. . . . Humanity is therefore confronted by a stark alternative: either the "destruction of culture"—or communism. There is no third possibility'.[21]

In the early months of the revolution Bukharin had proposed to accelerate capitalism's dissolution by launching a 'revolutionary war'. Both on that occasion and in his reading of *The Economics of the Transition Period* Lenin treated Bukharin's predictions with the usual scepticism. The 'impossibility' of reconstruction, he commented, could not be proven 'theoretically' but only in practice. In the margin of Bukharin's text he wrote, '*qui prouve trop* [*ne prouve rien*]'.[22] Bukharin had failed to 'pose the relation between theory and practice dialectically'.[23] He had not seen that further revolutionary advance would depend upon the success of Communist parties in adapting their tactics to changing circumstances. In July 1920 Lenin told the Comintern Second Congress that it was an 'error' to declare that capitalism's recovery was 'absolutely impossible'. The war had not inflicted equal damage on all countries; despite their present difficulties, the strength of America, Britain, and Japan remained considerable. A dialectical interpretation of the transition period did not include predictions of automatic collapse:

'There is no such thing as an absolutely hopeless situation. The bourgeoisie are behaving like barefaced plunderers who have lost their heads; they are committing folly after folly, thus aggravating the situation and hastening their doom. All that is true. But nobody can "prove" that it is absolutely impossible for them to pacify a minority of the exploited with some petty concessions. . . . To try to "prove" in advance that there is "absolutely" no way out of the situation would be sheer pedantry, or playing with concepts and catchwords. Practice alone can serve as real "proof" in this and similar questions.'[24]

[20] Ibid., p. 46.
[21] Ibid., p. 50.
[22] *Leninskii Sbornik*, XI, p. 362.
[23] Ibid., p. 357.
[24] Lenin, *Collected Works*, XXXI, p. 227.

However harsh Lenin's criticism may have been, Bukharin and Trotsky were not alone in their dismal appraisal of Europe's future. In 1919 John Maynard Keynes, a British Treasury representative at the Paris conference, published his sensational book, *The Economic Consequences of the Peace*. Keynes agonized over the possibility that the peace settlement with Germany would perpetuate the structural imbalances caused by the war. Europe had lost important export markets without which it would be unable to sustain prewar imports of food and materials. The recovery of internal European trade would similarly be impaired by Clemenceau's determination to impose what Keynes called a 'Carthaginian Peace'. Through his demand for exorbitant reparations the French leader was committing 'one of the most outrageous acts of a cruel victor in civilized history'[25] and would 'sow the decay of the whole civilized life of Europe'.[26] Motivated by 'imbecile greed', the peace would ruin Germany and subject the whole continent to an intolerable burden. The statesmen of Paris were undermining the capitalist order with as much inevitability as 'the bloodthirsty philosophers of Russia',[27] whose 'malady of the mind' could easily infect Central Europe:

'As I write', warned Keynes, 'the flames of Russian Bolshevism seem, for the moment at least, to have burnt themselves out, and the peoples of Central and Eastern Europe are held in a dreadful torpor. The lately gathered harvest keeps off the worst privations, and peace has been declared at Paris. But winter approaches . . . [and] who can say how much is endurable, or in what direction men will seek at last to escape from their misfortunes?'[28]

The forecasts of Bukharin, Trotsky, and Keynes appeared to be confirmed by the world economic crisis of 1920–21. Throughout 1919 the transition to peacetime production had gone surprisingly smoothly in the victor countries. By the spring of 1919 boom conditions prevailed, and during the following year British prices leaped upwards by nearly fifty per cent. Demand had accumulated during the war, and in many industries fixed capital had to be repaired and replaced as material inventories were rebuilt. In

[25] John Maynard Keynes, *The Economic Consequences of the Peace*, New York 1971, p. 168.

[26] Ibid., p. 225.

[27] Ibid., p. 238.

[28] Ibid., p. 251.

France price increases were dramatic as reconstruction began with the help of currency expansion and short-term borrowing to be repaid out of German reparations. But early in 1920 Japan encountered difficulties that rapidly spread to America and Europe. Retailers and processors, having acquired commodities and materials at high prices, now cancelled orders and waited for markets to clear. In America the slackening of European demand for food and war materials aggravated the problem of inventory accumulation. Agricultural incomes fell, industrial wages followed, and millions of workers were unemployed. Shipping, steel, textiles, and coal—all the key industries on both sides of the Atlantic were eventually driven into the crisis. Did the latest setback confirm the theory of systemic crisis, or was it merely a cyclical downturn and therefore a prelude to prosperity? In the effort to answer these questions Soviet views of the postwar world underwent a gradual revision.

The first sign of a more consistent effort to apply the approach of Marx's *Capital* came in the summer of 1921 with Trotsky's address to the Comintern Third Congress. The fact that capitalism possessed sufficient reserves to sustain an economic boom in 1919 suggested to Trotsky that Lenin had been right in disputing Bukharin's theory of unilinear collapse through *expanded negative reproduction*. Acknowledging the restoration of capitalism's cyclical dynamic, Trotsky now adopted a position mid-way between Lenin and Bukharin. His analysis turned on the concept of *equilibrium*. 'Capitalist equilibrium', he told the delegates, 'is an extremely complex phenomenon. Capitalism produces this equilibrium, disrupts it, restores it anew in order to disrupt it anew, concurrently extending the limits of its domination. . . . Capitalism thus possesses a dynamic equilibrium, one which is always in the process of either disruption or restoration. But at the same time, this equilibrium has a great power of resistance, the best proof of which is the fact that the capitalist world has not toppled to this day.'[29]

Trotsky's use of the term 'dynamic equilibrium', a concept borrowed from Bukharin and foreign to *Capital*, was careless and misleading. What sort of 'equilibrium' was it that was 'always in the

[29] Trotsky, *The First Five Years*, I, p. 174.

process of disruption or restoration'? In an attempt to clarify his meaning Trotsky differentiated between the long and short run, or between equilibrium in *secular* and in *cyclical* terms. Arguing that some form of cyclical equilibrium was definitely being restored, he warned against the assumption that 'we are . . . dealing with a corpse. So long as capitalism is not overthrown by the proletarian revolution, it will continue to live in cycles, swinging up and down. Crises and booms were inherent in capitalism at its very birth; they will accompany it to its grave.'[30] The real problem was to replace the previous assumption of unilinear collapse with a more concrete analysis of how close the grave might be: in other words, to 'determine the general conditions of the capitalist organism by [measuring] . . . the rate at which its pulse [the business cycle] beats'.[31]

For this purpose Trotsky referred to a table published in *The Times* (London). The table indicated that the pattern of the business cycle had not been uniform throughout capitalism's history but varied in accordance with different periods of capitalist development. 'In periods of rapid capitalist development the crises are brief and superficial . . ., while the booms are long-lasting and far-reaching. In periods of capitalist decline the crises are . . . prolonged . . . while the booms are fleeting, superficial, and speculative. In periods of stagnation the fluctuations occur upon one and the same level.'[32] To plot the cycles, which averaged between 8 2/3 and 9 years, would reveal a secular path of development with several distinct turning points. Up to the mid nineteenth century capitalism had expanded gradually; the revolution of 1848 inaugurated an interval of rapid growth, lasting until 1873; from 1873 to 1894 a period of depression prevailed; from 1894 to the eve of the war a sustained boom took hold. 'Then, finally, with the year 1914, . . . the period of the destruction of capitalist economy [begins]'.[33] In coming years a succession of weak recoveries and protracted setbacks would create a new pattern. The return to an unstable, cyclical equilibrium would signify the lack of

[30] Ibid., p. 200.
[31] Ibid., p. 202.
[32] Ibid., pp. 201–2.
[33] Ibid., p. 201.

secular equilibrium and a downturn in the aggregate 'curve of capitalist development'.

However confusing his terminology, Trotsky had defined a critical problem. Business cycles could not be considered in the abstract but had to be related to the distinctive stages of capitalist development. With this speech Trotsky effectively broke off his relationship with Bukharin. In October 1922, he recalled the event, commenting that his reassessment of the crisis of 1920–21 caused 'a flurry in our own ranks' during which 'N.I. Bukharin . . . vehemently rose up in arms against me'.[34] But the break with Bukharin did not yet signify a complete reconciliation with Lenin, or with the view that some countries might actually gain from the war. For Trotsky it seemed that all countries would suffer a period of historical regression. The differences between the imperialists would be *evened out in reverse*, this process supplanting uneven development. The cause of this new period of systemic contraction and irregular cycles would be chaos in international trade, along the lines suggested by Keynes. The war had 'severed' the world economy 'at its roots'.[35] Returning to his original emphasis on the world division of labour, Trotsky pointed out that America suffered from 'plethora', Europe from 'anemia'. From 1914 to 1918 Europe had been scorched by 'a sheet of fire . . . while the American bourgeoisie warmed its hands at the flames. America's productive capacity has grown extraordinarily, but her market has vanished because Europe is impoverished and can no longer buy American goods.'[36] America would now experience delayed retribution in the form of 'a prolonged epoch of depression'.[37]

In Europe the outlook was no better. Unable to unblock domestic bottlenecks by relying on imports, the European countries would have to live with chronic scarcities of key commodities. The European economy would 'have to level . . . out in accordance with the most backward, i.e., the most ruined areas and branches of industry. This will mean an economic levelling out in reverse, and consequently a prolonged crisis: in some branches of economy and

[34] Ibid., II, 198.
[35] Ibid., I, 180.
[36] Ibid., p. 196.
[37] Ibid., p. 206.

some countries—stagnation; in others—a weak development. Cyclical fluctuations will continue to take place, but in general the curve of capitalist development will not slope upwards but downwards.'[38] If the revolution were postponed another fifteen or twenty-five years, a new long-run equilibrium might be established. But in the meantime Europe would be 'thrown violently into reverse gear'. Millions of workers would perish 'from unemployment and malnutrition'.[39] An inevitable exacerbation of class contradictions would inaugurate the proletarian revolution long before a new secular equilibrium could materialize. At most, restoration of the business cycle would put off the day of capitalism's final reckoning.

2. The Bourgeois Professors Intervene

Trotsky's address to the Comintern in the summer of 1921 revised the revolutionary timetable without exaggerating the turn for the better in the West. A first attempt to apply Marx's theory of the business cycle to the postwar period, it erected a new framework for discussion over the next several years. But because of the ambiguities in Trotsky's reasoning, his analysis could easily be faulted. Having shown that the rate of capitalist expansion varied over the course of history, he had predicted a period of general stagnation. A perceptive critic might well inquire how and why stagnation would necessitate an eventual revolution. Had not Engels himself lived through just such a period of stagnation after 1873, arguing at that time that capitalism would never surmount its chronic depression? And had not that period been followed by sustained economic expansion from 1894 to 1914? Even if a new period of stagnation were at hand, where was the evidence that decades of renewed expansion might not ensue once again? These were the questions raised by Professor N.D. Kondrat'ev.

In his book *Soviet Economists of the Twenties*, Naum Jasny described Kondrat'ev as a 'brilliant' economist, a student of Tugan-Baranovsky, whom Jasny considered the 'greatest Russian economist of all time'.[40] Soviet Marxists' appraisal of both Kondrat'ev and

---

[38] Ibid., pp. 206–7.
[39] Ibid., p. 211.
[40] Naum Jasny, *Soviet Economists of the Twenties*, London 1972, p. 159.

his mentor was less enthusiastic. Tugan had served as a minister in the separatist government of the Ukraine during the civil war, having long before annoyed Marxists of all shades with his interpretation of *Capital*. He had contended that the entire working class might be displaced by machinery, but so long as proportionality were maintained in the market there could be no crises. Such an extreme view was unacceptable even to Lenin, who emphasized that 'a certain state of consumption is one of the elements of proportionality'.[41] The Bolsheviks would later find Kondrat'ev no less objectionable than Tugan. During the early years of the new government, however, Trotsky and Lenin both believed it imperative to draw upon the expertise of bourgeois 'specialists', to harness them to the service of the proletariat. Kondrat'ev worked in the Soviet government for an entire decade as a financial and agricultural adviser. But as a theorist of business cycles he provoked immediate distrust.

The antagonism flared up with publication of his book *The World Economy and Its Conjunctures*. 'Lost' by its Soviet publisher in 1921, the manuscript had to be rewritten from notes and was published in 1922. Kondrat'ev believed that the objective consequence of every business cycle was to restore equilibrium:

'In its most general form the essence of an economic crisis lies in the fact *that the national economies of separate countries and the world economy as a whole, taken as a moving system of elements, loses its equilibrium and experiences an acute, painful process of transition to the condition of a new moving equilibrium.* From the economic point of view, a crisis is always only an acute and painful process of liquidating the disparities that have arisen in the structure of a national economy and are destroying the equilibrium of its elements. [A crisis] is the process of establishing a new equilibrium among those elements in place of the one that has broken down.'[42]

Had Kondrat'ev set out with the deliberate intention of sowing confusion he could hardly have been more successful. Not only did he foresee more favourable prospects for capitalism than Trotsky had done, but he also buttressed his interpretation with a more

[41] Lenin, *Collected Works*, IV, 161.
[42] N.D. Kondrat'ev, *Mirovoe Khozyaistvo i evo Kon'yunktury vo Vremya i Posle Voiny*, Vologda 1922, p. 191.

exact usage of Trotsky's terminology, while invoking similar evidence of international disproportionalities. Although they drew conflicting conclusions, he and Trotsky often appeared to be saying the same thing. Kondrat'ev held that the loss of European productive capacity during the war had been compensated by gains in America and other countries. In 1919, when Europe set out to replace its losses, a crisis necessarily erupted: 'the intensification of the struggle over markets must be given particular emphasis: it is extremely important in explaining the essence and character of the crisis in the world economy that began in 1920'.[43] But Kondrat'ev's *tour de force* was his theory of *long waves*. By denying that capitalism's long-run equilibrium had been restored, Trotsky had kept alive the hope of systemic crisis. Kondrat'ev challenged this conclusion by taking the Comintern report one step further and reinterpreting the very same historical data.

Kondrat'ev believed that the movement of capitalism entailed not one cycle but two: a short cycle of approximately ten-year periods and a longer wave lasting up to fifty years or more. The long waves were divided into rising and falling moments, succeeding one another in an unbroken sequence and determining the peculiar pattern of uneven growth that Trotsky had discussed in terms of the Marxist thesis of distinct historical periods. According to Kondrat'ev, these were not separate periods at all; they were merely components of a broader pattern of historical continuity—or of a *systemic moving equilibrium*. Since 1789 two long cycles had already been completed. The years 1789 to 1809 saw a long wave of expansion, followed by a wave of slower growth between 1809 and 1849. In 1849 a new cycle began with an expanding wave that lasted until 1873 and then gave way to a slowdown until 1896. The expanding wave of the third long cycle began in 1896 and had continued until 1920.[44]

The theory of long waves at once affirmed that capitalism's 'moving equilibrium' remained intact and discounted the Marxist hope for systemic disintegration. A period of stagnation might indeed lie ahead, but it would be stagnation only in relation to an underlying and unbroken historical trend. In other words, a

[43] Ibid., p. 104.
[44] Ibid., pp. 242–3.

succession of lethargic ten-year cycles would represent nothing more than the fall to the trough of the third long wave; in no way would a change in the rate of growth denote impending collapse. As for further revolutions, they were most improbable. Social unrest occurred in times of economic turmoil. By restoring capitalism's moving equilibrium the crisis of 1920 would bring about 'a gradual reduction of the symptoms of shock and crisis'.[45] Kondrat'ev did not deny that the postwar crisis had been more severe than its immediate predecessors; he merely added that 'the cyclical movement of the conjuncture did not begin here, and there is no reason to suggest that it will end here'.[46] His entire analysis leaned towards undisguised optimism:

'Thanks to the crisis, thanks to the return of a relative correspondence between the level of prices and the purchasing power of the masses, between the supply of capital and the demand for it, between the productive capacity of the separate economic branches and the volume of the demands they make upon the commodities of other branches, the existing system, to a significant degree and for a certain period of time, will free itself of the disharmonies and lack of correspondence that are causing the crisis. . . . The world economic crisis, taking place on the basis of wartime exhaustion, was particularly severe, but it is ending and being left behind. . . . It was merely one link, admittedly a complex one, in the ongoing course of the postwar conjuncture.'[47]

Before Trotsky and Kondrat'ev could disentangle their respective positions both would have to clarify their use of the concept 'equilibrium'. In *Capital* Marx had avoided reference to a moving (or dynamic) equilibrium, speaking instead of proportionate growth that 'springs as a continual process from disproportionality'.[48] In the Soviet context, reference to moving equilibrium originated with Bukharin and would remain a source of confusion until the mid-1920s. In the meantime, Kondrat'ev's critics denounced the political implications of his theory. In the words of one author, Kondrat'ev had produced 'political contraband of an arch-

[45] Ibid., p. 240.
[46] Ibid., p. 254.
[47] Ibid., p. 241.
[48] Marx, *Capital* III, p. 251.

reactionary character' that implied 'super-optimistic' prospects for capitalism.[49]

If Kondrat'ev served as Trotsky's nemesis in these early debates, much the same could be said of Professor S.A. Fal'kner's relation to Bukharin. Fal'kner's career resembled Kondrat'ev's during the 1920s, leading him from a position in the Commissariat of Foreign Trade in 1920 to a post in the world-economy section of Gosplan (the State Planning Commission) in the closing years of the decade. A classical 'fellow-traveller', Fal'kner sympathized with Marxism but considered Marxists narrow-minded and intolerant. Narrow-mindedness, in Fal'kner's view, meant disagreement with bourgeois 'specialists' endeavouring to restrain Bolshevik excesses. In March 1921 Fal'kner reviewed Bukharin's *Economics of the Transition Period*. Singling out the same weakness Lenin had detected, he argued that 'statification' was merely a passing consequence of the war. A curtailment of state intervention after 1918 proved that 'the most centralized processes of the war period everywhere and always came into effect against the will of the bourgeoisie'.[50] The greatest 'distinction' of Bukharin's book appeared to be its extraordinary misjudgement of the entire nature of modern capitalist organization.

After criticizing Bukharin's 'state-capitalist trusts', Fal'kner challenged the claim that warfare had become the new mode of international competition. If wars had become cyclical, he inquired, how could Bukharin be so certain that the proletarian revolution would come after the *first* world war? Why not after the second, or the third? Indeed, there was no more reason to think that war would lead automatically to revolution than to argue that every crisis must lead to the expropriation of capital. By predicating revolution upon recurrent cycles of warfare, Bukharin would even defeat his own purpose. The 'cost' of social change would appear so great as to discourage the workers from daring to challenge the existing order. Abject surrender in the class struggle would become preferable to a revolution that would depend upon the slaughter of millions.

---

[49] M. Bronsky, 'Obzor Literatury po Mirovomu Khozyaistvu', *Vestnik Sotsialisticheskoi Akademii*, no. 2 (January 1923), p. 215.

[50] S.A. Fal'kner, 'Teoreticheskaya Ekonomika Sotsial'noi Revolyutsii', *Nauchnye Izvestiya: Sbornik Pervyi*, Moscow 1922, pp. 236–7.

Fal'kner held that Bukharin had been irrationally impressed by the events of 1914–18. 'The development of ideology', he remarked, 'always tends to lag behind the evolution of reality.'[51] Lacking any technical merit, Bukharin's arguments served a sole purpose; they offered 'a profound documentation of the psychology and teleology of the epoch in which we live'.[52] There was an obvious element of truth in this observation, although it would not endear Fal'kner to Bukharin or his supporters.

Fal'kner was equally unimpressed by Bolshevik writing on questions of a more strictly economic character. In particular he believed that colonies were of little benefit to metropolitan countries, an argument that prompted one of his own reviewers to write that 'Fal'kner believes, like Kautsky and others, that in their struggle to acquire colonies the capitalists misunderstand their own interests'.[53] In effect, Fal'kner rejected Marxist theories of imperialism, holding that the volume of trade in colonial markets was insignificant compared with domestic consumption in the capitalist countries. The search for the cause of crises had to begin here, and not with the struggle over world markets that figured so prominently in Bukharin's thought. Although critical of Kondrat'ev's work as well, Fal'kner agreed with the latter on one important point: there was nothing unique about capitalism's postwar crisis. Whereas Kondrat'ev upheld this argument by submerging the events of 1920–21 in the long wave, Fal'kner attributed capitalism's continuity to the persistence of the 'iron law of wages'. The most recent crisis, like its predecessors, had resulted from chronic underconsumption. Prior to 1913 inflation had eroded working-class incomes, thus creating the conditions for a crisis. The war had intervened, postponing contradictions for several years. Exacerbated by its delay, the postwar crisis was otherwise perfectly typical and would be followed by an equally typical recovery.

Fal'kner presented this analysis in *The Postwar Conjuncture of the World Economy*, written early in 1921. His next book, *The Turning Point in the World Industrial Crisis* (1922), proudly documented the revival of economic activity in the West. Party writers who had

[51] Ibid., p. 241.
[52] Ibid., p. 247.
[53] S. Chlenov, in *Narodnoe Khozyaistvo*, no. 3 (March 1921), p. 221.

expected total economic collapse were now treated to a lecture on the 'dynamic' and 'universal' tendencies of the business cycle. Unable to deny the quarrelsome professor the gratification of having issued a sound prediction, his critics pounced upon his spurious theoretical premises and charged him with holding a 'vulgar' underconsumptionist theory of crises and with ignoring the achievements of political economy 'during the past hundred years'.[54] As an economic theorist Fal'kner was never so formidable an adversary as Kondrat'ev. Until a new generation of Marxist economists could emerge, however, he did manage to intimidate most opponents, enliven the literature, . . . and commit the indiscretions that would ultimately contribute to his downfall. The only Marxist economist who offered a serious alternative to the 'counter-revolutionary' prognostications of the 'bourgeois professors' during the 1920s proved to be Eugen Varga.

3. Eugen Varga on the Postwar Cycle

A former professor of economics in Budapest, Varga possessed the training and knowledge of European affairs needed to add substance and a measure of respectability to Comintern pronouncements. During the brief lifespan of the Hungarian Soviet Republic he had served as chairman of the Supreme Economic Council and Finance Commissar. When the Republic fell he fled to Austria and thence to Moscow, where he soon acquired prominence as an expert on the world economy. In 1921 he worked closely with Trotsky, preparing the theses for the Comintern Third Congress. Until the mid-1920s he informally organized Soviet studies of international economics, thereafter becoming a member of the Communist Academy and director of its Institute of World Economics and World Politics. Varga held this post for the next two decades, then fell out with Stalin after the Second World War, only to return to favour under Khrushchev and establish a record of longevity in Soviet public affairs matched by few contemporaries.

Less imaginative than Trotsky or Kondrat'ev, Varga avoided theoretical innovations and strove to fit recent developments into

[54] Bronsky, 'Obzor Literatury . . .', *Vestnik Sotsialisticheskoi Akademii*, no. 3 (February-March 1923), p. 288.

the established Marxist categories. In Central Europe he saw many of the same phenomena as Bukharin: the discrepancy between financial and real values, the obstacles to renewed capital accumulation, and the crippling effects of shortages of vital commodities, especially food and fuel. But Varga also emphasized that Britain and America belonged to an entirely different group of countries, in which finance capital had survived the war more or less intact. Applying Hilferding's ideas to these two countries, he cautioned against hasty generalizations.

Bukharin had interpreted Hilferding's work in terms of expanded negative reproduction, the self-negation of finance capital. Varga concentrated instead on modern capitalism's capacity for self-protection. Although Britain was experiencing 'the gravest crisis' in history,[55] it was nevertheless dangerous to exaggerate the severity of recent events. Transition from the 'free capitalism' of Marx to the 'organized' capitalism of Hilferding[56] enabled finance capital to shift the burden of adjustment onto the shoulders of the working class more directly than ever. As Varga explained:

'There can be seen a general tendency of "organized" capital to regulate the partial overproduction arising from the anarchy of production by a very simple means—by stopping production. . . . The crises of competitive capitalism, as Marx described them, injured capital itself; they were onerous but comparatively brief. The crises of contemporary . . . capitalism involve no bloodshed on the part of the capitalists. The whole burden of the crisis comes down on the proletariat in the form of protracted complete or partial unemployment.'[57]

The new tactics of organized capitalism generated contradictory results: crises were lengthened, the number of unemployed would grow, and the greater suffering of the working class would merely testify to the stability of finance capital. American and British industrialists were *deliberately* intensifying unemployment in order to lower wages and enhance their competitive position in world

---

[55] E. Varga, 'Angliya', *Narodnoe Khozyaistvo*, no. 5 (May 1921), p. 812.

[56] Varga, 'Linii Razvitiya i Upadka Kapitalisticheskovo Khozyaistva', *Narodnoe Khozyaistvo* (December 1920), p. 76.

[57] Varga, 'Ekonomicheskoe Polozhenie Anglii', *Narodnoe Khozyaistvo* (November 1920), p. 78.

markets.[58] And how would this new form of cyclical crisis affect the capitalists? Varga predicted that 'the colossal organizations of American capital' would emerge unscathed for the most part.[59] 'The amalgamation of enterprises in enormous trusts and their nearly total subordination to large banking combinations have caused such a close integration that the loss of even a single member is impossible without bringing down the entire structure.'[60]

Like Trotsky, Varga believed it was the instability of world markets, or the world distribution of income, that posed the greatest threat to capitalism's survival. Widespread currency depreciation had transformed international trade into little more than specu-lation, tariff barriers had proliferated as a result of the national self-determination proclaimed at Versailles, and the previously in-tegrated international economy had fragmented into separate components facing contradictory problems. In Britain and the neutral countries of northern Europe commodities were overflow-ing warehouses for want of markets; in Germany, Poland, Austria, and Hungary recovery was being frustrated for want of the most essential types of capital and consumer goods. 'Relative over-production' in the first group of countries reflected the loss of demand, or 'absolute underproduction', in the second.[61]

The division of labour had been destroyed not only within Europe but also between Europe and the colonies. Britain had been unable to supply her dependencies with manufactured products during the war. Canada, Australia, New Zealand, and South Africa had been compelled either to develop their own industries or to turn to America for substitutes. Although America now stood at the centre of a vastly reduced volume of international trade, her difficulties were similar to Britain's. American industrial and agricultural capacity had swollen to meet the needs of the Entente war machine. Now the problem was to extract the resulting profits and transform paper debt obligations into real values. The transfer

[58] Varga, 'Ekonomicheskoe Polozhenie Severo-Amerikanskikh Soedinennykh Shtatov', *Narodnoe Khozyaistvo*, no. 3 (March 1921), pp. 169–70.

[59] Varga, 'Ekonomicheskii Bazis Imperializma Soedinennykh Shtatov Severnoi Ameriki', *Kommunisticheskii Internatsional*, no. 17 (7 June 1921), p. 4113.

[60] Varga, *Krizis Mirovovo Kapitalizma*, Moscow 1921, p. 24.

[61] Ibid., pp. 28–9.

could occur in one of two ways: either America could assume ownership of Europe, or Europe could send a return flow of commodities back to America. Harding's election to the presidency indicated that American capital was bent on isolating itself from European intrigues and repatriating its assets. Even if Europe were able to supply a return flow of real values, the inevitable consequence would be to create still greater 'relative overproduction' in the already glutted American market.

America's relationship to Europe paralleled the victorious Entente's to Germany. In both cases payments were being demanded on the one hand, while the means of making such payments were denied on the other. Only one solution was conceivable: America would have to follow Keynes's advice, foregoing collection of the war debts and permitting the Entente to abandon its claims against Germany. This would be but a first step. The Americans would then have to place substantial new credits at Europe's disposal. 'The wisest of capitalism's defenders', Varga wrote, 'see . . . that although the restoration of the world economy is in general possible on the basis of capitalism, this will occur only when the redundant means of production on hand in the United States are put at the disposal of ravaged Central Europe, and when the mad idea of restoring the economic life of France, Belgium, and Italy at the cost of Germany is set aside. However, every effort in this direction has proven a failure.'[62]

America was unwilling to cancel Europe's obligations because of the extraordinary political leverage they provided. Varga detected the seeds of the next imperialist war buried in the tangle of financial commitments. France was menacing Germany over reparations; the Anglo-Saxons were making ready to resolve their own differences through another trial of strength.[63] Should a second imperialist war break out so soon after the first, its result would be 'the destruction of capitalism throughout the entire world'.[64]

Separating the national from the international aspects of the postwar crisis, Varga played an important part in bridging the gap

[62] Ibid., p. 43.
[63] Varga, 'Ekonomicheskoe Polozhenie Severo-Amerikanskikh Soedinennykh Shtatov', pp. 177–80.
[64] Varga, *Krizis Mirovovo Kapitalizma*, p. 47.

between Lenin and Trotsky. He interpreted recent events as being *cyclical* in nature, thereby supporting Lenin's view that at least some countries would, as Varga put it, see 'better days';[65] he also agreed with Trotsky that the outstanding threat to contemporary capitalism lay in the disintegration of the *world economy*. Within a somewhat eclectic general analysis he incorporated elements of Hilferding's thought together with an essentially Luxemburgist view of the long-run problem of markets. In every previous crisis capitalism was said to have reacted successfully by adopting new technology with which to lower costs and penetrate foreign markets. But this avenue was no longer open: in 1914 capitalism had reached 'the limits of the available world market'.[66] To create new markets in India or China would require decades, and the capitalists had no such time at their disposal. By accentuating domestic unemployment they were undermining the labour aristocracy, provoking working-class resistance, and interfering with a normal cyclical recovery. Varga saw no reason to revise the outlook Engels had sketched more than twenty-five years earlier. Paraphrasing Engels's notes in *Capital*, he predicted: 'the intensive crisis will assume a chronic character and will be only briefly interrupted from time to time by weak improvements in the economic curve'.[67]

To illustrate his thesis Varga could point to the miners' strike in Britain. In April 1921 British coal companies locked out their employees in an effort to reduce wages and regain export markets. The miners resolved to fight to the finish. Railway and transport workers rejected a sympathy strike, but Belgian miners and dockers refused to load coal destined for Britain. The country's industry headed towards standstill. Four million workers were either unemployed, on strike, or working short hours. The class struggle, Varga reported, was becoming 'ever broader and more acute'. Unemployment was assuming 'a magnitude probably without precedent in the history of capitalism'.[68] Even *The Economist* described 1921 as 'one of the worst years of depression since the

[65] E. Varga and A. Lozovsky, *Mirovoi Krizis—Zadachi i Taktika Profsoyuzov*, Moscow 1921, p. 5.
[66] Ibid., pp. 10–11.
[67] Ibid., p. 5.
[68] Varga, 'Angliya', p. 180.

industrial revolution'. When the strike ended in defeat, Varga applauded the struggle as 'the most grandiose movement' in the history of the working class. Betrayal by trade-union leaders did not detract from a heroic precedent. 'With a few more such victories, English capital will perish.'[69]

Organized capital in America was mounting a similar offensive against the workers, aided by Samuel Gompers and other 'aristocrats' who considered themselves above the class struggle. The longer America refused to participate in restoring European markets, the more intensive would industrial conflicts become. The crisis had already taken on '*a permanent character, and one can speak only of a progressive deterioration, not of an improved situation*'.[70] In Germany another variant of the same process was under way, the country experiencing a bacchanalia of inflation, in an effort to stimulate exports by depreciating the international value of its currency. In reality, the decline in the exchange rate would merely ensure a unilateral exodus of real values, thereby preventing any renewal of capital accumulation. There was no sense, Varga concluded, 'in talking either of the reconstruction of equilibrium in the world economy or even of the signs of such an equilibrium'.[71] Both the capitalists and such Bolshevik sympathizers as Professor Fal'kner were being carried away by marginal improvements. On the central issue, Trotsky had been correct. The 'immanent', self-regulating mechanism of the market economy could never close the abyss between Europe and America. That would require 'conscious' leadership in the form of an international plan.[72] The policies currently applied would simply erect new obstacles to trade.

4. From the Crisis of 1920–1921 to the Genoa Conference

By 1920–21 Soviet economists and political leaders (with the

[69] Varga, 'Angliya', *Narodnoe Khozyaistvo*, no. 6–7 (June–July 1921), p. 228.

[70] Varga, 'S-Amer. Soed. Shtaty. Khozyaistvennoe Polozhenie v Pervoi Polovine 1921g.', *Narodnoe Khozyaistvo*, no. 8–9 (August-September 1921), p. 209.

[71] Varga, 'Polozhenie Mirovovo Khozyaistva i Khod Ekonomicheskoi Politiki za Poslednie Tri Goda', *Narodnoe Khozyaistvo*, no. 3 (March 1922), p. 6.

[72] Ibid., p. 10.

exception of Bukharin) generally agreed that the chief threat to capitalism lay in the disintegration of international trade. A corollary of this view appeared to be that capitalism's plight could be converted into a Soviet advantage. Keynes had written, 'If trade is not resumed with Russia, wheat in 1920–21 . . . must be scarce and very dear . . . we are blockading not so much Russia as ourselves.'[73] An increase in the productivity of the Soviet peasant, Keynes added, would require the import of technology and consumer goods, which could best be managed 'through the agency of German enterprise and organization'.[74] 'It is in our own interest', he concluded, 'to hasten the day when German agents and organizers will be in a position to set in train in every Russian village the impulse of ordinary economic motive. This is a process quite independent of the governing authority in Russia.'[75] Clearly delighted with the suggestion that political differences need not interfere with trade, Lenin had adopted the same attitude in December 1920:

'Germany cannot exist from the economic standpoint following the peace of Versailles; neither can all the defeated countries, such as Austria-Hungary. . . . These countries form, in Central Europe, a vast group with enormous economic and technical might. . . . [But] for the world economy to be restored, Russian raw materials must be utilized. [It is impossible to] get along without them—that is economically true. It is admitted even by a bourgeois of the first water, a student of economics, who regards things from a purely bourgeois standpoint. That man is Keynes.'[76]

In the spring of 1921 a commercial agreement was concluded between Britain and Soviet Russia. A year later the Soviet government was represented at the Genoa conference, a first international attempt to co-ordinate Europe's postwar reconstruction. All signs suggested that Soviet Russia's reintegration with Europe was inevitable. The capitalists needed food and materials: let them assist in reactivating the Soviet factories and mines laid idle during the civil war and allied intervention. European industrialists

[73] Keynes, *Economic Consequences*, pp. 292–3.
[74] Ibid., p. 293.
[75] Ibid., p. 294.
[76] Lenin, *Collected Works*, XXXI, p. 450–51.

needed markets: let them provide the Soviet government with a loan and see how quickly orders would be placed. L.B. Krasin, who had negotiated the agreement with Britain, believed European goods would pour into Russia once the obstacles were removed. In September 1921 he wrote:

'There are now in France, England, and America hundreds of thousands of automobiles, hundreds of thousands of tractors, and all sorts of transportation machinery, locomotives, tools, scientific instruments, supplies of iron, steel, etc., for which there is no outlet at all . . . the idea has begun to work itself into the minds of the most far-sighted capitalist leaders that without an economic reconstruction of Russia, there is no possibility of attaining a healthy circulation of the blood of this great world economic organization.'[77]

Grigory Sokol'nikov, commissar of finance and a leading exponent of Russia's return to the world economy, agreed with Krassin. The 'common wail' of the German bourgeoisie, he reported, was: 'Our salvation lies in Russia.'[78] Capitalism was not experiencing any kind of recovery and 'cannot manage without us'.[79]

Although Varga and Trotsky had helped encourage the view that a *modus vivendi* with Russia would be in the capitalists' interest, neither shared the current enthusiasm. On the eve of the Genoa conference Varga observed that the capitalists 'will not be able to resist the necessity of restoring the Russian market by means of credit. But they will do so on such a modest level as to have no significance in terms of restoring the equilibrium of the world economy'.[80] Trotsky thought European capital would look after its own needs before contemplating assistance to revolutionary Russia. Genoa would provide Soviet workers and peasants no respite unless several demands were met, including removal of the Comintern headquarters from Russian territory, forfeiture of oil supplies in the Caucasus, and the disbanding of the Red Army. Renewed military

[77] Lyubov Krassin, *Leonid Krassin, His Life and Works*, London n.d., pp. 180-81.
[78] *Pravda*, 4 December 1921.
[79] *Vserossiiskaya Konferentsiya R.K.P. (B): Byulleten'*, no. 5, p. 37.
[80] Varga, 'Polozhenie Mirovovo Khozyaistva i Khod Ekonomicheskoi Politiki . . .', p. 18.

intervention was a distinct possibility unless the Soviet government surrendered on all these issues.[81] In the event, Europe's demands were not quite as exigent as Trotsky expected. In April 1922 the French and Belgian representatives told Soviet delegates at Genoa that they would settle for repayment of the Tsarist debts and complete restitution of private property. Rejecting the opportunity to lease Soviet enterprises, they argued it was absurd to ask foreign nationals to lease back their own property, which had been nationalized in 1918. The British position was slightly less rigid: London would agree to leasing arrangements provided control over Soviet oil was ceded to Britain.

Unable to reach a compromise, the Russians left Genoa with one accomplishment—the Rapallo Treaty with Germany and a secret understanding concerning military co-operation. Soviet Russia would free Germany from the military restrictions imposed at Versailles in exchange for armaments factories, whose output the two governments would share. From the standpoint of the restoration of international trade, the Genoa conference was a failure. On that account Varga even expressed satisfaction. He had worried that by financing the Russian market the imperialists might reverse 'the current extraordinarily favourable period for the shaking up of capitalism'.[82] Although the summer of 1922 brought a cyclical upturn in some countries, most notably the United States, Varga remained confident that nothing essential had changed since 1920. The colonial countries were still industrializing; in Britain, America, and Japan excess industrial capacity persisted; in Central Europe underproduction showed no sign of abating. All these themes re-emerged in Varga's new book, *The Decline of Capitalism*, issued simultaneous with the Comintern's Fourth Congress in October 1922.

Updating Trotsky's address to the Third Congress, Varga remarked that the recovery in America proved there would be no automatic collapse, as 'certain comrades of the "left" hoped'.[83] On the other hand, it was equally certain that there was no prospect of a

[81] *Vserossiiskaya Konferentsiya*, no. 5, pp. 48–9.
[82] Varga, 'Povorot v Ekonomicheskoi Politiki Sovetskoi Rossii', *Kommunisticheskii Internatsional*, no. 18 (8 October 1921), p. 4602.
[83] Varga, *Le Déclin du Capitalisme*, Hamburg 1922, pp. 5–6.

return to capitalist equilibrium. Although arguing a familiar point, Varga now adopted a novel approach. Marx, he pointed out, had shown in *Capital* that even during the period of geographic expansion the equilibrium of the capitalist system was 'always unstable'. If this was true in Marx's time, it was all the more obvious now that Soviet Russia had left the world capitalist economy, the colonies had been cut off from the metropolitan centres, and a period of systemic contraction was in progress. In contrast to Fal'kner and Kondrat'ev, who saw normality in the beginnings of a cyclical upturn in 1922, Varga made a critical distinction between a cyclical 'phase' and a historical 'period': '*We are no longer in a phase of crisis . . . however, we continue to be in the period of the crisis of capitalism.*'[84] By the mid-1920s this distinction would evolve into the concept of capitalism's 'general crisis', interpreted in a manner quite similar to Luxemburg's approach. A harbinger of that development could already be detected in *The Decline of Capitalism*, in which Varga obliquely criticized Marx's reproduction schemes.

The problem with the schemes, Varga maintained, lay in their high degree of abstraction. Marx had worked with the flow of exchanges between the two departments of a self-contained, 'pure' capitalist economy, one without 'third parties'. 'But in reality, the conditions of equilibrium in the world capitalist economy [are] infinitely more complex, for the system [is] not uniformly developed in all of its parts. Equilibrium [has] . . . other bases than those indicated by Marx.'[85] It would be more useful, Varga suggested, to think in terms of the two main sectors of the world economy, the imperialist and the colonial, which together constituted an interdependent system. Then it would be clear that a normal cycle was now impossible: 'In both regions there is relative overproduction and therefore disequilibrium.'[86] Aware that these comments might associate his thinking with that of Luxemburg, Varga added that capitalist accumulation was indeed *theoretically* possible without non-capitalist consumers.[87] But the disclaimer was not entirely convincing. In a review of the literature in January

[84] Ibid., p. 11.
[85] Ibid., p. 12.
[86] Ibid., p. 14.
[87] Ibid., p. 28.

1923, M. Bronsky noticed that *The Decline of Capitalism* was 'inclined towards the views of Rosa Luxemburg both in the sense of its appraisal of the role and significance of imperialism and in the sense of its understanding of the conditions of capitalist bankruptcy'.[88]

By the time of the next world economic crisis in 1929, Varga's rapprochement with Luxemburgist ideas would become much more obvious. In 1923, however, Bronsky had to phrase his judgement carefully, for Varga drew upon many views of imperialism, with little regard for their mutually exclusive assumptions. Thus in *The Decline of Capitalism* he also adopted a Leninist perspective on the question of unevenness. One of the weaknesses of Trotsky's report to the previous Comintern congress had been the prediction of 'a prolonged period of depression' in America, 'an economic levelling out in reverse' in Europe. The recent recovery in America permitted Varga to avoid a like error and to cite the localization of the American success—its failure to spread to continental Europe—as further evidence of the rupture of international economic relations. 'The distinctive feature of the period of the decline of capitalism is that the homogeneity of the capitalist world has disappeared.'[89] When Trotsky discussed the conclusions of the Fourth Congress he admitted that he had previously misjudged America, overlooking the ability of American capital to penetrate Europe's former colonial markets. The 'Babylonian Tower' of American industry had been propped up by further aggravating the contradictions in the older capitalist countries, where the outlook continued to be one of 'stagnation and even disintegration'.[90]

Notwithstanding its theoretical eclecticism, Varga's latest work delivered one very clear message: a truly international recovery from the war would not materialize unless the complementary sectors of the world economy were reintegrated. The key to reconstruction still lay in the relation between Europe and America: 'Only a *pro-European* policy [in America], annulment of the allied

[88] Bronsky, 'Obzor Literatury . . .', *Vestnik Sotsialisticheskoi Akademii*, no. 4 (April–July 1923), p. 415.
[89] Varga, *Le Déclin du Capitalisme*, p. 17.
[90] Trotsky, *The First Five Years*, II, p. 308.

debts, and large credits to continental Europe, that is, a transfer of part of the excessive means of production from America to the impoverished areas of Europe, would in the more or less near future make possible the establishment of a new equilibrium . . . assuming the proletarian revolution allows capitalism the time required for this evolution.'[91] When the Dawes Plan eventually provided Germany with American credits, the question of capitalism's 'stabilization' logically arose. For the moment, however, Varga saw no possibility of enlightened international action. Having settled their own rivalry over naval armaments at the Washington conference of 1921, the Americans and the British were now bent on creating 'a world Anglo-Saxon empire'.[92] The Anglo-American plot would lead directly to revolution. With perfect accuracy, Varga expected the Americans to collect war debts from the British, the British to demand payment from the French, the French to squeeze reparations out of Germany, and Germany to collapse.

5. From the Ruhr Invasion to 'Socialism in One Country'

Of all the capitalist countries, Germany had most in common with Soviet Russia. Both had been devastated by the war; both were ordered by the Entente to compensate for Western wartime losses; and, by virtue of their inability to pay, both had become international pariahs. The Rapallo Treaty of 1922 reflected the belief of many Bolsheviks that Germany's 'national' interest required an eastern orientation. The Ruhr invasion of 1923 and the Dawes Plan shattered this hope and provided a model of what the imperialists might also have in store for Soviet Russia. After the Bolsheviks had been rebuffed at Genoa and 'betrayed' by the German bourgeoisie, Stalin devised the slogan of 'socialism in one country' and began to reshape the entire Soviet perception of postwar relations.

Initially, Soviet observers expected that Germany would escape French impositions by following the Soviet strategy of playing one imperialist against the other. The French insisted that Germany pay for reconstruction and the discharge of French debts to Britain

[91] Varga, *Le Déclin du Capitalisme* pp. 35–6.
[92] Ibid., p. 58.

and America; the British replied just as forcefully that reparations must be tailored to Germany's ability to pay. A struggle for continental hegemony seemed to loom between British and French imperialism. When the Americans endorsed the British position, Varga reiterated his view that 'the outlines of an Anglo-American alliance, of an Anglo-Saxon world imperialism', were becoming ever more distinct.[93] The British bourgeoisie hoped to refinance German payments by invoking the assistance of American capital, thus subjecting Europe to the joint financial dictatorship of London and New York.

The prize in the struggle was control of Germany's economy. Within its present frontiers France was responsible for 40 per cent of Europe's production of iron ore, but only 7 per cent of European coal output.[94] By *de facto* annexation of German coal, the French would reinforce their military superiority in Europe with industrial hegemony. Intent upon thwarting French designs and preserving good relations with the Reichswehr, the Bolsheviks in the early months of 1923 encouraged German tactics of 'passive resistance'. The embattled German government hoped to sabotage the French operation by subsidizing a halt to production in the occupied areas. Instead the mark collapsed, effectively expropriating the middle class and arousing fears of a right-wing coup against the Stresemann government. As of August of 1923 it was clear that Stresemann would either come to terms with the French or be dismissed. In Moscow plans were set in motion to pre-empt either possibility.

Karl Radek, the Comintern representative most responsible for German party affairs, viewed the options this way: 'There are only two alternatives for Germany: with Russia against France or with France against Russia . . . only if Germany, in its fight against the imperialism of the Western powers, joins hands with Russia, will German nationalism have a chance. But to join the struggle of all the oppressed involves a complete break with capitalism.'[95] Looking at

---

[93] E. Pavlovsky (Varga), 'Germany and the End of the Entente', *International Press Correspondence*, III, no. 8 (1 March 1923), p. 116.

[94] Varga, 'Ruhr Occupation—German and French Economics', *International Press Correspondence*, III, no. 12 (29 March 1923), p. 187.

[95] Quoted in Franz Borkenau, *World Communism*, Ann Arbor, Michigan 1962, p. 246.

the Ruhr from another perspective, Varga warned the Soviet leaders of the strategic implications of a French victory:

'Is Germany to be dismembered and her most important industrial areas absorbed by France, the rest being divided up into vassal states, and French hegemony in Europe finally established from the Atlantic Ocean to the frontiers of Soviet Russia, across Czechoslovakia and Romania and into Asia Minor? Is France at the same time to become the greatest country of heavy industry in Europe? Or—and this is the meaning of [the British reparations policy]—is a Germany to arise, under an Anglo-American protectorate, playing the part of an economic and political counterweight to France's design of gathering the whole continent of Europe under her sway? The policies of the great bourgeoisie of France and England clash on this point.'[96]

The French had sabotaged Soviet objectives at the Genoa conference and organized a system of alliances in Eastern Europe directed against both Germany and Russia. By October 1923, a German revolution appeared to be the only effective guarantee against French militarism. On Moscow's advice, German Communists joined the left-wing socialist governments of Saxony and Thuringia, planning to acquire arms and launch a general strike.[97] The socialists wavered, the Reichswehr deposed them, and after two days of fighting in Hamburg the revolution collapsed. To make matters worse, Germany then received the financial assistance Soviet Russia had been refused.

Work began on the Dawes Plan in December 1923. According to Varga, the French had no option but to accept the solution proposed by the Anglo-American bankers. Protracted involvement in the Ruhr had eroded French resolve and inspired a flight of capital. Reconstruction expenditures had been financed by short-term borrowing, and stringent conditions in the money market now imperilled government finances. In March 1924 Varga wrote that J.P. Morgan had assured French acquiescence with a loan of $100 million to defend the franc. France was 'at the mercy of the

[96] E. Pavlovsky, p. 116.
[97] Trotsky spoke of the 'guidance and help' given to Heinrich Brandler, leader of the German Party, during his trip to Moscow in September, 1923. See Louis Fischer, *Russia's Road from Peace to War*, New York 1969, p. 115.

American bourgeoise'.[98] For Germany the Dawes Plan provided a loan of 800 million marks and a substantially reduced schedule of payments. Should Germany's balance of payments be too feeble to effect the transfer of sums involved, the Reparations Commission would give priority to currency stability and postpone the transfer. Varga believed the German economy would never reach a level of exports sufficient to pay reparations in foreign currency. The Dawes Plan would at most retard the advent of a new crisis that would wreak further havoc on capitalism's systemic equilibrium: 'At present the whole of Western Europe cannot find a market for its full productive capacity . . . such a great export of German goods would lead, with the present reduced absorptive capacity of the world market, to a severe disadvantage for French and English industry. We are therefore of the opinion that the whole payments can neither be made by Germany nor be accepted by the Entente.'[99]

The alternative to a new reparations crisis would be for Germany to export titles to productive assets instead of commodities, or to accelerate its import of foreign capital. In that case the colonization of Germany would be complete. The French would indeed receive reparations, but would surrender at least half their plunder to Britain and America in settlement of war debts. British and American capitalists would transform Europe into a colony. Anglo-Saxon ambitions seemed even more transparent when in 1924 the European press began to consider the possibility of the imposition of a Dawes Plan on France as well. The logic of a French Dawes Plan led directly to the financial 'sanitation' of Soviet Russia.[100] Clearly the French would be in a better position to forward tribute to London and New York if they could collect on the securities they had purchased from the Tsar. British Prime Minister Stanley Baldwin was already casting his glance eastward, proposing that Germany earn her export surplus in the Soviet market rather than competing with Britain elsewhere.[101] Baldwin, like Keynes, be-

---

[98] Varga, 'Economics and Economic Policy in the First Half Year 1924', *International Press Correspondence*, IV, no. 63 (4 September 1924), p. 673.

[99] Varga, 'The Meaning of the Report of the Experts' Commission', *International Press Correspondence*, IV, no. 28 (8 May 1924), p. 270.

[100] Varga, *Plan Dauesa i Mirovoi Krizis 1924 Goda*, Moscow 1925, p. 68.

[101] Ibid., p. 70.

lieved that the ideal solution would be for Soviet Russia to purchase German manufactures in exchange for agricultural products and raw materials. In 1921 Lenin had been prepared to contemplate such an arrangement in an effort to escape from economic and political isolation. Conditions in the Soviet domestic economy had significantly improved since that time. Varga reflected the consequent change of attitude when he warned that implementation of the Anglo-Saxon grand design would reduce Russia to the status of 'a German agricultural colony'.[102]

Mention of this possibility at once imparted a dramatic new dimension to internal Soviet politics. Lenin had died in January 1924, leaving Stalin and Trotsky as the principal contenders for the succession. Stalin saw the opportunity to outmanoeuvre Trotsky by abandoning the main lines of foreign policy originally set down by Lenin. Shortly before the Genoa conference Lenin had declared that the revolution must pass one final test, 'the test set by the . . . international market, to which we are subordinated, with which we are connected, and from which we cannot isolate ourselves'.[103] With the slogan 'socialism in one country' as a synonym for self-sufficient industrialization, Stalin converted the necessity of isolation from Europe into a virtue. In a defiant address to the party congress of 1925 he vowed that he would never accept the 'Dawesization of our country'. The Land of Soviets would never become 'an agrarian country for the benefit of some other country'. In a resolution prepared for the congress Stalin argued: '[We must] conduct our economic construction in such a way as to convert the USSR from a country that imports machines and equipment. . . . In this manner the USSR . . . will become a self-sufficient economic unit building socialism.'[104] Stalin's programme of industrial autarky, which would end in forced collectivization and the Five-Year Plan, brought one period in the development of Soviet political economy to a close. The years of waiting for a revolution in Europe, for a breach in the capitalist encirclement, had ended. Now the problem was to determine whether or not the Dawes Plan embodied capitalism's final 'stabilization'.

[102] Ibid., p. 72.
[103] Lenin, *Collected Works*, XXXIII, p. 276–77.
[104] *Chetyrnadtsatyi S'ezd Vsesoyuznoi Kommunisticheskoi Partii (Bol'shevikov): Stenograficheskii Otchet*, Moscow 1926, p. 958.

3
The Debate Over
Capitalist 'Stabilization'

With its promise of rescuing Germany from economic and political collapse, the Dawes Plan raised the question of capitalist equilibrium in a new and unexpected context. Neither Marx's *Capital* nor Lenin's *Imperialism* had used the concept of equilibrium, except as a momentary pause in the continual reproduction of contradictions. In *Capital* Marx argued that fluctuations in social demand could be absorbed only by a planned economy, which would protect itself against the uneven reproduction of fixed capital through a deliberate policy of planned surpluses, or 'continuous relative overproduction'. Lenin agreed with Marx that in theory the entire social product could be realized within a self-contained capitalist system; in practice, however, crises of disproportionality were inevitable.

Applying Marx's logic to the emergence of finance capital and imperialism, Lenin showed that domestic disproportions were projected into the world economy. Each capitalist country strove to dump surpluses in the world market and to sustain the domestic rate of profit by exporting capital. Thus the law of uneven (or disproportionate) development was the most universal law governing the reproduction of capital both within and between countries. In Lenin's work neither the national nor the international sphere of economic activity assumed logical priority; instead the two spheres were related in a dialectical interaction that magnified and universalized contradictions. Military conflicts might briefly alleviate disproportionalities and create the conditions for a temporary equilibrium, much as classical crises did in Marx's interpretation. But the idea that capitalism might transcend the law of unevenness was as foreign to Lenin's reasoning as it had been to Marx's.

The Soviet debate over capitalist stabilization, which lasted from 1924 to 1929, reflected a disintegration of Lenin's theoretical synthesis and a new polarization in Marxist economic thought. Trotsky and Varga believed that by disrupting the world market the imperialist war had radically altered what Trotsky referred to as the *external conditions* of capitalist development. American hegemony and the weakening of Europe's hold over former colonies deprived the older capitalist countries of markets and prevented the resumption of capital accumulation, investments, and a normal business cycle. In a new debate with Kondrat'ev, Trotsky explained the anti-Marxist implications of the theory of moving equilibrium and held that even the temporary stabilization of European capitalism was then impossible.

As the leading exponent of stabilization, Bukharin reasoned from entirely different premises, lending logical priority to the *internal conditions* of reproduction. For Bukharin, the predominant tendency of modern capitalism was towards state intervention and economic planning. 'State capitalism' enabled finance capital to protect itself against external disruptions by controlling the flow of commodities and capital across national frontiers. Within these more or less organized national economies—or imperialist blocs—Bukharin saw the possibility of regulating production in accordance with demand, and even of moderating demand fluctuations. In *Imperialism and the Accumulation of Capital* (1925), he refuted Luxemburg's theory that expanded reproduction required access to 'third-party' markets. 'How is a mobile equilibrium possible', he asked, 'in a growing system?' The answer was simple: Marx had demonstrated in his reproduction schemes that 'along with the growth of . . . production, the market . . . grows too. . . . In other words, here the possibility is given of both an equilibrium between the various parts of social production and an equilibrium between production and consumption'.[1] The fact that Marx had used the reproduction schemes to illustrate the sources of *disequilibrium* (or disproportionalities) seems to have escaped Bukharin's notice.

Since 1920 Bukharin had been adjusting his views on the subject of capitalism's moving equilibrium. In *The Economics of the Transition Period* (1920) he had predicted systemic crash as a result

[1] Luxemburg and Bukharin, *Imperialism and the Accumulation of Capital*, p. 160.

of expanded negative reproduction. Trying to dampen this enthusiasm, Lenin pointed out that 'a certain equilibrium' had emerged by 1921. In *Historical Materialism* (1921) Bukharin replied with an elaboration of the 'law of mobile equilibrium'. Expanded negative reproduction, it now turned out, was itself a form of moving (or dynamic) equilibrium—an 'unstable equilibrium with a negative indication'.[2] Two other variants of equilibrium were possible: simple reproduction, 'a constant reestablishment of equilibrium . . . on the old basis'; and expanded reproduction, or what Bukharin called an 'unstable equilibrium with a positive indication'.[3] Societies had now become 'social systems', interacting with their external 'environment' and preserving their integrity by virtue of their internal adaptive capacity. In 1925 Bukharin used Hilferding's 'universal cartel' to illustrate the theoretical ability of capitalism to organize an internal equilibrium.

'Let us imagine', he wrote, '. . . the *collective-capitalist social order* (state capitalism), in which the capitalist class is a unified trust and we are dealing with an organized, though at the same time, *from the standpoint of classes*, antagonistic economy. . . . Is accumulation possible here? Of course it is. Constant capital grows, the consumption of the capitalists grows, new branches of production continually arise in response to new needs, the consumption of the workers grows even though it is confined within definite limits. *Despite* this "underconsumption" of the masses, crises do not occur because the demand of *each branch of production in relation to the others*, the *consumer demand* of the capitalists, and that of the workers, is determined in advance (there is no "anarchy of production", but a rational plan from the viewpoint of capital). . . . Thus *no crisis of overproduction can occur here*. The course of production, in general, is planned.'[4]

The unifying focus of Bukharin's thought throughout the 1920s was Hilferding's concept of 'organized capitalism'. It was therefore perfectly understandable that Bukharin endorsed the slogan of

[2] Bukharin, *Historical Materialism*, Ann Arbor, Michigan 1969, pp. 119–20.
[3] Ibid., p. 119.
[4] Bukharin, *Imperializm i Nakoplenie Kapitala*, third edition, Moscow and Leningrad 1928, p. 82; cf. Luxemburg and Bukharin, p. 226.

socialism in one country: an isolated socialist state was the obvious analogue of the 'collective-capitalist social order', the sole difference having to do with property relations. Trotsky's objection to the programme of economic self-sufficiency was likewise related to his view of capitalism's equilibrium: just as the capitalist states could not escape the external conditions of reproduction, so the Soviet state could not free itself of international economic dependencies. The issues of capitalist stabilization and socialism in one country represented two aspects of a single theoretical disagreement.

Trotsky believed external conditions would govern the pace of socialist construction through the action of the world law of value. Were the Soviet state to strive for autarky, building its own capital equipment and flouting the world division of labour, productivity gains would be sacrificed and high domestic prices would attract contraband imports to satisfy peasant demand. The answer to this threat was to continue the policy initiated by Lenin: having lost major markets to America, the European countries must be persuaded to develop a Soviet market by extending credits. Bukharin was unimpressed by Trotsky's argument on several grounds. To start with, he saw no reason why a socialist economy could not maintain its internal equilibrium by using the same organizational techniques as finance capital.[5] Second, he believed that Europe's stabilization would lessen the capitalists' interest in foreign markets. Finally, he was appalled by Trotsky's endorsement of the theory of 'primitive socialist accumulation'.

When Marx described 'primitive capitalist accumulation' he was referring to the expropriation of the peasant: 'great masses of men are suddenly and forcibly torn from their means of subsistence, and hurled onto the labour-market as free, unprotected, and rightless proletarians. The expropriation of the agricultural producer, of the peasant, from the soil is the basis of the whole process.'[6] Fearful that Trotsky's taxation policies would estrange the peasants at a time when the capitalist countries were growing stronger, Bukharin sided with Stalin, whom he thought could be more easily restrained.

[5] See Day, 'Dialectical Method . . .'
[6] Marx, *Capital* Volume I, p. 876.

Distorting Trotsky's real objections to the programme of industrial self-sufficiency, Bukharin and Stalin jointly declared that their enemy had lost confidence in the Russian revolution.[7]

Marxist and bourgeois economists alike became involved in the stabilization debate, with little interest in or understanding of its political dimension. Fal'kner and Kondrat'ev thought stabilization was a fact; their Marxist counterparts found scant evidence to justify a complete reversal of past Comintern decisions. The longer the debate went on, the more impatient the economists became to have done with it. While the party leadership plunged into confusion, Varga and his associates scurried for evidence to prove Bukharin wrong. By 1928 this tension had given rise to 'Varga's Law', a unique neo-Luxemburgist challenge to Marx's theory of internal market creation and an ideal justification for forced collectivization. By forecasting the end of stabilization, Varga provided theoretical support for Stalin's announcement of a new period of wars and revolutions. The threat of a capitalist attack served as the rationale for the quest for industrial self-sufficiency— and helped Stalin rid himself of Bukharin in the bargain. The debate over stabilization thus provides a mirror image of the more familiar struggle over the fate of the New Economic Policy.

1. The Political Leaders on Stabilization

The first reference to stabilization appears to have come at a meeting of the Soviet Communist Party just before the Comintern Fifth Congress, scheduled to meet in June 1924. At that meeting Bukharin proclaimed that the 'general crisis of the capitalist system', although continuing, had become a 'creeping crisis'.[8] The 'creeping crisis' entailed recovery in England and Germany and a relapse in America. Generalizing his analysis, Bukharin argued that capitalism had entered an equilibrium phase, which most Marxists had hitherto thought of as stagnation: 'in general and on the whole, we have a position that points to a certain stabilization of

---

[7] See Day, *Leon Trotsky and the Politics of Economic Isolation*, London 1973, pp. 105–52.

[8] *Trinadtsatyi S'ezd Rossiiskoi Kommunisticheskoi Partii (Bol'shevikov): Stenograficheskii Otchet*, Moscow 1924, p. 323.

internal capitalist relations, in which fluctuations in one area are compensated by fluctuating movements in other geographical points. That is the general position.'[9] As titular head of the Comintern, Zinoviev was instructed to carry these tidings to the full congress. At first Zinoviev struck a reassuring posture: 'Capitalism continues to find itself in a period of decline. In America we see the beginnings of a new economic crisis.'[10] But Zinoviev also noted that in view of recent developments, 'events have not proceeded as rapidly as we supposed'.[11] Varga was more frank. After summarizing the 'general crisis' of world capitalism and the 'special crisis' of Europe, he recalled Lenin's comment that the 'inevitable' collapse could not be taken for granted. Allowance had still to be made for subjective conditions: 'The possibility cannot be excluded—perhaps even the probability—that capitalism will succeed in prolonging its agony for a considerable time, and will perhaps even extricate itself from the crisis at the expense of the proletariat.'[12]

A German delegate immediately denounced Varga, claiming that he was suggesting the restoration of 'normal' capitalism and even a whole new era of 'ultra-imperialism', the old error of Karl Kautsky.[13] Now the issue was in the open, and Zinoviev came to Varga's rescue: 'The situation is very complicated, and it is not Varga's fault that certain symptoms of the strengthening of capitalism exist. Unfortunately, it is so, and we cannot simply shut our eyes.' Varga's critic had insisted that 'we are as much in the epoch of world revolution now as we were before . . . the next stage of the world revolution will be in Germany'. Zinoviev answered that even in Germany there were recent signs of consolidation. Since the Third Congress in 1921, he continued, 'we have learned much . . . and we have . . . come to understand that we must handle the term "collapse of capitalism" very carefully. The downfall of capitalism is inevitable; capitalism is doomed, but we must see things in their real light and interpret the times more rationally than

[9] Ibid., p. 318.
[10] Pyatyi Vsemirnyi S'ezd Kommunisticheskovo Internatsionala: Stenograficheskii Otchet, 2 vols., Moscow and Leningrad 1925, I, 56.
[11] Ibid., p. 57.
[12] Ibid., p. 112.
[13] International Press Correspondence, IV, no. 47 (23 July 1924), p. 290.

we have hitherto done.'[14] In his preparation of a new Comintern programme, Bukharin was having his own difficulties with another German representative, who thought Luxemburg had given the only consistently revolutionary account of imperialism. Explaining the disagreement, Bukharin warned that 'we must be more cautious. . . . We already see the empirical fact that on the whole we are facing a process of capitalist decay, but within this great process we also see partial processes of regeneration.'[15]

'Regeneration', 'consolidation', 'stabilization'—in this new vocabulary Trotsky saw apologies for the way his enemies had mismanaged the German revolution a year earlier. Although he did not participate in the congress, Trotsky found other forums in which to express himself while the meetings were in session. 'Up to now', he told one gathering on 21 June 1924, 'it is quite impossible to observe any phenomena that would provide evidence for believing that the capitalist economy of Europe and the world is near to finding a new mobile equilibrium.' The Dawes Plan could never lead to 'the final restoration of the stability of the capitalist system.'[16] Four days later, Trotsky asserted that the American capitalists, 'the bourgeoisie of bourgeoisies', had conceived the loan to Germany in order to accord Europe sufficient leeway to make debt payments. But Europe would be permitted to recover only 'within limits set in advance, with certain restricted sections of the world market allotted to it. American capitalism . . . will slice up the markets; it will regulate the activity of European financiers and industrialists. . . . *It wants to put capitalist Europe on rations.*'[17] The most that could be expected was 'a rotten equilibrium' and a 'lean existence upon standardized American rations'.[18]

Trotsky's unexpected intervention brought a spirited rebuke from Bukharin, who claimed that 'American rations' smacked of Rudolf Hilferding's 'organized capitalism'. Citing Hilferding's latest publications, Bukharin declared that Social Democrats

[14] *Pyatyi Vsemirnyi S'ezd*, I, 439–41.
[15] Ibid., p. 494.
[16] Trotsky, *Through What Stage Are We Passing?*, translated by Brian Pearce, London 1965, p. 26.
[17] Trotsky, *Europe and America*, translated by John G. Wright, Colombo, Ceylon n.d., p. 16.
[18] Ibid., p. 31.

expected the German 'Lazarus' to be resurrected by 'the American Christ'.[19] Trotsky, he said, was following in Hilferding's footsteps, thinking the Americans could 'organize' capitalism on a world scale and create a 'supranational trust' to allocate markets. Not to be outdone by Bukharin, Stalin equated 'American rations' with a period of reformist 'pacifism'. Disagreeing with Varga's projection of an Anglo-American alliance, Stalin believed the real goal of the Dawes Plan was to secure American control over German heavy industry and to drive the British out of world markets. 'But to believe that Britain will resign herself to such a situation means not to know ... how greatly Britain values the interests of her metallurgical industry.'[20] Trotsky would do well, suggested Stalin, to remember Lenin's strictures on the law of uneven development, which 'remains in force today more than ever before'.[21]

For the next several months the politicians trumpeted the new doctrine of 'relative', 'temporary', 'partial' stabilization. Zinoviev began to see that capitalism's good fortune might well prove handy. Comintern misadventures, often criticized by Trotsky, could be excused by the change in objective conditions, the 'collapse of the revolutionary wave' and consequent absence of a 'direct revolutionary situation' in Europe.[22] In May 1925 Zinoviev announced that stabilization might last for 'several years'.[23] Within six months, as Stalin made ready to oust Zinoviev from the leadership, the latter decided that socialism in one country was a mistake after all. He now came to the conclusion that the timetable of stabilization had to be revised: 'That this stabilization is partial, that it is relative, that it would be the greatest error to overestimate it, that it is temporary and even short-lived—all of this is absolutely clear after all the events we have experienced in the past year.'[24]

As Zinoviev entangled himself in his own inconsistencies, Stalin

[19] Bukharin, 'Protivorechiya Sovremennovo Kapitalizma', Bol'shevik, no. 10 (5 September 1924), pp. 8–9.

[20] J. Stalin, Works, 13 vols., Moscow 1953–5, VI, p. 303

[21] Ibid.

[22] Pravda, 22 March 1925.

[23] G. Zinoviev, 'Chastichnaya "Stabilizatsiya" Kapitalizma i Zadachi Kominterna i RKP (B)', Kommunisticheskii Internatsional, no. 5 (42) (May 1925), p. 12.

[24] Zinoviev, '8 Let Revolyutsii', Kommunisticheskii Internatsional, no. 11 (48) (November 1925), p. 10.

scored points against Trotsky. In 1921 Trotsky had told the Comintern Third Congress that an epoch of stagnation was at hand. But Trotsky was again mistaken: 'Stabilization', insisted Stalin, 'is not stagnation. Stabilization is a strengthening of the current position and a further development. World capitalism . . . is moving forward, even expanding its sphere of influence and multiplying its wealth. It is not true that capitalism cannot develop, that the theory of capitalist decay given by Lenin in his *Imperialism* excludes the development of capitalism.'[25] Underscoring the connection between stabilization and socialism in one country, Stalin pointed to a simultaneous stabilization in 'two camps'—'the camp of capitalism, headed by Anglo-American capital, and the camp of socialism, headed by the Soviet Union'.[26] Having inspired this confusion with his report in preparation for the Fifth Congress, Bukharin was not yet ready to follow Stalin in speaking of capitalism's wealth. He believed capitalism remained in a condition of simple reproduction: 'in the course of this epoch there will be periods of ebb and flow, periods of decay and periods of expansion. . . . This means that when we speak of the stabilization of capitalism we understand a comparative stabilization.'[27]

2. Marxist and Bourgeois Economists

Viewing this spectacle from the sidelines, Soviet economists were initially at a loss as to how to react. Dm. Bukhartsev supported Stalin's claim that America would use German heavy industry as a 'battering ram' with which to penetrate Britain's overseas markets: Germany would become an industrial hinterland of American capital.[28] Modest Rubinshtein, a specialist on American affairs, thought the Dawes Plan symbolized the formation of a 'capitalist international' ranged against the world proletariat.[29] He suspected

[25] Stalin, *Works*, VII, p. 95.
[26] Ibid.
[27] Bukharin, 'The Stabilization of Capitalism, the Second International and Ourselves', *International Press Correspondence*, V, no. 53 (2 July 1925), p. 718.
[28] Dm. Bukhartsev, 'Sotrudnichestvo i Protivorechiya Anglo-Amerikanskovo Kapitalizma v Plane Dauesa', *Bol'shevik*, no. 1 (17) (15 January 1925), pp. 82–3.
[29] M. Rubinshtein, ' "Kolonizatsiya" Evropy Amerikanskim Kapitalom', *Bol'shevik*, no. 12–13 (20 October 1924), p. 29.

that German imports would be used to undercut prices and reduce wages in other industrial countries. Another writer, E. Gol'denberg, maintained that Germany would experience 'de-industrialization'. Unable to pay reparations through industrial exports, she would have to turn to agriculture and become an 'agrarian appendage' of America.[30] Professor Fal'kner found these appraisals silly and predicted there would be no difficulty with the transfer of reparations for at least another four or five years.[31] Professor Y. Bukshpan claimed that the recent consolidation was merely a continuation of the trend towards expansion that had begun in 1920–21.[32]

What annoyed Marxist economists most was Bukharin's suggestion that stabilization might last for an entire 'epoch'. There might be room for disagreement over immediate prospects. But where was the evidence for a total reversal of long-term expectations? This was the question addressed to N. Lapinsky, who early in 1925 published *The New Phase of Imperialism and Its Economic Sources*. Although Lapinsky's conclusions were anything but positive, the title and theme of his book galvanized party economists into action. By suggesting that stabilization would be far more than an interlude, Lapinsky offered other Marxists the opportunity to say to a peer what could not be said to members of the Politburo. Varga indicated that he was already having second thoughts. Characterizing Lapinsky's book as 'interesting', he proceeded to argue that stabilization was nothing more than a 'subjective' phenomenon with no basis in production. The bourgeoisie had momentarily regained confidence; the spirit of revolt among the masses had subsided. But there was no 'thought whatever of "normal" production; that is, of production increasing at the prewar rate'.[33] In spite of all the fuss made over the Dawes Plan, the recovery in Germany would be 'a brief, transitory episode'.

[30] E. Gol'denberg, 'Germanskoe Khozyaistvo i Reparatsii', *Sotsialisticheskoe Khozyaistvo*, no. 5 (November 1924), p. 214.

[31] Fal'kner, 'Ekonomicheskie Osnovy Plana Dauesa', *Planovoe Khozyaistvo*, no. 1 (January 1925), pp. 208–9.

[32] Y. M. Bukshpan, 'Mirovoe Khozyaistvo v 1924g.', *Ekonomicheskoe Obozrenie*, no. 23–24 (December 1924), pp. 181–2.

[33] Varga, 'Economics and Economic Policy in the First Quarter of 1925', *International Press Correspondence*, V, no. 44 (21 May 1925), p. 573.

Bukhartsev adopted a more aggressive tone. He blamed Lapinsky for sowing doubts in the party ranks and described *The New Phase of Imperialism* as 'the basic work substantiating the notorious "stabilization" of the world economy'[34]—a gross exaggeration of the book's importance. Referring to local party officials (surrogates for Stalin, Bukharin, and Zinoviev), he decried the way stabilization was being touted as scriptural truth: 'Comrade Lapinsky is the father of stabilization, which in its "relative", "temporary", and other variations is becoming a virtual canon. What self-respecting secretary of a cell does not demonstrate his erudition by beginning his report with this canon of stabilization? To a large extent the responsibility for this falls to Comrade Lapinsky.'[35] Spektator (M.I. Nakhimson) denied that even the most elementary task of currency stabilization could be taken for granted. Every Marxist knew that a stable currency presupposed stability in the realm of production.[36]

In June 1925 another scapegoat appeared in the person of I. Litvinov, an occasional book reviewer and journalist with the party newspaper, *Pravda*. In one of his *Pravda* surveys Litvinov wrote that the Dawes Plan had restored order in Europe, that French and German industrialists were espousing pacifism, and that Anglo-American co-operation was flourishing.[37] Varga lost patience and described the article as 'a model of how not to . . . write about the world economy'. Litvinov was charged with deliberately misleading his readers and portraying 'a good world conjuncture when it does not exist'.[38] At a meeting of the State Planning Commission Varga lamented the tendency to confuse stabilization with 'stability': 'To my knowledge of the Marxist and Leninist literature, this is neither a Marxist nor a Leninist term; I suggest, moreover, that it is a term that has been most unfortunately chosen.'[39] The

---

[34] Bukhartsev, 'O "Novoi Faze" i Stabiliziruemykh "Revolyutsionerakh" ', *Bol'shevik*, no. 13–14 (30 July 1925), p. 103.

[35] Ibid.

[36] Spektator, ' "Stabilizatsiya" Kapitalizma ili Shatanie Mysli', *Bol'shevik*, no. 13–14 (30 July 1925), pp. 99–100.

[37] *Pravda*, 10 June 1925.

[38] *Pravda*, 23 June 1925.

[39] Varga, 'K Voprosu o "Stabilizatsii" Mirovovo Kapitalizma', *Planovoe Khozyaistvo*, no. 6 (June 1925), p. 154.

complaint aptly summarized the sentiment of the Soviet community of economists, with the notable exceptions of Fal'kner and Kondrat'ev.

In October 1925 Fal'kner incensed Marxist economists with an unusually pretentious article. As an academic, Fal'kner thought facts had nothing to do with the observer's political viewpoint. And the facts, in his judgement, incontestably spoke in favour of stabilization. Negotiations were under way to match the reparations settlement with a European political settlement. Acceptance of the Locarno Treaty would guarantee Germany's frontiers with France and Belgium and create just the right atmosphere for investor confidence. In the spring of 1925 the pound sterling had been restored to its prewar parity; the French, Belgians, and Italians were also planning to stabilize their currencies in the near future. In America the contraction of 1924 had given way to a new boom based on residential and industrial construction and growth in the automotive industry. In Britain unemployment remained   high, but the figure had been constant for some time; in that respect the British economy was also stable.

Fal'kner expressed bewilderment at the imperviousness of Marxists to these facts: 'In the daily press we are continually told that the depression is intensifying or an economic crisis beginning in one country or another. Such *conjunctural* descriptions are significant only in relation to a certain level of economic activity, from which the deviations occur. . . . The question is: *on what level* of activity . . . have these transitory and successive crises and depressions taken place?'[40] Fal'kner introduced a whole new system of concepts in the interests of greater realism; they included 'dynamic processes' of degradation, reconstruction, deformation (and their negative variants), as well as general-evolutionary processes. The elaborate system of neologisms was far more difficult to understand than the modest conclusions it generated. In essence, Fal'kner agreed with Bukharin that an international process of readjustment had seen the growth of some countries compensate for the weakness of others. Europe was converging towards equilibrium at the prewar level; the Americans, with a far higher rate of capital

[40] Fal'kner, 'Dinamicheskie Protsessy v Sovremennom Mirovom Khozyaistvo', *Planovoe Khozyaistvo*, no. 10 (October 1925), pp. 173–4.

accumulation, would soon surpass all records. In America and Britain two three-year cycles had occurred; elsewhere the pattern was one of smooth reconstruction.[41]

Fal'kner's reference to a *three-year business cycle* touched on an issue that would spark a serious conflict among Marxists in 1929–30 over the likely outcome of the American stock-market crash. In the early months of 1924 Varga had written of a new cyclical crisis in America, one that would confirm his own expectations and console the Comintern. But the brevity of the American pause led many Soviet observers to speak of 'business stagnation' rather than a genuine 'crisis'. Even Varga admitted that because of the modern forms of capitalist organization the American bourgeoisie had again succeeded in averting price reductions and serious bankruptcies.[42] A year later Varga professed uncertainty about the postwar cyclical pattern, particularly with regard to Europe: 'I must admit that I have no answer to this question.'[43] The answer came only in 1929, when Varga took issue with the theory of the three-year cycle. With the benefit of hindsight, he then argued that a 'normal' cyclical crisis—separated from that of 1920 by nine years—was being superimposed on the chronic 'general crisis' of the capitalist system. Varga would then face the task of explaining how a 'normal' cycle and a chronic crisis could possibly co-exist.

But in October 1925 it was not Fal'kner's mention of the three-year cycle that annoyed his critics; on the contrary, it was his tendency to treat cycles as inconsequential compared to 'levels' of economic activity. Most party economists thought stabilization was at best a conjunctual moment, an interlude between feverish oscillations. The first of many rebukes in an affair that lasted six months came from Spektator, who reiterated that 'capitalism has yet to regain its prewar stability . . . the last word still belongs to the proletariat'. Fal'kner had diminished the significance of the conjuncture by adopting an incorrect methodology. Spektator inquired:

'What would we say of an economist who declared that he studies the history of capitalism not by means of annual data, but with

[41] Ibid., pp. 212–13.
[42] Varga, *Plan Dauesa i Mirovoi Krizis 1924 Goda*, p. 17.
[43] Varga, 'K Voprosu o "Stabilizatsii" . . .', p. 163.

averages for ten or fifty years, and who concluded on that basis that "the reconstruction process" of capitalism develops smoothly, that there are no crises, that everything points upward and so on? . . . If a doctor were to diagnose a man sick with fever not in terms of the continuous rise and fall of his temperature, but from the point of view of an *average* temperature, then he would obviously understand nothing about the patient's condition. Fal'kner is exactly that sort of doctor when it comes to capitalism.'[44]

At this point Fal'kner would have been well advised to hold his tongue. Instead he drew attention to the apparent contradiction between Marxist economists and the leaders of the party. Had not Stalin recently declared that 'capitalism has succeeded in extricating itself from the quagmire of the postwar crisis'? Had not Zinoviev decided that completion of the revolution would require decades? Why then would an 'irresponsible journalist' like Spektator—who, incidentally, later proved to be one of the more skilful Soviet economists—say the opposite, if not merely to prove his 'r-r-revolutionary zeal with cries about the "destruction" of capitalism'?[45] By proclaiming a collapse every six months Marxists were arguing that 'the sun revolves around the earth'.[46]

The bouquet of insults was promptly returned. A. Aizenshtadt, another Marxist, commented on the similarity between Fal'kner's and Kondrat'ev's methodology. Both professors were engaged in empty scholasticism; both were idealists who thought their 'reason' would organize reality; and both hoped to bury the conjuncture in long-term trends and averages. An objective study would have emphasized the very fact Fal'kner treated as unimportant, 'that the *waverings* of capitalist production are becoming more frequent . . . and that crises therefore succeed one another at shorter intervals . . . of three to three and a half years instead of seven'.[47] Fal'kner was a Kantian 'idealist' whose new concepts

---

[44] Spektator, 'Skazka pro Vosstanovitel'nye i Degradatsionnye Protsessy', *Planovoe Khozyaistvo*, no. 10 (October 1925), p. 226.

[45] Fal'kner, 'O Teoreticheskoi Bespomoshchnosti i Polemicheskoi Razvyaznosti', *Planovoe Khozyaistvo*, no. 11 (November 1925), p. 190.

[46] Ibid., p. 184.

[47] A. Aizenshtadt, 'K Voprosu o Stabilizatsii Kapitalizma', *Mezhdunarodnaya Letopis' Politiki*, no. 10–11 (November-December 1925), p. 33.

painted capitalism in a 'rosy light'; they marked him as a deliberate apologist. Or as A. S. Mendel'son remarked, Fal'kner saw the world in terms of isolated facts because he was a fetishist: 'To analyse economic phenomena in this manner is to fetishize them, to turn them into things—the relations between people and classes are replaced by relations between things.'[48]

3. Kondrat'ev and the Problem of Equilibrium

Fal'kner's political difficulties at the end of 1925 were partly of his own making, partly a reflection of a more general trend. In most academic disciplines the years 1925–6 saw the beginnings of a class differentiation through which theoretical research would eventually be transformed into a 'fighting front' in the class struggle. As the most prominent of all the bourgeois economists, Kondrat'ev too was caught up in this process. Fal'kner was an irritant to Marxist economists; Kondrat'ev, however, was something of an enigma and therefore a threat. Fal'kner presented his findings in a language of his own invention, whereas Kondrat'ev applied the laws Marx had discussed in *Capital* and used the term 'equilibrium' in much the same sense as Bukharin. Trotsky was the first to see that the theory of long waves depended on belief in a 'moving equilibrium' and to challenge Kondrat'ev on that point. In 1925–6 Kondrat'ev responded to Trotsky's criticisms and landed himself in the middle of the internal party dispute over stabilization.

It will be recalled that when Trotsky first acknowledged the possibility of a postwar recovery he thought of equilibrium in two ways: a *secular* equilibrium, or long-term trend of development, and a *cyclical* equilibrium, or the temporary elimination of disproportions in the wake of a crisis. It was Trotsky's view that the long-term trend had followed an erratic course since the early nineteenth century, periodically changing direction (or its slope when portrayed on a graph). The year 1914 brought the final turning point, inaugurating the period of capitalism's decline. 'Levelling out in reverse' would result from domestic bottlenecks in each country that could not be removed through trade. The level of investment

[48] A. Mendel'son, 'K Voprosu o Dinamicheskikh Protsessakh v Sovremennom Mirovom Khozyaistve', *Planovoe Khozyaistvo*, no. 1 (January 1926), p. 249.

would therefore decline as well, and the classical business cycle would give way to irregular spasms. Following his Comintern address of 1921, Trotsky decided that the problem of equilibrium might best be conceived in terms of two 'curves': the cyclical and the basic curve. The latter was the one with an 'uneven upward curvature' reflecting separate historical periods: 'There are decades when it rises by a hair's breadth, then follow decades when it swings sharply upwards, only in order later, during a new epoch, to remain for a long time at one and the same level.' The relationship between the two curves could be compared to the vibrations in a string of wire—provided one remembered that the string of wire was not really a curve at all, but was divided into separate segments.[49] This emphasis on the unevenness of the trend is crucial for understanding Trotsky's reaction to both Kondrat'ev's view of long cycles and Bukharin's position on stabilization. It indicated that there was no single moving equilibrium—or smooth curve with a single equation—that described the history of capitalism's growth. Thus Trotsky offered the further analogy of capitalism's heartbeat: in a healthy organism the cyclical pulse was regular; with the advance of senility it becomes convulsive.

In June 1923 Trotsky published a stylized diagram of the two curves. This schema made two points: first, it again showed the basic curve as a segmented line; second, the breaks in the line were connected with *external* events. In the latter category Trotsky included wars, social reforms, revolutions, the rise of new political parties, and even new philosophical or literary schools—in other words, events that could not be linked mechanically to the business cycle *per se*. Cyclical fluctuations resulted from capitalism's internal contradictions, but the overall pattern of cycles had been altered from time to time by external conditions. Because these external conditions were in part fortuitous, the historical periods they shaped were likewise lacking in cyclical rhythm. They could not be confused with the presumed waves of Kondrat'ev's long cycle:

'One can reject in advance the attempts by Professor Kondrat'ev to assign to the epochs that he calls long cycles the same "strict rhythm" that is observed in short cycles. This attempt is a clearly mistaken generalization based on a formal analogy. The periodicity of short cycles is conditioned by the internal dynamic of capitalist

[49] Trotsky, *The First Five Years*, II, pp. 80–81.

forces, which manifests itself whenever and wherever there is a market. As for those long (fifty-year) intervals that Professor Kondrat'ev hastily proposes also to call cycles, their character and duration is determined not by the internal play of capitalist forces, but by the external conditions in which capitalist development occurs. The absorption by capitalism of new countries and continents, the discovery of new natural resources, and, in addition, significant factors of a "superstructural" order, such as wars and revolutions, determine the character and alteration of expansive, stagnating, or declining epochs in capitalist development.'[50]

During 1923 Kondrat'ev made his own distinction between the two curves, calling the one 'reversible' (or cyclical), the other 'irreversible' (meaning that it was not periodically interrupted as Trotsky claimed). In 1925 Kondrat'ev completed a new essay entitled 'The Long Cycles of the Conjuncture'. Here, and also in a report dated February 1926, he explained the statistical methods used to produce a graph of the long cycle. (Kondrat'ev's techniques, as well as a comparison of his graphs with Trotsky's, will be found in the appendix). By plotting a continuous curve with a single equation in place of Trotsky's segmented trend-line, Kondrat'ev made manifest the ideological assumption implicit in the concept of moving equilibrium: the lack of unevenness in the historical development of capitalism.

Although they clarified one aspect of the debate, Kondrat'ev's newest findings confounded another. By 'internalizing' Trotsky's external conditions, he produced an ultra-deterministic theory of history that few Marxists could contemplate. Wars, revolutions, technological innovations, agricultural depressions, changes in the money supply, the absorption of new markets, and all manner of social and political transformations were reduced, in Kondrat'ev's approach, to 'regularities' of the long cycle. Kondrat'ev conceded that with respect to the 'strict rhythm' of the long cycle his research was still incomplete. Nevertheless, present evidence seemed to indicate that the long cycle was even more rhythmical than the short.[51] This conclusion was to be expected, for in Kondrat'ev's opinion the long cycle was governed by factors perfectly analogous

---

[50] Trotsky, 'O Krivoi Kapitalisticheskovo Razvitiya', *Vestnik Sotsialisticheskoi Akademii*, no. 4 (April-July 1923), p. 9.

[51] N.D. Kondrat'ev, ed., *Voprosy Kon'yunktury*, Moscow 1925, p. 59.

to those Marx had discussed when explaining the classical cycle:

'[Just as] Marx asserted that the material basis of crises, or of average cycles repeating themselves each decade, is the material wearing out, replacement, and expansion of means of production in the form of machines lasting an average of ten years, it can be suggested that the material basis of long cycles is the wearing out, replacement, and expansion of fixed-capital goods that require a long period of time and enormous expenditures to produce. *The replacement and expansion of these goods does not proceed smoothly, but in spurts, another expression of which are the long waves of the conjuncture.* . . . Thus the long cycles of the conjuncture constitute the processes of the deviation of the real level of the elements of the capitalist system from the equilibrium level . . . of this system; processes in the course of which the equilibrium itself changes [as shown by the unbroken-trend line].'[52]

Trotsky did not deny that economic fluctuations resulted from variations in fixed-capital investments. But he did argue that it was precisely the failure of investments to recover in Europe that explained the current unevenness of development on the opposite sides of the Atlantic. Thus even in its proper (segmented) form, the trend had to be recognized as a mathematical abstraction that obscured Europe's problems in the world market and the consequent inability to achieve even a modicum of stability. With its limited access to world markets Europe was experiencing contradictions of prewar intensity even before reaching prewar levels of output.[53] Not only was there no stabilization such as Bukharin had suggested and Kondrat'ev appeared to confirm; there was not even a regular cycle—only 'twitches, spasms, sudden and acute fluctuations, with no periodization of the economic conjuncture'.[54] The Ruhr occupation exemplified the military and political disturbances—or external conditions—that were disrupting capitalism's internal dynamic and preventing 'the free or semi-free play of economic forces'.[55] Kondrat'ev had attempted to reduce all these

[52] N.D. Kondrat'ev and D.I. Oparin, *Bol'shie Tsikly Kon'yunktury*, Moscow 1928, pp. 60–61.

[53] See the comment on Varga's report in *Planovoe Khozyaistvo*, no. 6 (June 1925), p. 173.

[54] Ibid., p. 176.

[55] Trotsky, 'K Voprosu o Tendentsiyakh Razvitii Mirovovo Khozyaistva', *Planovoe Khozyaistvo*, no. 1 (January 1926), p. 188.

external conditions to manifestations of the long cycle, to the 'regularities' of capitalism's immanent processes. Here, declared Trotsky, 'is Professor Kondrat'ev's error'.[56]

Other Marxists were equally sceptical of Kondrat'ev's findings. S. Guberman, who specialized in cycles and the theory of markets, charged that the unbroken-trend line served as an apologetic 'natural law' of capitalist growth: 'the secular movement is the sort of fiction that inevitably leads to distortion of the real dynamic of capitalism if its different epochs are not taken into consideration'.[57] A.G. Gertsenshtein, author of the book *Do Long Cycles of the Conjuncture Exist?* (1929), took the same view: Kondrat'ev's 'cycles' resembled a 'fly-wheel in empty space'.[58] In reality separate countries developed at different rates according to natural and geographic conditions, changes in economic organization, and the deforming influences issuing from the world market.[59] L. Eventov, who would later himself win notoriety over the issue of the three-year cycle, accused the professor of posing as a 'priest' of mathematics in order to conceal his intellectual poverty behind 'statistical probabilities and mathematical formulae'.[60] Not even the other professors were sympathetic. Fal'kner could find no long-run decline in output to substantiate a falling wave of the long cycle.[61] Professor D.I. Oparin proved to be a remorseless and often petty critic of Kondrat'ev's statistical methods. Professor Y. Dimanshtein quoted the findings of Harvard economists in support of a three-and-a-half year cycle.[62] And Professor S. Pervushin, although he accepted the existence of long, wave-like movements, denied that they were cyclical or even had anything to do with capitalism. In his opinion they originated in agriculture and had

[56] Ibid., p. 190.

[57] S. Guberman, 'Problemy Malykh i Bol'shikh Tsiklov', *Sotsialisticheskoe Khozyaistvo*, no. 1 (1927), p. 41.

[58] A. Gertsenshtein, *Sushchestvuyut li Bol'shie Tsikly Kon'yunktury?*, Moscow 1929, p. 55.

[59] Ibid., p. 14.

[60] L. Eventov, 'O Prirode Dlitel'nykh Kolebanii v Kapitalisticheskom Dinamike', *Problemy Ekonomiki*, no. 1 (January 1929), p. 65.

[61] Kondrat'ev and Oparin, p. 177.

[62] See *Gospodarstvo Ukrainy*, no. 5–6 (1926), p. 164.

operated for centuries: 'They characterize the economic dynamic as such, and from this point of view the distinction between capitalist and pre-capitalist economy is simply obliterated.'[63]

Kondrat'ev was shocked by the hostile response. When Marxist economists imputed bourgeois motives to his work he protested that he was dealing with 'scientific generalizations' that might be correct or incorrect but certainly had nothing to do with motives.[64] 'We do not understand', he wrote, '. . . how critics . . . can see any particular optimism in our conclusions. . . . In order to be an optimist or pessimist in scientific work one must employ it to defend a specific political, socio-economic idea. There is nothing of the kind in our book; it stands on a theoretical plane, and therefore our views are completely indifferent to pessimism or optimism.'[65] On the question of methodology Kondrat'ev defended himself as follows:

'Crossing through different stages, capitalism remains capitalism and maintains its basic features and regularities. Otherwise how could these stages be stages of capitalism? The law of value and prices, the tendencies of the norm of profit and production, the waverings of the conjuncture and crises, might manifest themselves with one distinction or another at different stages, but I am not aware that Marxism or any other trend in economics has asserted that the law of value and prices, or the law of profits and of conjunctural fluctuations, is *absolutely different* at diverse stages of capitalist development so as to preclude generalizations. Likewise, I am not aware of any physiology that asserts that the laws of the blood's circulation and of respiration are *absolutely different* at the different stages of an organism, and do not admit of generalizations.'[66]

Try as he might to defend his views by appropriating Marxist terminology, Kondrat'ev failed to halt the torrent of criticism Trotsky had unleashed. Trotsky attacked the theory of long waves for the same reason as he disputed Bukharin's talk of equilibrium and capitalist stabilization. In both cases inadequate attention was

[63] S.A. Pervushin, *Khozyaistvennaya Kon'yunktura*, Moscow 1925, p. 20.

[64] Kondrat'ev, 'Spornye Voprosy Mirovovo Khozyaistva i Krizisa', *Sotsialisticheskoe Khozyaistvo*, no. 4–5 (June-July 1923), p. 58.

[65] Ibid., p. 75.

[66] Kondrat'ev, 'K Voprosu o Bol'shikh Tsiklakh Kon'yunktury', *Planovoe Khozyaistvo*, no. 8 (August 1926), p. 171.

paid to the external conditions that determined the contours of conjunctural changes. 'For example', he told a meeting in January 1926, 'the United States of America is a new, powerful country—is it able to impose stagnation on Europe? Of course it is. And does this have anything to do with the internal rhythm of Europe's economic development? No, it does not.'[67] When the external conditions were favourable, when 'new continents, colonies, and new markets' were being opened up, capitalism grew rapidly (and vice versa). Kondrat'ev considered expansion into new markets one of the 'regularities' of the long cycle; Bukharin thought the internal market of a 'state-capitalist trust' could guarantee expanded reproduction and the maintenance of equilibrium.

Through sheer persistence Trotsky discovered the anti-Marxist implications of the theory of moving equilibrium. A more succinct criticism might have concentrated on a single issue, the incompatibility between Marx's theory of disproportionalities and any notion of equilibrium as more than a passing moment of the cycle. One Marxist who understood the question perfectly was N. Osinsky. In *The World Economy and Crises* (1925) Osinsky pointed out that moving equilibrium implied the 'harmonization', 'rationality', and 'stability' of a system in which equilibrium really required the senseless destruction of capital in a crisis.[68] 'Throughout the entire remainder of the capitalist cycle the contradictions of capitalism . . . create a constant lack of equilibrium.'[69] It was not hard to find evidence to support this interpretation of Marx. In *Capital* Volume 3 Marx said quite explicitly that the 'crises are always but momentary and forcible solutions of the existing contradictions. They are violent eruptions which for a time restore the disturbed equilibrium'.[70] In the same volume Marx also described equilibrium as an 'accident', as the *post facto* imposition of rationality upon an irrational system. In *Theories of Surplus-Value* he referred to capitalism's 'permanent disproportionality' and 'permanent disharmony'.[71] A genuine moving equilibrium

---

[67] Trotsky, 'K Voprosu o Tendentsiyakh Razvitii . . .' p. 190.
[68] N. Osinsky, *Mirovoe Khozyaistvo i Krizisy*, Moscow 1925, pp. 51–52.
[69] Ibid., p. 53.
[70] Marx, *Capital* Volume 3, p. 244; cf. Osinsky, p. 43.
[71] Osinsky, p. 54.

would require nothing less than planned capitalism, or the ability to organize production and anticipate social demand.

By emphasizing the uneven character of capitalism and the inevitability of fresh economic crises, Osinsky and other Marxists made it clear that they would no longer be intimidated by the bourgeois professors. From 1925–6 both Kondrat'ev and Fal'kner lost whatever influence they once possessed. Varga expressed the new attitude when he complained that the teachings of Marx and Lenin had bounced off the 'blank wall' of Fal'kner's 'bourgeois class consciousness'. The latest incidents were 'a reminder of how much remains to be done on the ideological front'.[72] The professors of the old regime might protest all they wished that they were not 'politicians', that they were concerned only with 'purely economic' questions. 'But that kind of answer would be a lie. Whoever declares himself to be a "disinterested party" in the class struggle between the bourgeoisie and the proletariat actually stands on the side of the bourgeoisie. Whoever asserts that he looks at the contemporary world in a "purely economic" way is actually engaged in politics and serves the interests of the bourgeoisie.'[73]

Raising the demand for political limitations on the scope of economic discourse, Varga helped to inaugurate a process he would later regret. In 1929 he would find himself in a position similar to that of Fal'kner and Kondrat'ev, defending what appeared to be objective truth against the distortions of Stalinist party functionaries. The wide-ranging character of economic debates in the interim can be attributed to the disunity that continued to exist at the highest levels of the Communist party during the 1920s. Until the leadership struggle was resolved there could be no 'official' party position. In the years 1926–7 Stalin gradually dislodged Trotsky from power and simultaneously moved the stabilization debate into a new phase.

Determined to promote the expansion of heavy industry at the expense of the peasantry, Stalin eventually realized that his alliance with Bukharin had to end. The threat of imperialist war provided a more plausible rationalization for industrial self-sufficiency than

[72] Varga, 'Dinamicheskie Protsessy v Sovremennom Mirovom Khozyaistve', *Planovoe Khozyaistvo*, no. 11 (November 1925), p. 191.
[73] Ibid., p. 194.

the prospect of continued international stability. Trotsky's defeat was therefore accompanied by a widening rift between Stalin and Bukharin over the fate of stabilization and its implications for Soviet domestic policy. Bukharin decided that new investments in the West were restoring capitalism's internal markets and might soon provide a solid foundation for expanded reproduction. Stalin saw only the practical difficulties the imperialists faced in their struggle over external markets. The new battle lines were drawn when Stalin adopted what Bukharin must have considered a Trotskyist thesis: stabilization had become 'rotten' and the 'problem of markets' had emerged as a necessary consequence of the restoration of capitalist production to prewar levels. The hardening of Stalin's view took Bukharin by surprise, but it could have been detected in his response to three new developments during and after 1925: the progress of the Chinese revolution, the general strike in Britain, and the onset of what Varga termed the 'stabilization crisis'.

4. The Chinese Revolution

Soviet involvement in China during the early 1920s had been the result of an uneasy alliance between the Chinese Communist Party and Sun Yat-sen, organizer of the nationalist Kuomintang. After Sun's death in the spring of 1925, the Kuomintang divided into left- and right-wing factions over the issue of continued co-operation with the Comintern. Within a year Chiang Kai-shek gained the upper hand and turned on his erstwhile allies. The fact that Chiang betrayed the Communists before they could betray him upset Comintern strategy and imposed a difficult choice: should local Communists be sacrificed in order to unify China and deny the imperialists control over a vast market? Or should the Comintern now attempt to radicalize the peasantry and overthrow Chiang? Stalin decided it was more important to close the Chinese market than to press for an immediate socialist revolution.

The strategy of undermining stabilization in the West by promoting anti-imperialist (or nationalist) uprisings in the East evoked supportive commentary and advice from Varga and a number of other economists. Originally Varga had thought the development of capitalism in Asia would require decades. By July

1925, he was reconsidering that view, noting that '*Asia is making rapid progress in capitalist development.* It is passing from the stage of natural economy to that of commodity economy, from handicrafts to capitalist large-scale industry, from self-sufficiency to integration in the world economy. . . . *The importance of the Asiatic market for the imperialist world powers is rapidly increasing.*'[74] Asia offered 'enormous possibilities for the development of capitalism', including a huge population of potential consumers and 'great stores of unexploited natural wealth'. Hitherto Varga thought stabilization a pious hope. But if the capitalists plunged into China with the construction of new railways and communications facilities, the whole future of imperialism might be altered. 'The events in China have become the centre of world politics. . . . It is upon Asia . . . that the bourgeois economists are concentrating all their hopes for a fresh revival of capitalism.'[75] The clear implication was that the integration of China into the imperialist world economy had to be thwarted at any cost. By excluding foreign capital from the East it would be possible to revolutionize workers in the West. Soviet policy in China had to be subordinated to the goal of generating instability in Europe. Varga explained it this way:

'*It appears as if the fate of world capitalism is going to be decided in Asia.* Either the imperialist powers, suppressing their mutual antagonisms for the moment, will succeed in establishing and extending their dominance in Asia, and in thus isolating the Soviet Union from the South and the East, . . . or the *Asiatic peoples will emancipate themselves*—perhaps at the outset under the hegemony of the proletariat—*from the yoke of the imperialist exploiters*, thus depriving . . . the bourgeoisie of . . . the possibility of employing colonial surplus profits for the purpose of buying over sections of the upper strata of the proletariat at home. . . . These are the most important possibilities of further development.'[76]

To Varga and other opponents of stabilization the *market question* had become decisive. Political unrest in China was seen as an insuperable obstacle to the restoration of a European labour

[74] Varga, 'Economics and Economic Policy in the Second Quarter of 1925', *International Press Correspondence*, V, no. 66 (26 August 1925), p. 191.
[75] Ibid.
[76] Ibid.

aristocracy. In April 1925 Bukhartsev referred to the 'organic crisis' of postwar capitalism and maintained that the 'problem of contemporary capitalism is the problem of markets. Until the key to this problem is found, the equilibrium of capitalism cannot be restored'.[77] Spektator wrote: 'we have clear evidence of overproduction in the sense that the productive apparatus [of the capitalist countries] exceeds the purchasing power of the population.'[78] Even Lapinsky, whom Bukhartsev had recently called 'the father of stabilization', believed that the 'organic' problem of inadequate domestic markets would cause Asia to become 'the centre of the world politics of imperialism'.[79]

While Bukharin pondered the achievements of 'organized capitalism', Stalin predicted that 'the process of capitalism's "recovery" contains within itself the germs of its inherent weakness and disintegration'. As early as March 1925, he balanced Europe's partial stabilization against the growth of colonial unrest:

'The growth and consolidation of the national-liberation movement in India, China, Egypt, Indonesia, North Africa, etc., . . . is undermining capitalism's rear . . . for its "recovery" imperialism must enlarge its sphere of influence in the colonies and dependent countries, whereas the struggle of these countries against imperialism is undoubtedly becoming intensified.'[80]

At a party meeting in Moscow Stalin held that the further expansion of capitalism was theoretically possible—Lenin's *Imperialism* allowed for uneven improvements—assuming both the success of the Dawes Plan and suppression of revolt in the colonies. But neither assumption was reasonable. 'To think that a cultured nation like the German nation . . . will consent to bear this . . . yoke without making repeated serious attempts at a revolutionary upheaval means believing in miracles.'[81] As for China, Stalin asked: 'Does not the growth of the revolutionary movement in China show that the machinations of the foreign imperialists are doomed to

[77] Bukhartsev, 'O "Pafose" Vosstanovleniya Mirovovo Khozyaistva', *Bol'shevik*, no. 8 (30 April 1925), p. 108.

[78] Spektator, ' "Stabilizatsiya" Kapitalizma . . .', p. 100.

[79] N. Lapinsky, *Novaya Faza Imperializma i ee Ekonomicheskie Istochniki*, Moscow 1925, p. 51.

[80] Stalin, *Works*, VII, p. 52–53.

[81] Ibid., p. 99.

failure?'[82] In December 1925, Stalin told the Fourteenth Congress of the Soviet Communist Party that stabilization was 'rotten':[83] the great powers were faced with 'the danger of losing their chief [support in the] rear, i.e., the colonies. Here the stabilization of capitalism is in a bad way.'[84]

In March 1926, when Chiang Kai-shek declared martial law in Canton, imprisoned his Soviet advisors, disbanded trade unions, and began to arrest local Communists, Stalin resisted pressures to make a complete break. The fate of Europe appeared to be at stake, and in the summer of 1926 the Soviet government supported Chiang's Northern Expedition to unify the country. By March 1927 Trotsky began to attack Stalin's betrayal of the Chinese revolution and his failure to encourage the creation of soviets. Ignoring Trotsky's protest, Stalin ordered the revolutionary workers of Shanghai to bury their weapons and welcome Chiang's advancing army. On 12 April 1927 Chiang entered the city and promptly massacred every Communist he could find. Even after the Shanghai massacre, Stalin hoped to 'reorganize' the Kuomintang and replace Chiang with left-wing nationalists still in touch with the Comintern. Had Trotsky shared the prevailing Soviet concern over stabilization, he might have been more sympathetic to Stalin's preemptive policies. As it was, the Opposition accused Stalin of clinging to the Kuomintang in order to disguise the previous errors of Comintern policy.

5. The 'Stabilization Crisis' and the British General Strike

Besides the Chinese events, the second factor that encouraged Stalin's ambivalent view of capitalist prospects was the contention of the economists that stabilization was already growing over into a 'stabilization crisis'. Varga repeatedly pointed to the absence of a normal business cycle in any of the leading countries.[85] There was

[82] Ibid.
[83] Ibid., p. 274.
[84] Ibid., p. 276.
[85] Varga, 'World Economics at the End of 1925', *International Press Correspondence*, VI, no. 12 (11 February, 1926), p. 173.

no reason to alter the judgement passed upon Fal'kner in November 1925: 'all prophecies regarding a fresh revival of European capitalism' were merely 'idle predictions' and 'counter-revolutionary apologetics'.[86] Europe would continue to experience 'rapidly recurring and lengthy crises, interspersed with brief intervals of better conditions [and] . . . acutely revolutionary situations'.[87]

In Germany the 'stabilization crisis', or the deflationary adjustment required to restore confidence in the currency, was plainly visible in the early weeks of 1926. A restrictive monetary policy had resulted in sensational bankruptcies. The Frankfurt Chamber of Commerce had estimated the nation's productive potential at 120 per cent of prewar levels, while the market was able to absorb only 70 per cent of prewar output.[88] American credits had provided the circulating capital needed to revive German industry—only to create an 'exceedingly acute economic crisis', with up to 3 million workers unemployed. In response to the problem of markets German industrialists were rationalizing production, shutting down the least efficient plants and transferring the burden of contraction to the working class in the form of chronic unemployment. As other countries sought to stabilize their currencies, they too would pass through the 'stabilization crisis'. Adaptation 'in a downward direction'—or what Trotsky had called the 'levelling out in reverse'—continued to typify the epoch of capitalist decline, with no sign of expanded reproduction or a restored moving equilibrium. Varga foresaw massive unemployment in France: 'We are . . . of the opinion that after the stabilization [of the franc]the newly established productive apparatus will fall into disuse even more rapidly than in Germany; the stabilization crisis will cut even more deeply, and the class struggle will be more severe.'[89]

The norm towards which all the European countries appeared to be moving was chronic stagnation of the sort prevalent in Britain. Here there had been no rapid inflation, the export interests of industrial capital being sacrificed since 1921 to demands by

[86] Ibid., p. 176.
[87] Ibid., p. 178.
[88] Ibid., p. 176.
[89] Varga, 'Economics and Economic Policy in the Fourth Quarter of, 1925', *International Press Correspondence*, VI, no. 15 (25 February 1926), p. 224.

financial institutions for a stable pound. Britain had been suffering a stabilization crisis for the past five years. For the sake of a stable currency, several leading industries had been chronically depressed. Iron and steel output at the beginning of 1925 stood below the monthly average for 1913; shipbuilding had fallen to its lowest level since 1909; and the cotton textile industry, afflicted by a boycott in China, had been on short hours throughout 1925.[90] Endorsing Varga's assessment, Spektator claimed that far from being stabilized in the sphere of production, Britain had been in the grip of an 'organic crisis' ever since the war.[91] Mary Smit, of the Soviet Central Statistical Office, pointed out that the level of British unemployment even in the best postwar years was higher than in most previous cyclical crises: 'From this point of view it is clear that the current crisis, which began in 1921, is still far from over, and that its general dimensions . . . cannot be compared to any previous crises.'[92] Eventov noted that British exports had stagnated far below the prewar volume while productive capacity was actually shrinking.[93] Bukharin had implied that the resumption of investments would restore capitalism's internal market. But the majority of Soviet economists still agreed with Trotsky that new investments made little sense so long as the European countries were unable to employ the productive potential already at their disposal.

The deterioration of British exports was especially pronounced in the coal industry, where petroleum products and electrical energy were providing new competition. Chaotically organized in comparison to their Ruhr competitiors, British mine owners complained they would be ruined unless wages were drastically reduced. The Conservative government of Baldwin attempted to defuse the crisis by subsidizing the industry and appointing a committee of inquiry. In the spring of 1926 the committee reported its agreement with mine owners on the need for wage cuts. The

[90] Varga, 'Economics and Economic Policy in the Fourth Quarter of 1925', *International Press Correspondence*, VI, no. 16 (4 March 1926), p. 245.

[91] Spektator, 'K Polozheniyu Khozyaistva v Anglii', *Kommunisticheskii Internatsional*, no. 3 (March 1926), p. 113.

[92] N. Osinsky, M. Spektator, M. Smit, and Politikus, *Istoricheskii Krizis Angliiskovo Kapitalizma*, Moscow and Leningrad 1926, p. 69.

[93] L. Eventov, 'Mirovoe Khozyaistvo v Pervom Kvartale 1926 Goda', *Planovoe Khozyaistvo*, no. 6 (June 1926), pp. 143–45.

political consequences were better than Soviet leaders had dared hope. The miners' union rejected the committee's recommendations, the owners imposed a lock-out, and in May 1926, Britain was briefly paralysed by a general strike of 5 million workers.

The response of British labour to the new wage-cutting offensive provoked an unprecedented display of international solidarity. A year earlier, in anticipation of the clash, Soviet trade unions had formed an Anglo-Russian Committee with British labour leaders. Now a strike fund of 2 million rubles was collected in the Soviet Union and supplemented by contributions from workers in Holland, Switzerland, Denmark, France, Germany, and Austria. Dock workers in Europe again imposed a coal blockade, supported by railway workers and seamen, and for nine perilous days Britain hovered on the brink of civil strife. Caught up in the excitement, Soviet party leaders momentarily reached unanimous agreement that the outlook for stabilization had suddenly turned bleak.

On the verge of being eased out of Comintern affairs as a result of his dispute with Stalin, Zinoviev grasped at the general strike in the hope of last-minute vindication. The Anglo-Russian Committee went the way of the alliance with Chiang Kai-shek when the British TUC rejected the offer of Soviet gold and abandoned the miners after their refusal to compromise; but Zinoviev promised that the opportunists were signing their own death warrants: 'The English working class . . . a giant, sees its hands and feet being bound with cords by the dwarfs who call themselves its leaders. The English working class will shake off these gentlemen with a single shrug of its shoulders. These people have sung their last song . . . the revolutionary impetus . . . will grow more than ever after this strike.'[94]

Lest Zinoviev's enthusiasm be discounted as politically suspect, let us note that Bukharin spoke in the same terms. Prone to hyperbole as ever, he compared the strike to events in Petrograd during the summer of 1917. In the Russian revolution the soviets had sprung up alongside the provisional government, creating a situation of 'dual power'. The TUC had similarly become involved in the distribution of supplies and administration of public services,

[94] Zinoviev, 'The International Significance of the General Strike in Great Britain', *International Press Correspondence*, VI, no. 48 (17 June 1926), p. 791.

prompting the British Communist Party to issue the slogan 'All power to the General Council'—just as Lenin had called for 'All power to the soviets'. Had British workers compelled the TUC to transform industrial action into a political attack on the state, Bukharin thought Baldwin's government and indeed British capitalism as a whole would have collapsed. 'Some comrades' (including Trotsky) were demanding withdrawal from the Anglo-Russian Committee (just as they would criticize the alliance with Chiang Kai-shek a year later). But Bukharin insisted on continuing support for trade-union reactionaries 'in just about the same way that a rope supports the person being hanged from it'.[95]

For Stalin, the British general strike afforded the most imposing evidence of all against stabilization. The leftward movement of the working class had resulted from the loss of colonial profits and the consequent need to reduce proletarian living standards. The stabilization of capitalism was intensifying international competition, restoring commercial contacts, and thereby having the paradoxical effect of advancing the world revolution. 'The struggle for a market', Stalin announced, 'has again arisen with fresh force.' Choosing his words carefully, Stalin described the significance of the strike this way:

'The strike in Britain has shown that the resolution of the Communist International on the temporary and insecure character of stabilization is absolutely correct. The attack of British capital upon the British miners was an attempt to transform the temporary, insecure stabilization into a firm and permanent one. That attempt did not succeed and could not have succeeded. The British workers . . . have shown the whole capitalist world that the firm stabilization of capitalism . . . is impossible, that experiments like the British one are fraught with the danger of the destruction of the foundations of capitalism.'[96]

6. Industrial Rationalization and 'State Capitalism'

Stalin's appraisal of stabilization grew steadily more negative after

[95] Bukharin, 'Questions of the International Revolutionary Struggle', *International Press Correspondence*, VI, no. 52 (8 July 1926), p. 852.
[96] Stalin, *Works*, VIII, pp. 175–76.

the spring of 1926. Cracks in the alliance against Trotsky widened and simultaneously undermined Bukharin's position within the party leadership. The beginnings of a decline in Bukharin's influence were accompanied by a resurgence of Varga's. Serious disagreement arose between the two over how to interpret recent changes in industrial organization. The dispute closely paralleled that which had divided Marxists prior to the First World War. Traditionally, Luxemburgists had subordinated the emergence of trusts and cartels to the problem of capitalism's chronically inadequate market. In the absence of 'third-party' demand, capitalism leaned in the direction of a permanent crisis of overproduction. Hilferding had taken the opposing view that organization created the potential for internal capitalist stability—at the cost, as Bukharin inferred, of more acute international conflicts. Although Lenin had shown that this division could be reconciled through Marx's theory of the business cycle, by the mid-1920s a similar polarization occurred within the Soviet Communist Party. Varga gravitated in the direction of neo-Luxemburgism; Bukharin resurrected his earlier theory of 'state-capitalist' organization.

An accelerated centralization of industrial capital had been under way in Europe since 1925. Reporting on attempts to form cartels and restrict output in several branches of production, Varga contended that the Dawes Plan was 'rendering the *question of finding markets* more acute than ever'.[97] Each step towards recovery in industrial production aggravated the shortage of markets and imparted a new impetus to the opposing tendency of limiting industrial operations. The 'feverish' tempo of concentration reached its apogee in 1927 with conclusion of a European iron and steel cartel. Made up of Germany, France, Belgium, and Luxembourg, the new cartel was to put the finishing touches to the reparations settlement with Germany. Both the French and German governments covertly sought to resolve the problem of Ruhr coal and Lorraine iron ore by postponing a trade agreement until private industrialists worked out their own arrangements for heavy industry. This inter-state collusion made a lasting impression. According to Varga, it demonstrated 'more clearly than ever

[97] Varga, 'Economics and Economic Policy in the First Quarter of 1925', *International Press Correspondence*, V, no. 45 (28 May 1925), p. 587.

that the state apparatus . . . with all its ministries, parliaments, etc., is merely the executive organ of the bourgeoisie'.[98]

But Varga did not go beyond this observation to make a more positive statement about capitalism's organizational potential. For him as for most other economists, the real question raised by concentration was whether it would eventually pass from adaptation 'in a downward direction' to a new phase of expanded reproduction. Would the capitalists install new equipment in the organized industries and raise the *productivity* of labour? Or would they rely upon 'Fordization', piece-work wages, and other forms of industrial 'speed-ups' to raise the *intensity* of labour without creating a corresponding market? To the majority of economists it seemed clear that the capitalists were adopting the second course: intensification was serving as a *substitute* for new investment, and its final result would be greater unemployment and even more acute overproduction. Spektator's comments reflected the prevailing opinion:

'. . . one can say that although capitalism in 1926 is different from what it was in 1920–21, it still has not created a stable basis for itself in the form of *the expanded reproduction of fixed capital*. . . . The expansion of output, the better use of productive forces, organizational improvements and so forth, are without doubt successes on the part of postwar capitalism; but taking place in the restricted context of a severely narrowed market, they have the consequence of worsening the position of the working class as a whole and must evoke protests which again and again will hurl the capitalists back from the social positions they occupy.'[99]

When the 'curve of development' had tended upwards, industrial rationalization had not displaced workers; on the contrary, the introduction of new technology coincided with the growth of employment resulting from the opening of new markets and a rise in investments in heavy industry. However, with the advent of 'monopolistic' and 'organized' capitalism, Spektator believed that rationalization had become merely 'the intensification of labour

[98] Varga, 'Economics and Economic Policy in the Third Quarter of 1926', *International Press Correspondence*, VI, no. 81 (30 November 1926), p. 1409.

[99] Spektator, '"Ratsionalizatsiya" i Kartelirovanie', *Kommunisticheskii Internatsional*, no. 1 (15 September 1926), p. 30.

using the existing means of production'.[100] In many industries, including the entire engineering sector, existing productive capacity was already excessive. In order to safeguard the value of existing plant, the owners would do everything possible to postpone the introduction of new technology. There could be no doubt whatever that 'a long period of economic stagnation' lay ahead.[101]

Soviet economists held that the regressive content of rationalization was defined by the suffocating problem of markets. Bukharin, on the other hand, suspected that a new surge of investment was about to alleviate working-class impoverishment and create a new flow of internal demand. In his address to the Fifteenth Congress of the party in October 1926, he admitted that stabilization was still 'relative': the fluctuations in economic activity still took the form of 'jumps and spurts'; as yet there was no regular periodicity.[102] But Bukharin also believed the economists had underestimated the extent of investment in new technology: 'In the literature of the Soviet Union . . . it is frequently assumed that this rationalization is restricted exclusively to the organization of work, and that technological changes play no part whatever. I believe this view to be wrong, however excellent the intentions of those who hold it. Were it really the case, the position of the capitalist world . . . would be much worse than it really is.' In the German coal industry introduction of new equipment had caused a considerable increase in labour *productivity*. The same was true of the steel, potash, and chemical industries. Entirely new branches of production were also growing up, including 'the conversion of coal into a liquid state, the production of benzine by means of hydration, the manufacture of artificial silk by new methods, etc'.[103] Product innovation was 'part and parcel of the system of stabilization tendencies' and inevitably suggested 'a new phase of capitalist development' in the direction of expanded reproduction.[104] Stalin and Varga expected colonial revolutions to lower the income of the working class and eliminate

[100] See Spektator's comments in *Mirovoe Khozyaistvo i Mirovaya Politika*, no. 10–11 (October-November 1926), p. 25.

[101] Ibid., p. 28.

[102] Bukharin, 'Questions of International Politics', *International Press Correspondence*, VI, no. 72 (4 November 1926), p. 1246.

[103] Ibid., p. 1249.

[104] Ibid., p. 1250.

the Social Democratic labour aristocracy; Bukharin insisted that new technology required new job skills and would create a new stratum of privileged workers. 'I do not go so far as those comrades who are of the opinion that the labour aristocracy is . . . abolished, for . . . the process of rationalization itself forms certain groupings of a new labour aristocracy.'[105] At the seventh plenary meeting of the Comintern's Executive Committee (the ECCI) in November 1926, Bukharin placed even greater emphasis on recent technological innovations, which were 'qualitatively modifying' industrial production:

'The rapid increase of the application of electrical energy with a tendency towards construction of tremendous central stations, the transition from hydro to thermal stations with the utilization of coal waste products, the increased power of turbines and the tension of the current, methods to produce liquid fuel, new methods of treating metals, the preparation of artificial silk and various salts by chemical means, experiments in the production of artificial cotton, the extraction of benzine from coal, wide application of Diesel engines in water transportation, the wide application of automobile transportation, etc., etc.—all these factors qualitatively change the technical basis of the productive process.'[106]

Varga's address to the same meeting of the ECCI testified to the strains that were mounting. In his judgement, Bukharin's reference to working-class impoverishment was ambiguous and 'inadequate'. A proper account of 'chronic unemployment and chronic overproduction' must explain the narrowing of the internal market on a class basis, with particular attention to the negative effects of industrial rationalization: 'We can see what the capitalists are actually doing: wage cuts, rationalization. This means that they are trying to get for themselves a still greater share of the values produced, by which means, of course, they still further cut down the possibilities of the internal market. . . . And how do the capitalists think they are going to escape from this situation? They want to dispose of their goods on the world market. . . . As far as the formation of cartels is concerned . . . these mean exactly the same

[105] Ibid., p. 1254.
[106] Bukharin, 'The World Situation and the Tasks of the Comintern', *International Press Correspondence*, VI, no. 85 (3 December 1926), p. 1464.

thing: artificial raising of the prices of commodities, viz., the narrowing of . . . the internal markets. So we see that we travel around in the same circle.'[107] Rather than holding forth the prospect of stability, the contradictions of capitalism were reproducing themselves 'through and within the stabilization'.[108]

During the early months of 1927 the differences simmered. Economic conditions improved in most European countries, the boom in America continued, and Varga and Spektator grudgingly acknowledged the beginnings of European investment, all the while arguing that the major production increases came from labour intensification. In the hope of sustaining the upward trend, a World Economic Conference was held in Geneva in May 1927, under the auspices of the League of Nations (and minus the United States). French representatives proposed to dismantle direct barriers to trade and replace them with international cartel agreements. Speaking for the Soviet Union, Osinsky proposed instead that the capitalists expand their market by granting credits to facilitate Soviet imports. Mutual relations between the capitalist and Soviet governments were to be based on 'recognition of the inevitable co-existence of two opposing systems', leaving room for a variety of economic agreements.[109] But even before the conference ended the British made it obvious that their interest in economic co-operation with Soviet Russia was strictly limited. A police raid on Arcos Ltd., the Soviet trading company in London, was justified by the charge that Soviet activities in China violated the commercial agreement signed by the two countries in 1921. On 26 May 1927 the British severed diplomatic relations.

With his customary zeal, Bukharin now exclaimed that the Chinese revolution was 'the dynamic force throwing out of balance everything upon which our Soviet Union was depending for its breathing-space'.[110] The war scare of 1927 proved helpful in expelling the Trotskyist Opposition from the party, for it was clear

[107] See Varga's comments in *International Press Correspondence*, VI, no. 88 (20 December 1926), p. 1530.

[108] Ibid., p. 1531.

[109] Osinsky, 'Mirovoe Ekonomicheskoe Polozhenie', *Ekonomicheskoe Obozrenie*, no. 5 (May 1927), p. 29.

[110] Bukharin, 'The Results of the Plenary Session of the ECCI', *International Press Correspondence*, VII, no. 37 (30 June 1927), p. 775.

that in time of crisis party 'unity' was crucial. At the same time, however, Bukharin's exaggerated remarks ran counter to all he had recently been saying concerning stabilization. Having assumed Zinoviev's Comintern responsibilities, Bukharin told the eighth ECCI plenum in Moscow that 'we are rapidly moving towards an epoch which will put an end to our breathing-space . . . a period involving wars and attacks upon the Soviet Union. We do not know when the storm will break over our heads, but we do know that it is approaching, dark and threatening.'[111]

Tiring of Bukharin's volatility, the economists were no more convinced of the proximity of war than of his interpretation of rationalization. Varga cited low interest rates and stable share prices to show that 'the behaviour of the capitalist class in the leading imperialist countries demonstrates . . . that war in the near future is considered by these circles to be most improbable'.[112] The British bourgeoisie was currently divided between 'diehard' and 'liberal' groups, the latter being committed to free trade and pacificism: 'in the immediate future . . . the liberal tendency will prevail'.[113] In August Osinsky told the party's Central Committee that the chances of war were remote.[114] As late as November 1927, Spektator took the same position, asking why the capitalists would jeopardize the possibilities of expanded reproduction by embarking upon military adventures.[115]

By this time Stalin realized that the way to humiliate Bukharin and press ahead with his own plans for heavy industry was to play the war danger to the limit. 'It can scarcely be doubted', he wrote in July 1927, 'that the main issue of the present day is the threat of a new imperialist war. It is not a matter of some vague and immaterial war "danger" . . . but of the real and actual *threat* of a new war in general, and of a war against the USSR in particular.' The Conserva-

[111] Ibid., p. 777.

[112] Varga, 'Polozhenie Mirovovo Khozyaistva', *Ekonomicheskoe Obozrenie*, no. 5 (May 1927), p. 192.

[113] Varga, 'Obzor Kon'yunktury po Stranam', *Mirovoe Khozyaistvo i Mirovaya Politika*, no. 8 (August 1927), p. 148.

[114] See A.I. Rykov, 'The Joint Plenum of the CC and CCC of the CPSU', *International Press Correspondence*, VII, no. 51 (1 September 1927), p. 1136.

[115] Spektator, 'Mirovoe Khozyaistvo za Poslednie Desyat' Let', *Planovoe Khozyaistvo*, no. 11 (November 1927), p. 171.

tive government in Britain, the 'most malignant strangler of peoples' revolutions', was engaged in a 'frantic struggle' over markets. Rallying Europe for an attack upon the USSR, the British were subsidizing the *émigré* 'government' of the Ukraine and 'financing bands of spies and terrorists, who blow up bridges, set fire to factories and commit acts of terrorism against USSR ambassadors'.[116] In August Stalin delivered a speech on 'The International Situation and the Defence of the USSR', insisting that China and the Soviet Union had attracted the attention of the imperialists because the restoration of production in the West made clear the need for new markets. 'Is it difficult to understand that the excessive growth of capitalism's productive potentialities, coupled with the limited capacity of the world market . . . intensifies the struggle for markets and deepens the crisis of capitalism?'[117] The rhetorical question might well have been addressed to Bukharin, for by the time of the Fifteenth Congress in December 1927, Bukharin was already retracting his forecast of hostilities.

Internal Soviet politics had become as tense at the end of 1927 as at any moment since the introduction of the NEP in 1921. The first phase of the industrialization drive, accompanied by several errors of policy, was causing peasants to hoard their grain rather than sell it for cash that could not readily be transformed into low-cost consumer goods.[118] From Stalin's perspective, the class enemy— the *kulak*, or wealthy peasant—was launching a 'grain strike' in order to paralyse industrialization and hold the working class to ransom. To break the strike agriculture would have to be collectivized (by means of 'demonstration and persuasion'). The peasant would be compelled to sell to the state by strict measures of revolutionary legality. Stalin added that revolutionary legality 'does not, of course, preclude the taking of certain necessary administrative measures'.[119]

Bukharin's hope of conciliating the peasant and avoiding the renewal of class warfare was at last beginning to unravel. The only

[116] Stalin, *Works*, IX, p. 333.
[117] Ibid., X, p. 52.
[118] E.H. Carr and R.W. Davies, *Foundations of a Planned Economy*, 3 vols., London 1969–78, I, pp. 244–45. For the investment data see pp. 291–2.
[119] Stalin, *Works*, X, p. 319.

alternative to grain requisitions was the diversion of domestic capital investments into light industry: 'If we were to invest capital . . . in the light industries, where returns are more quickly realized . . . in the form of finished products, thus speeding the turnover of capital . . . and alleviating the goods famine—this would provide a way out of the present situation . . . investments in very large-scale factories, for example in metallurgy and so forth, yield a return only after several years. As a result, we collect money and invest it; but the market for consumer goods does not feel the effects as quickly or as directly as we would wish.'[120]

The more desperate Bukharin became to avoid the final crisis of the NEP, the greater was his need to argue that the threat of war was not immediate after all, that capitalism, after a brief detour, was returning to the path of continuing stabilization. Conversely, Stalin would free his own hand by emphasizing the war danger and the need to devote all available resources to heavy industry, without which the USSR would be caught militarily unprepared. Under the influence of these domestic concerns, the two finally parted company on the matter of stabilization.

Stalin told the congress that current plots against the USSR proved that stabilization was drawing to a close. The fact that capitalism had regained prewar levels of output, was implementing new technology, and was now experiencing a new upsurge of industrial concentration could not be interpreted to mean that stabilization was 'firm and lasting': 'On the contrary, this very stabilization, the fact that production is growing, that trade is growing, that technological progress and production possibilities are increasing, whereas the world market, the limits of that market, and the spheres of influence of the individual imperialist groups remain more or less stable—precisely this is giving rise to a most profound and acute crisis of world capitalism, a crisis which is fraught with new wars and which threatens the existence of any stabilization at all.'[121] The failure of the World Economic Conference to reduce customs barriers proved that capitalism had become 'cramped in the framework of the present markets. . . . Peaceful attempts to solve the problem of markets have not produced results, nor could they

[120] *Pravda*, 24 November 1925.
[121] Stalin, *Works*, X, p. 280.

do so.'[122] Stabilization was becoming 'more and more rotten and unstable'.[123]

When Stalin defined the current *epoch* as one of 'general crisis' and the *period* in terms of wars and revolutions, Bukharin replied that the epoch would see wars and revolutions, but the period was one of stabilization.[124] The difference was significant: an epoch of wars and revolutions might include years or even decades of tranquility; a period would locate hostilities in the more or less immediate future—no more than a five-year plan away at best. During an epoch of wars and revolutions, according to Bukharin, there was an irresistible tendency towards state capitalism. The First World War had organized the whole of capitalist society into 'state-capitalist trusts' resembling Hilferding's 'universal cartel'. A *second round of state capitalism* would ensure that no change of period was at hand, that 'a partial stabilization of capitalism is in progress on the basis of the greater exploitation of the workers; its champion is the trust form of capital.'[125] To Stalin's quasi-Luxemburgist emphasis on the chronic 'problem of markets' Bukharin counterposed the ability of modern capitalism consciously to organize and regulate production and sales:

'I might sum up this position as follows. While on the one hand there is an accentuation of the conflicts among the capitalist state organisms in spite of all attempts at conciliation, this very development forces the bourgeoisie on the other hand to tighten the screws of concentration and centralization of capital within their individual countries. In other words: at present the tendency of development is towards state capitalism. . . . I have in mind the astounding growth in . . . the last few years . . . of great trusts. . . . The concentration and centralization of economic life is advancing with seven-league boots. We might even affirm that there is taking place a "trustification of the state power itself", i.e., that the state power of the bourgeoisie is becoming more than ever dependent upon the

[122] Ibid., p. 282.
[123] Ibid., p. 292.
[124] Bukharin, 'The International Position and the Tasks of the Communist International', *International Press Correspondence*, VII, no. 73 (29 December 1927), p. 1671.
[125] Ibid., p. 1673.

great and powerful capitalist concerns or combinations of concerns.'[126]

The party's Fifteenth Congress at the end of 1927 made explicit for the first time the polarization that had gradually been developing in Soviet Marxism since the beginning of the stabilization debate. In the first chapter of this study it was suggested that Marxist theories of imperialism broadly divided into two groups: those that attributed capitalist expansion to cyclical disproportionalities and a declining rate of profit (the work of Hilferding and Lenin), and those that stressed instead what Stalin and Varga called the chronic 'problem of markets' (as in the case of Kautsky and Luxemburg). The theoretical division of prewar Marxism had now become a personal division within the leadership of the Soviet Communist Party. Bukharin was applying the arguments of Hilferding (or his own version of them) to defend the concept of stabilization; Stalin, with the support of Varga and several economists, was approaching a Luxemburgist understanding of the 'general crisis' of the capitalist system. Within months, Varga would acknowledge his own affiliation with Luxemburg's approach, and 'Varga's Law' would contribute to the further erosion of Bukharin's political stature. As Stalin moved to resolve his own quarrel with Bukharin over the fate of the NEP, the years 1928–9 brought a definitive collision in the analysis of capitalist prospects between Varga's neo-Luxemburgism and Bukharin's 'Hilferding tinge'. The significance of the Varga-Bukharin relationship will become more apparent if we now interrupt the historical narrative briefly and locate the two men on a broader map of Marxist economic theory.

[126] Ibid., p. 1672.

4
Hilferding and Luxemburg: Ambiguous Legacies

By resurrecting the theory of 'state-capitalist' organization at the end of 1927 Bukharin stumbled into a political trap. In his early writings he had gone far beyond Hilferding's predictions to provide his critics with an inventory of self-incriminating remarks which could now be collected and used against him. In *The Economics of the Transition Period* he had described the income of capital as 'a unique kind of dividend, paid out by a single joint-stock company and trust, that is, by the imperialist state'. Through the sale of war bonds, planned prices, and various taxation instruments, the state consciously appropriated and redistributed the social surplus-value. Imposing a coherent plan upon the ruling class, the state had enabled capital to make its appearance as 'a single finance-capitalist clique', or what Hilferding had speculatively referred to as a 'unified force'. According to Bukharin, the proletarian state would merely complete the organizational tendencies initiated by the capitalists: it would represent state capitalism 'turned inside out'.[1] Through 'statification' of property, the dictatorship of the proletariat would emerge as the organized consciousness and 'collective reason' of the working class. The style of Bukharin's thought emerges clearly from some of his more provocative comments at the time of his dispute with Lenin:

'In our epoch competition between capitalists has changed its form to a significant degree. For the leading capitalist countries it has been transferred exclusively to the arena of external competition, that is, competition with foreign capitalists on the world market.'

[1] Bukharin, *Ekonomika Perekhodnovo Perioda*, pp. 63–4.

'The economic property of each country is more and more being converted into the collective (common) property of a small class of the large capitalists. The former diverse and unorganized capitalism is being replaced by organized capitalism.'

'In the arena of the internal relations of capitalist society the place of unorganized enterprises and "free competition" is being taken by organized, monopolistic capitalism.'

'Not only has free competition died out . . . but there has developed as well a strong tendency towards the regulation of production by way of its statification.'

'The intermediate stratum and the small producer have disappeared. . . . All the means of production are concentrated in the hands of the capitalist state. State capitalism is growing up as the last conceivable form of capitalism.'[2]

In his response to the Franco-German trade negotiations Bukharin had slightly revised his earlier opinions, speaking now of the 'trustification of the state' rather than the 'statification' of capital. During the years of the imperialist war, he told one critic at the Fifteenth Congress of the Soviet Communist party, state-capitalist measures had been imposed from above in the creation of a war economy. By 1927 the organizational process had been reversed: now the chief tendency was 'a process of growing together between the economic organs of capital and the organs of state power "*from below*" '.[3] In either case, the end result was the same: an economy more or less free of cyclical crises and capable of economic planning. So long as the stabilization debate had been limited to differing interpretations of the available evidence, Bukharin could be suspected of short-sightedness and errors of judgement. Once the discussion moved from an empirical to a more ideological plane, he left himself open to charges of a 'Social Democratic' deviation.

1. Early Criticisms of Bukharin

An early portent of what should have been expected came in 1925,

[2] Quoted in M. Ioel'son, 'Monopolisticheskii Kapitalizm ili "Organizovannyi" Kapitalizm', *Bol'shevik*, no. 18 (30 September 1929), pp. 27–8.

[3] Bukharin, 'The International Position and the Tasks of the Communist International', *International Press Correspondence*, VIII, no. 1 (5 January 1928), p. 31.

when Bukharin was still at the peak of his political influence. In an article entitled 'Lenin and the Problem of Imperialism' B.S. Borilin recalled that the theory of 'organized capitalism' had caused the German Social Democratic Party to degenerate 'from a party of proletarian revolution into a party of state order, of evolution'.[4] More than any other individual, Rudolf Hilferding had been the architect of betrayal. Borilin expressed a widespread Soviet ambivalence towards Hilferding in the following comment:

'The name of Hilferding is connected with one of the best works in Marxist economic thought. But that was a long time ago. . . . Those small sections in *Finance Capital* that were opportunistic but could not fundamentally alter the significance of the book have [now] been raised to a higher power, supplemented and developed into a system by the Hilferding of today. The modest "theoretical" assumption of the old Hilferding concerning the possibility of a general world cartel [sic] has become a reality in the view of the Hilferding of "postwar formation". Monopolies have led Hilferding directly to . . . organized (!) capitalism.'[5]

From rebuking Hilferding Borilin turned to documenting the influence of *Finance Capital* upon Bukharin. The theory of 'state-capitalist' trusts was a reiteration of Hilferding's errors and had provoked Bukharin's clash with Lenin. On numerous occasions Lenin had explained that 'imperialism is characterized not by the domination of monopolies alone, but by struggle, by a profound, cruel, insoluble struggle between monopolies and the competition, anarchy, and lack of organization that exist side by side with them'.[6] Lenin had repeatedly explained to Bukharin that 'imperialism does not and cannot reconstruct capitalism from top to bottom', that it was 'incapable of eliminating exchange, the market, competition [and] crises'. Yet Bukharin had learned nothing from Lenin's comradely advice. In 1925 he published his critique of Rosa Luxemburg and revived all the old errors. In *Imperialism and the Accumulation of Capital* he invited his readers to imagine an 'ideal' variant of state capitalism that would organize both production and distribution, resolve the problem of markets, and eliminate the

---

[4] B.S. Borilin, 'Lenin i Problema Imperializma', *Pod Znamenem Marksizma*, no. 5–6 (May–June 1925), p. 117.
[5] Ibid., p. 118.
[6] Ibid., p. 119.

business cycle. 'But what is the need in economic science', demanded Borilin, 'for such an "ideal" type of "organized but antagonistic society"? What cognitive value does it have for us? Such an "abstraction" would make sense only if it corresponded to *the basic tendency* in contemporary capitalist society. But that is precisely what it does not do. . . . *The basic tendency of capitalism is [towards] an ever-greater intensification of economic contradictions.*'[7]

Even more remarkable than the inflammatory tone of Borilin's article was its stony reception by the economic journals. An issue of explosive potential had been raised, only to be greeted by a single, belated response. In *Bol'shevik*, of which Bukharin was the main editor, K. Rozental' endeavoured to pour oil on troubled waters. Bukharin's indiscretions could be excused, maintained Rosental', since the study of imperialism was a complex matter and involved modification of the laws of 'pure' capitalism. Two opposing tendencies had to be reconciled: the sharpening of economic contradictions and 'the transition from free competition to monopoly, from anarchy to a certain "planned character" '.[8] Bukharin had done nothing more than repeat Hilferding's oft-quoted opinion that a state-capitalist trust was 'abstractly and theoretically possible'.[9] While Rozental' attempted to exonerate Bukharin, more direct pressure was brought to bear on the editors of *Pod Znamenem Marksizma*, the journal that had published Borilin's article. In an apologetic letter to *Bol'shevik* the editors explained that they did not agree with 'certain positions of Comrade Borilin, in particular with his position on state-capitalist trusts'.

The timing of Borilin's article was premature, but it did symbolize the mistrust of Bukharin prevalent in the economic community. A second indicator of this same hostility came in 1927 with E. Khmel'nitskaya's 'historical' study of the German war economy. Khmel'nitskaya argued that Bukharin's references to the 'New Leviathan' were historically inaccurate and politically misleading. Bukharin had helped to create 'a widespread misconception in the postwar economic literature of a "single national-

[7] Ibid., pp. 124–5.
[8] K. Rozental', 'Ob Odnoi Umnoi Teorii i Neumnom Kritike', *Bol'shevik*, no. 17–18 (30 September 1925), p. 21.
[9] Ibid., p. 27.

economic trust". Moreover, to the organized influence of the state
. . . was attributed the elimination of the anarchy of production
within national limits. United by the economic policy of the state
into a single trust, the national economy is supposed to have
overcome the contradictions arising from the commodity form and
the spontaneous structure of the economy; the realm of spontaneity
is transferred beyond the frontiers of the state-capitalist economy
and is preserved only in the sphere of the world economy, in world-
economic relations.'[10] In Khmel'nitskaya's estimate this interpretation required an 'essential correction': the ruling circles of
Germany had actually failed miserably in their attempt to function
as the 'economic reason' of the nation. Instead of planning the war
economy, the German state had reacted spontaneously to inter-
departmental rivalries and shifting military needs. In both industry
and agriculture the facade of planning at best disguised, at worst
promoted, the growth of anarchy.

In *The Economics of the Transition Period* Bukharin had described
the disappearance of market 'commodities' and their replacement
by planned 'products' subject to orderly distribution by way of
price controls. Khmel'nitskaya argued that state manipulation of
prices in fact drove the German peasant to set his own real prices in
the black market. A subsequent attempt to control the physical
movement of agricultural commodities was no more successful: the
market, following its own laws, invariably 'slipped away' from state
control. By 1918 the 'single economic organism' of prewar Germany had been fractured into 'a series of local markets with their
own price movements'; the linkages between town and country had
been ruptured; several commodities had disappeared altogether.
These were the *'typical features of the breakup of the German
economy by the end of the war'*.[11]

In the industrial sector similar conditions had prevailed. Inter-
capitalist rivalries were simply transferred from the market-place to
the state apparatus itself, where the spokesmen of industry—
frequently the biggest industrialists—quarrelled over political
position and access to scarce materials. Driven to frustration, by

---

[10] E. Khmel'nitskaya, 'Planovoe Regulirovanie v Voennom Khozyaistve Ger-
manii', *Vestnik Kommunisticheskoi Akademii*, no. 19 (1927), p. 137.

[11] Ibid., p. 158.

1918 the bourgeoisie wanted nothing more than an end to the whole affair. With his bourgeois class instinct, Professor Fal'kner had long ago pointed out to Bukharin that the capitalists were the first to demand the end of state interference.[12] For Khmel'nitskaya Bukharin's theory represented 'a significant overestimation of the tendencies towards overcoming the anarchy of production'. The wartime experience proved conclusively that the 'single state-capitalist trust' was a chimera; the bourgeoisie was quite incapable of converting 'an irrational economic system into a rational one'.[13]

2. Social Democrats on 'Organized Capitalism'

Bukharin's return to the notion of 'state capitalism' reminded Soviet economists not only of his dispute with Lenin but also of the similarity between his current views and those traditionally expounded by Social Democratic 'revisionists'. German socialists had become infatuated with the power of the state long before Hilferding. Formed in 1875 when Marx's followers united with those of Ferdinand Lassalle, the German party had adopted a programme that Marx himself vilified for including 'the Lassallean sect's servile belief in the state'. When the programme suggested that 'under the democratic control of the toiling people' the state might 'aid' the growth of co-operative production, Marx replied: 'It is worthy of Lassalle's imagination that with state loans one can build a new society just as well as a new railway!'

Had Bukharin been more astute he might have protected himself by tracing the origin of his ideas to the (presumably) more orthodox view of the state expounded by Engels. In *Anti-Dühring* (1878) Engels had argued that the contradiction between social production and private appropriation impelled the capitalists, in their own interests, to adopt a policy of state ownership of the means of production. Each industrial crisis gave impetus to 'the socialization of huge means of production', until the rise in the organic composition of capital finally made state ownership unavoidable. 'Many of these means of production and communication', observed

[12] Khmel'nitskaya, 'Gosudarstvenno-Monopolisticheskii Kapitalizm', *Vestnik Kommunisticheskoi Akademii*, no. 24 (1927), p. 157.
[13] Ibid.

Engels, 'are from the outset so colossal that, like the railways, they exclude all other forms of capitalist exploitation. At a certain stage of development even [the joint-stock form of organization] no longer suffices; the official representative of capitalist society, the state, is constrained to take over their management. This necessity of conversion into state property makes itself felt first in the vast institutions for communication: the postal service, telegraphs and railways.'[14] While Engels did not use the term 'state capitalism' to describe this collective form of capitalist ownership, he did mention that it deprived individual capitalists of their entrepreneurial function. The difference between Bukharin's description of state-capitalist 'dividends' and Engels's account of the distribution of surplus-value was hard to discern. According to Engels, the 'capitalist no longer has any social activity save the pocketing of revenues, the clipping of coupons and gambling on the stock exchange'.[15] Through its intervention in production, the state had become 'the ideal collective body of all capitalists. The more productive forces it takes over, the more it becomes the real collective body of all capitalists'.[16] What other label, Bukharin might well have asked, should be applied to state regulation of capitalist society, if not 'state capitalism'?

In their own assessment of capitalism's postwar stabilization German Socialists typically translated the prospect of gradual socialization into one of peaceful transition to socialism. The experience of the war years had proven that the state could 'plan' the economy in pursuit of military victory. There appeared to be no reason why the democratic state could not similarly manipulate the institutions of finance capital for the achievement of 'economic democracy'. Hilferding had demonstrated that the direction and control of production was 'a question of power'. Were the workers to accede to power democratically, the state would become an instrument of inter-class co-operation. The representatives of labour and capital had worked alongside one another from 1914 through 1918: both prices and wages had been administratively

---

[14] Engels, *Herr Eugen Dühring's Revolution in Science [Anti-Dühring]*, translated by Emile Burns, C.P. Dutt, ed., London n.d., pp. 311–12.

[15] Ibid., p. 312.

[16] Ibid., p. 313.

determined. The interlude of 'class peace' provided a model for postwar political tactics and restored traditional faith in the efficacy of state power. Prominent Social Democratic journals regularly recorded government decisions under the heading of 'state capitalism'. In *The Monopoly Question and the Working Class* (1917) Heinrich Cunow predicted that 'state socialism' would impose restrictions on private property and ease the social strains of the transition period.[17] Using the same terminology as Bukharin, Karl Renner (a prominent Austrian Socialist) declared that capitalist society had become an 'organic unity'; the private economy of *laissez-faire* individualism had evolved into a genuine 'national economy'. 'This statification of the economy constitutes the specific distinguishing feature of recent developments. It entails a radical innovation . . . that Marx did not experience and about which he could not write.'[18]

Bukharin spoke of trade unions becoming the 'labour departments' of a militarist machine. Social Democrats used the political framework of the Weimar Republic to consolidate the 'citizenship' organized labour had won from the Kaiser. The Factory Council Law provided for the participation of council representatives in factory management. With trade-union officials playing a prominent role, the Ministry of Labour was charged with settling the most fractious industrial disputes through binding arbitration. In *The Theory of the Modern State* (1923) Rudolf Abraham found no reason to alter the view that 'state capitalism' could with equal justification be called 'state socialism'.[19] Karl Kautsky emphasized the need for working-class participation in state institutions, saying 'statification . . . is socialist only in a *fully democratic* state'.[20] At the Heidelberg Congress of 1925, Rudolf Hilferding summarized the official party position this way:

'After the revolution in all countries in which power came into its hands either fully or in large measure, the working class found itself for a time facing the question of realizing socialism.

[17] See Khmel'nitskaya, 'Gosudarstvenno-Monopolisticheskii Kapitalizm', p. 144.
[18] Ibid., pp. 145–6.
[19] Quoted in A.S., 'K Kharakteristike Ideologii Sovremennoi Sotsial-Demokratii', *Bol'shevik*, no. 7–8 (15 April 1927), p. 14.
[20] Ibid.

'From the outset we . . . realized . . . that *we would achieve the process of socialization only if it were simultaneously a process of democratization.* Making a decisive break with the view that the state bureaucracy is able to control the economy [on its own], we came to the conclusion that control of the national economy must be the affair of the producers themselves. . . . *Thus we arrived at the construction of a social organism that must replace the large concentrated capitalist branches of production . . . and which must be managed by the representatives of the producers,* the consumers and the democratic state.'[21]

In 1924 Hilferding had written that the transition 'from freely competitive capitalism to organized capitalism' would still lead to an economy that would be organized 'hierarchically, in an antagonistic form'.[22] Three years later, he told the Kiel Congress, 'Organized capitalism means . . . replacement of the capitalist principle of free competition with the socialist principle of a planned economy'.[23] 'Our generation', he said, 'faces the task of transforming . . . this economy, organized and controlled by the capitalists, into an economy controlled by the democratic state. Thus it follows that the problem confronting our generation is nothing other than socialism.'[24] Hilferding's strategy had become one of *democratizing* the state from above and below: from above through a parliamentary majority, from below through the factory councils. The workers had no choice but to reform the state from within, for an organized economy would assign 'political prices' to all commodities, including labour-power: 'We have, thanks to the principle of collective agreements and the conciliation offices, the political regulation of wages and the political regulation of the working day. The personal fate of the workers is determined by the policy implemented by the state.'[25]

By the mid-1920s there was little to choose between Hilferding and Kautsky. In *The War Question and Social Democracy* (1928)

[21] Ibid., p. 20.
[22] Quoted in M. Ioel'son, 'Monopolisticheskii Kapitalizm . . .', pp. 31–2.
[23] Ibid., p. 32.
[24] Ibid., p. 34.
[25] Quoted in P. Lapinsky, 'Sotsial'noe Gosudarstvo. Etapy i Tendentsii Razvitiya', *Bol'shevik*, no. 13–14 (31 July 1928), p. 14.

Kautsky combined the theory of organized capitalism with his earlier commitment to 'ultra-imperialism'. The international organization of finance capital would dramatically alter relations between states. With the League of Nations and Franco-German economic co-operation, the 'finance capitalists have other, less costly and less dangerous methods than war between the great powers for achieving their aspirations'.[26] Having tasted political power, Social Democrats were convinced both that they could plan capitalism and that planning would eliminate crises as well as the need for revolution. When the Socialist International met in Brussels in 1928, Otto Bauer revelled in the opportunity Bukharin had provided to pour scorn upon the Comintern. Ten years ago, he exclaimed, the European dynasties were collapsing and it was doubtful whether capitalism would survive. At that time, 'there could be debates with the Communists *about how to achieve socialism*: either by the path of *democracy*, as we said, knowing that the working class can find within itself the strength to build a new society only in an atmosphere of freedom, or by the path of *dictatorship and force*, as the Communists thought. At that time there was a debate between us concerning the historical perspective. . . . But now, when the Bolsheviks themselves talk of the stabilization of capitalism, can there really be any debate over which perspective proved to be correct?'[27]

Under the pressure of his political struggle with Stalin, Bukharin had allowed himself to be driven into the position of speaking the same language as Western Socialists. In European usage 'state capitalism' had become the equivalent of 'economic democracy', and 'economic democracy' was seen as the substitute for proletarian revolution. Beginning with the same theoretical concepts as Hilferding, Bukharin appeared to have followed the logic of *Finance Capital* to the same 'revisionist' conclusions. By 1927–8, the emerging dilemma of Soviet Marxism was the seeming impossibility of finding an alternative explanation of recent developments without moving in the direction of Rosa Luxemburg. The scope of this dilemma, as well as the tenacity of the Hilferding tradition, can

[26] Quoted in M. Ioel'son, 'Monopolisticheskii Kapitalizm . . .', p. 36.

[27] Quoted in A. Leont'ev, ' "Organizovannyi Kapitalizm" i "Khozyaistvennaya Demokratiya" ', *Problemy Ekonomiki*, no. 4–5 (April–May 1929), p. 5.

be most effectively documented by comparing Hilferding's fate in Soviet economic literature with Luxemburg's.

3. The Soviet Appraisal of Rosa Luxemburg

The obstacles to a significant Luxemburgist trend amongst Soviet economists had always been formidable. S. Dvolaitsky, who translated Luxemburg's work into Russian, once remarked that Hilferding's approach to imperialism was 'shared by the best representatives of the Bolsheviks'[28] and 'on the whole was taken over by Russian Communist literature'.[29] Few Bolsheviks had ever taken Luxemburg's ideas seriously. The person most responsible for keeping interest alive was August Thalheimer, a collaborator with Luxemburg before her assassination and later secretary of a Comintern commission charged with preparing a new programme. Thalheimer had been a thorn in Bukharin's side since 1922, when he had created a furor by asserting that any theory of imperialism other than Luxemburg's necessarily led to opportunism. Acknowledging that Lenin had been an exception to this generalization, Thalheimer ascribed this to Lenin's 'lack of consistency'.[30] In 1923 S. Bessonov assessed the validity of Thalheimer's remarks and anticipated the arguments Varga would soon employ in defence of his new 'law'.

On the main issue in contention Bessonov held that Thalheimer was correct: Luxemburg had proven 'the inevitability of the collapse of capitalism'.[31] The link between her theory of accumulation and genuinely revolutionary tactics was so close that 'recognition of the one without the other is possible only at the price of theoretical inconsistency'.[32] While agreeing with Thalheimer in principle, Bessonov yet attempted to rescue Lenin. In his view,

[28] S. Dvolaitsky, 'Teoriya Realizatsii R. Lyuksemburg', *Vestnik Sotsialisticheskoi Akademii*, no. 4 (August-September), p. 49.

[29] Dvolaitsky, 'K Teorii Rynkov', *Vestnik Sotsialisticheskoi Akademii*, no. 3 (February-March 1923), p. 112.

[30] Quoted in S. Bessonov, 'Teoriya Rynkov V.I. Lenina', *Sputnik Kommunista*, no. 23 (June-July 1923), p. 46.

[31] Bessonov, 'Programma Kominterna i Teoriya Rozy Lyuksemburg', *Sputnik Kommunista*, no. 21 (23 April 1923), p. 154.

[32] Ibid., p. 161.

Lenin had been 'one of the very earliest . . . exponents of the conception of Rosa Luxemburg'.[33] But the most forceful reference Bessonov could find to support this claim said something quite different. Lenin explicitly denied the chronic 'problem of markets' and insisted that realization crises were cyclical: 'I have nowhere said that this contradiction [between production and consumption] must *systematically* give a surplus product. I underline *systematically*, for the non-systematic production of a surplus product (crises) is *inevitable* in capitalist society due to the disruption of proportionality between the different branches of industry. *And a certain state of consumption is one of the elements of proportionality.*'[34]

Lenin had told the Narodniks that the market expands in pace with the division of labour and the progress of technology. The first stage in the process was the class stratification of the peasantry. Bessonov interpreted this to mean that it was only the *process* of stratification that created a market: once the peasantry was *already divided* into a rural proletariat and bourgeoisie—the condition Marx had described as 'pure' capitalism—no further market creation was conceivable. Then the contradiction between production and consumption would 'inevitably lead capitalism to a speedy collapse'.[35] To be more precise, capitalism depended on access to 'third-party' markets at every stage of development: 'The non-capitalist milieu and its disintegration—this is not only the starting point of primitive capitalist accumulation . . . but also the indispensable condition for the existence and development of capitalism during its entire history, right up to the transition to its highest form.'[36] When Lenin did define the most universal contradiction of capitalist society, he spoke of the antagonism between 'the social character of production (socialized by capitalism) and the private, individual mode of appropriation'. Bessonov dismissed this remark as an artful polemic: 'If the Narodniks had seized upon the contradiction between the social character of production and the individual character of appropriation, . . . Comrade Lenin would

[33] Ibid., p. 162.
[34] Quoted in Bessonov, 'Teoriya Rynkov . . .', pp. 60–61; cf. Lenin, *Collected Works*, IV, p. 161.
[35] Ibid., p. 78.
[36] Ibid., p. 84.

probably, with equal zest, have defended . . . the contradiction between production and consumption.'[37] In his effort to bridge the abyss between Lenin and Luxemburg—and by implication between Lenin and the Narodniks—Bessonov entirely missed the significance of these early writings as a link between Marx's *Capital* and Lenin's *Imperialism*.

The majority of Luxemburg's Soviet critics, like Bukharin, had been schooled in the Hilferding tradition. To these writers it was clear that Luxemburg's *Accumulation of Capital* had misconstrued Marx's account of internal market creation. L.N. Kritsman—more generally known for his economic history of War Communism[38]— protested that the function of new investment in capitalist society was to circulate the purchasing power needed to realize previous rounds of production. Moreover, when the capitalist exported his commodities to 'third-party' markets, his objective was to purchase raw materials and other goods in exchange, not merely to accumulate a cash hoard, as Luxemburg had assumed. Buying from 'third parties', the capitalists automatically renewed demand. 'As far as the demand from "third parties" is concerned, the capitalists can live in peace with no fear of crises.'[39] From Kritsman's viewpoint Luxemburg had gone astray by failing to focus her analysis on institutional change and the emergence of finance capital: 'Whoever wishes to understand imperialism as a specific historical category must begin with monopoly capitalism' as a unique phase of capitalist development.[40]

S. Dvolaitsky was even more emphatic in criticizing Luxemburg from the perspective of 'organized capitalism'. His comments were indistinguishable from Bukharin's. The modern state was said to have entered an organic union with finance capital to become a 'state capitalist' and 'the most universal socio-economic organization of the capitalist class'. Through its construction of railways, harbours, and provision of other public services, the state created employment and became 'involved in accumulation in the economic sense

[37] Ibid., p. 86.
[38] L.N. Kritsman, *Georicheskii Period Velikoi Russkoi Revolyutsii*, Moscow n.d.
[39] Kritsman, 'O Nakoplenii Kapitala i "Tret'ikh Litsakh"', *Vestnik Sotsialisti-cheskoi Akademii*, no. 4 (August-September 1923), p. 59.
[40] Ibid., p. 66.

of the term. . . . The problem of capitalism's growth, it turns out, is in this way resolved.'[41] As far as cyclical crises were concerned, Dvolaitsky saw the theoretical possibility of their transcendence. The great banking concerns had taken over the 'basic organizational functions of the capitalist class', acquiring the potential of eliminating internal contradictions through an anti-cyclical policy of consumer loans or through the deliberate fiscal intervention of public authorities.[42] When private hoarding drained purchasing power from the market, the state had only to tax the capitalists and press idle savings back into circulation, creating a multiple expansion of effective demand.[43] Once the state acquired the power to regulate total demand there could be no doubt that 'even in conditions of "pure" capitalism a simultaneous expansion of both production and effective demand is possible'.[44] Luxemburg had failed in her attempt to prove the 'automatic-mechanistic' necessity of breakdown.[45] She had ignored the 'enormous transformation process through which capitalism has passed, being converted from an anarchic, freely-competitive economic system into one that is *monopolistic* and more or less organized, at least as far as separate countries are concerned'.[46]

Although Dvolaitsky saw a weakness in the tendency of monopolies to postpone investment until existing plant was fully amortized, E. Leikin believed the deceleration of technological change was simply another expression of capitalist planning. As a secondary theme, Luxemburg had argued that a rise in the organic composition of capital created overproduction in Department II, a deficit in Department I. An obvious reply would be that relative prices would change and restore a balanced flow of values at the expense of Department II's rate of profit. Leikin believed this spontaneous adjustment process had been replaced by conscious regulation with the advent of organized capitalism:

'Contemporary capitalism, developing internal methods of regulation completely foreign to the classical capitalism of the nine-

[41] Dvolaitsky, 'Teoriya Realizatsii . . .', pp. 18–19.

[42] Dvolaitsky, 'Nakoplenie Kapitala i Problema Imperializma', *Krasnaya Nov'*, I (June 1921), p. 97.

[43] Dvolaitsky, 'K Teorii Rynkov', p. 122.

[44] Ibid., p. 124.

[45] Ibid., pp. 32–3.

[46] Dvolaitsky, 'Nakoplenie Kapitala . . .', p. 97.

teenth century, possessing even the embryo of planned regulation (albeit in the irrational and contradictory form of combinations and monopolies), and perfecting all the forms of credit by leaps and bounds . . .—this contemporary capitalism is opening up in our own day (and we are still far from "pure" capitalism!) broad possibilities for anticipating . . . forthcoming technological developments and therefore for preventing—more or less—the lack of correspondence between branches I and II referred to by Rosa Luxemburg . . . one must not brush aside the organizational and regulative perfection of capitalism . . . which to a colossal extent increases its elasticity as an economic system.'[47]

As if to underline the historical and logical antithesis between the Hilferding and Luxemburg traditions, Leikin quoted *Finance Capital* to show that the theoretical limit to capitalist organization was indeed a 'universal cartel'. Luxemburg's fascination with 'third parties' reflected her 'lifeless and schematic construction . . . with respect to the impossibility of pure capitalism'.[48] 'The view of the working class and its party', concluded Leikin, 'must be free of any [attraction to theories] of the mechanical destruction of capitalism. That is how we reply to the question posed by Thalheimer.'[49]

The most frequent charge levelled at Luxemburg was that she had committed exactly the same error as Kondrat'ev by failing to distinguish between separate historical periods. Bukharin commented that Luxemburg's 'whole definition of imperialism suffers from the basic fault that it treats the problem without any regard to the necessity of the specific characterization of capital as *finance capital*. Trade capitalism and mercantilism, industrial capital and liberalism, finance capital and imperialism—all these phases of capitalist development disappear or dissolve into "capitalism in general".'[50] What was the point, Bukharin asked, 'of all this talk about imperialism if one does not understand its specific historical characteristics? It means a misunderstanding of the demands of Marxist methodology.'[51]

[47] E. Leikin, 'Zametki o Teorii Nakopleniya Rozy Lyuksemburg', *Vestnik Kommunisticheskoi Akademii*, no. 7 (1924), p. 189.
[48] Ibid., p. 210.
[49] Ibid., p. 223.
[50] Luxemburg and Bukharin, *Imperialism and the Accumulation of Capital*, p. 253.
[51] Ibid., p. 257.

Making the same point as Bukharin, A.G. Gertsenshtein more cautiously adopted a Leninist perspective. The problem of imperialism, he affirmed, could not be detached from 'the natural and historic conditions in which the uneven development of the process of reproducing capital occurs'.[52] But Gertsenshtein also differentiated himself from Bukharin, noting that a 'balanced equilibrium' within any single economy could only be an accident: 'The constant deviation of the various branches of the national economy from the norms of productive proportionality . . . *creates . . . structural discontinuity and leads to the objective impossibility of . . . distributing the social product in the absence of external markets.*'[53] Spektator replied that Gertsenshtein's argument required one qualification: the theory of imperialism must include 'the struggle of state-organized monopoly capital of different countries with one another'.[54] 'On the world market contemporary capital now comes forth . . . as the representative of a particular state . . . the struggle is no longer one between individual entrepreneurs but between *states*.'[55]

These preliminary skirmishes over the validity of Luxemburgist theory helped to establish the battle lines of 1928–9. To judge from the anti-Luxemburg literature—with the exception of Gertsenshtein's contribution—two mutually exclusive interpretations of imperialism were presented. One position held that capitalism was becoming 'organized' and moving in the direction of 'state capitalism', which implied that the process of stabilization was likely to continue. The other held that the chronic 'problem of markets' would interrupt capitalism's recovery in mid-stream, prevent the restoration of a moving equilibrium, and inaugurate a new struggle for imperialist conquest of colonial markets.

The problem with this dichotomy was that it depended on a restrictive and misleading interpretation of Hilferding's *Finance Capital*. With few exceptions, Soviet economists had forgotten Lenin's warning that Hilferding must be treated with discretion.

[52] A. Gertsenshtein, *Teoriya Kapitalisticheskovo Rynka*, Moscow 1928, p. 184.
[53] Ibid., p. 160.
[54] Spektator, *Vvedenie v Izuchenie Mirovovo Khozyaistva*, Moscow and Leningrad 1928, p. 53.
[55] Ibid., p. 25.

Finance Capital's speculative references to the 'universal cartel' had to be balanced against Hilferding's clear opinion that in the real world trusts and cartels created only partial plans. And 'partial regulation', as Lenin and Hilferding agreed, had the effect of intensifying disproportionalities within industry as a whole. In other words, Lenin understood *Finance Capital* to demonstrate that capitalism's newest organizational forms actually enhanced the likelihood of *cyclical crises*. The most significant element missing from the Luxemburg debate was reference to Marx's theory of the business cycle. It was not until 1927–9 that a small group of Soviet economists began to consider the possibility that stabilization was really nothing more than a cyclical recovery of the sort Marx had described in *Capital*.

4. The Renaissance of Soviet Cycle Theory

The barriers to a renaissance of business-cycle theory in the Soviet Union were at least as imposing as those impeding the growth of a deliberate Luxemburgist trend. The theoretical paralysis induced by the concept of 'organized capitalism' was compounded by psychological unwillingness to contemplate a return to cyclical 'normality'. In these conditions, business-cycle theory was abandoned during the early years to the bourgeois professors. Professors Kondrat'ev and Pervushin made their own gratuitous contribution to the debate over 'organized capitalism' by encouraging the impression that cycles could be regulated by astute monetary policies. From Tugan-Baranovsky Kondrat'ev had learned that the immediate triggering mechanism of a crisis was the exhaustion of credit.[56] It followed that the function of the crisis was to restore the supply of loanable funds and create fresh incentives to borrow by bringing the interest rate into line with prevailing profit norms. In *The Economic Conjuncture* (1925) Pervushin maintained that 'general overproduction and crises . . . can only be explained on the basis of developments in the circulation of money, and of credit in particular.'[57] The way to eliminate crises was to restrict credit late in

---

[56] Kondrat'ev, *Mirovoe Khozyaistvo i evo Kon'yunktury*, p. 196.
[57] Pervushin, *Khozyaistvennaya Kon'yunktura*, p. 66.

the expansion and thus prevent the speculative accumulation of unsaleable inventories.

Among Marxists influenced by the bourgeois *kreditniki*, or monetarists, the most prominent was V.A. Bazarov. Sharing many of Bukharin's theoretical concepts, Bazarov believed that state control over credit would be tantamount to an indirect form of economic planning: production would 'at all times and in all its components find itself under the control of real [as opposed to speculative] demand and thus would satisfy the latter in a *smooth manner* . . . without crisis'.[58] P.V. Maksakovsky commented on the implications of Bazarov's position this way: 'The state organization of credit, in the context of Bazarov's thought, means "planned" capitalism—a capitalism in which there will be no crises arising from the *internal* structure itself. . . . For Bazarov a *state* organization of credit is enough to put an end to crises. . . . This is a non-marxist and frivolous position.'[59]

In his occasional comments on monetary policy Lapinsky went even further than Bazarov. In his judgement the economic apparatus of the modern state had become so pervasive as to make it 'impossible to discern where the [economic] "base" ends and the [political] "superstructure" begins'. The explosive growth of state budgets since 1914 had made any thought of a return to classical capitalism 'a reactionary, Manchesterian utopia'. The state had become 'all-embracing' and functioned as 'the fundamental "regulating" organ' of capitalist society.[60] Whereas Social Democrats viewed unemployment relief and social welfare programmes as examples of 'economic democracy', Lapinsky saw them as expressions of 'Napoleonic myths' of state responsibility—'legends and myths in accordance with which the state is "obliged" to guarantee all strata of the population, in all circumstances, a certain tolerable standard of living, a certain minimum'.[61] Through its manipulation

[58] V.A. Bazarov, ' "Krivye Razvitiya" Kapitalisticheskovo i Sovetskovo Khozyaistva', *Planovoe Khozyaistvo*, no. 4 (1926), p. 114.

[59] P. Maksakovsky, 'K Teorii Tsikla i Dinamiki Sovetskovo Khozyaistva', *Bol'shevik*, no. 6 (31 March 1928), p. 21.

[60] P. Lapinsky, 'Sud'by Poslevoennovo Gosudarstva. Pererozhdenie Burzhuaznovo Gosudarstva, Vyrozhdenie Burzhuaznoi Demokratii', *Bol'shevik*, no. 7 (17 April 1928), p. 21.

[61] Ibid., p. 31.

of money markets, the 'Napoleonic' state exerted control over the movement of wages, prices, and investments: 'without any exaggeration it can be said that there is no other area in which the contemporary capitalist state has assumed such incomparable influence over the whole course of economic life, over the level of prices . . . over the degree of expansion or contraction of unemployment—and, consequently, to a certain extent over the tension of class antagonisms—than through the mechanism and resources of its monetary and credit policy.'[62]

Although omnipotent within its own frontiers, the 'Napoleonic' state was not yet the last word in capitalist power, for it was in turn subordinated to 'the hegemony of international finance capital'.[63] If the directors of national banks in effect constituted a parallel government, Benjamin Strong of the New York Federal Reserve exercised the prerogatives of 'an "international" government'. Working in total secrecy, the international bankers could decide 'the rain and the weather' in the world economy.

In the works of Lapinsky and Bazarov monetary policy became one more instrument for the achievement of organized capitalism. Just how far these arguments diverged from *Finance Capital* can be illustrated quite graphically. Traditionally, Marxists had considered the availability of credit *subordinate* to the normal fluctuations of the cycle. When industrial capital was idled, money-capital would accumulate for want of profitable investment outlets. The growth of speculative inventories *resulted from* the growth of money-market liquidity, and in that sense was merely a symptom of the mounting crisis in the sphere of production. As Hilferding wrote: 'The same cause that immobilizes industrial capital equally immobilizes money-capital. Money does not enter into circulation and does not function as money-capital, because industrial capital is not functioning; it is idle because industry is idle.'[64] To lower the interest rate artificially in these circumstances would do precisely nothing to stimulate an economic recovery. Over the course of an industrial cycle it was not unusual for prices to vary by as much as 50 per cent or more. A drop in the interest rate from 7 to 2 per cent—

[62] Ibid., p. 33.
[63] Ibid., p. 34.
[64] Hilferding, *Das Finanzkapital*, p. 385.

the traditional range of variation—would be of minuscule significance compared to such drastic changes in price levels.[65]

In the final analysis, the whole case for 'organized capitalism' depended on the ability of trusts and cartels to adjust production to the market and thereby to regulate prices. The recovery of Soviet cycle theory began when attention turned to Hilferding's comments about the *law of value*, or the price mechanism of capitalist society. According to Hilferding, periodic violations of proportionality had to be explained by 'a perturbation in the formation of prices such that the latter no longer make it possible to recognize the requirements of production. In so far as this perturbation is periodic, it must be shown that what occurs with the law of prices is equally so.'[66]

In *Finance Capital* Hilferding had argued that uneven price movements were caused by differences in the organic composition of capital across industries. In heavy industry adjustment to an expanding market required large capital expenditures and a considerable time lag. The price of means of production tended to rise disproportionately and to siphon profits away from other industries. 'There is thus a tendency towards excessive investment, towards a surplus accumulation of capital in those spheres having a high organic composition.'[67] By overinvesting in the first phase of the cycle the capitalists contributed to overproduction at a later phase. Hilferding believed that organized capital, far from offsetting this irregular movement, would in fact forestall the restoration of proportionality. In their attempt to maintain prices above values, trusts and cartels would undertake a dramatic curtailment of output and intensify the contraction elsewhere, until 'outsiders' ultimately intervened and captured the once 'regulated' market. The law of value might be a poor guide to economic performance, but every interference with its operation would increase the amplitude of cyclical variations in both output and prices. The partial regulation of industry was a substitute neither for the classical law of value nor for a 'universal cartel' and a comprehensive plan.

The first Soviet attempt to apply Hilferding's reasoning came in

[65] Ibid., p. 387.
[66] Ibid., p. 348.
[67] Ibid., p. 356.

1928 with Spektator's article 'Marx's Theory of Crises'. The article showed that in addition to squeezing profit margins in Department II, artificially high prices for the means of production also prompted capitalists in the light industries to postpone investments and use their existing capital more intensively. Intending to compensate for a low rate of profit by enlarging the volume of sales, the capitalists in Department II defeated their own purpose: at the same time as they threw a larger volume of commodities onto the market they disrupted the process of market creation. *The expansion of investments created a market; the withholding of new capital expenditures brought on the crisis.* This article implied that both Bukharin and Stalin were wrong in their appraisal of stabilization. Neither an 'organized' expansion nor a chronic depression was possible. The realization crisis could not be attributed to working-class impoverishment, for wages developed dialectically: 'at first they lag behind the rise in the general level of prices; then, when the demand for labour-power grows rapidly, they *surpass* the rise in prices on finished goods, causing a sharp reduction in the norm of surplus-value . . . and serving as a . . . cause of the crisis.'[68] The Marxist theory of the cycle left no room for a chronic 'problem of markets': 'This is not a crisis due to "underconsumption", it is not the result of a lack of correspondence between the limited purchasing power of the masses and the ability of capitalist production to undertake unlimited expansion, but the result of an attempt by entrepreneurs to offset a fall in the norm of profit through an increase in the volume of production . . . which in practice only leads to a further fall in the norm of profit and to a glut of the market.'[69]

In P.V. Maksakovsky's *Capitalist Cycles* (written in 1928 and published posthumously in 1929), Hilferding's influence was even more direct than in Spektator's work. Contrary to the Luxemburg tradition, Maksakovsky also believed that 'the expansion of social production, being expressed in the growth of incomes, simultaneously creates the necessary base of effective demand'.[70] Prob-

[68] Spektator, 'Teoriya Krizisov Marksa', *Pod Znamenem Marksizma*, no. 2 (February 1928), p. 109.

[69] Ibid., p. 113.

[70] Maksakovsky, *Kapitalisticheskii Tsikl*, Moscow 1929, p. 62.

lems arose because the volume of demand developed unevenly over the course of the cycle. During the phase of expansion a massive surge of investment resulted in new jobs and a new stream of working-class incomes. As prices began to rise, particularly in Department I, a discrepancy appeared between market prices and prices of production, or the equilibrium prices that would prevail in the absence of the business cycle. As Maksakovsky wrote: 'the expansion is "oriented" not to the price of production, to a value that guarantees receipt of the "lawful" average profit, but to a *high* market price, which in itself expresses not the "proportions" of social production but a specific phenomenon—that is, the impossibility of production's growing at the same tempo as demand, which is fuelled by the massive renewal of capital.'[71]

By creating production disproportionalities between the two Departments of industry, the upward distortion of prices precluded any possibility of a 'moving equilibrium'. 'Thus on the basis of the divorce of price from the price of production—or from values— there takes place a process whereby the "proportionality" of social production is disrupted.'[72] In pursuit of superprofits new plants would be constructed, at some point creating the potential for a 'production' equilibrium. But until these plants came into operation the potential equilibrium would not be reflected in market prices. The law of value would therefore cause the capitalists to overshoot equilibrium. Consciousness of the requirements of proportionality would lag behind changes in productive capacity. The cohesion of the aggregate reproduction process would subsequently have to be imposed, in Marx's words, as a 'blind law' in the form of general overproduction and a crisis. Disputing the claim that capitalist anarchy could be replaced by 'organization', Maksakovsky summarized his study of the law of value as follows:

'*The market mirror* ("demand" and "supply") *ceases to reflect production movements.* The market links of capitalist competition cannot reflect the results [of competitive investments] . . . until the newly-created productive apparatus begins to function. . . . That which the market language [prices] designates as *underproduction*,

[71] Ibid., pp. 63–4.
[72] Ibid., p. 68.

is, in the language of production, an approaching establishment of "equilibrium". That condition which in the language of the market will constitute "equilibrium"—that is, supply catching up with demand—in the language of the system will represent matured "overproduction". Supply on the market will catch up with demand only when the newly constructed factories and works become "subjects of supply" and throw their products onto the market. But that will mean inevitable overproduction.'[73]

Taking account of the 'official' view of the 'problem of markets', A.G. Gertsenshtein attempted to join the theories of disproportionality and underconsumption in a 'theoretical synthesis'. In his account of price differentiation he followed Maksakovsky to the conclusion that the 'market does not control, but provokes a growth in the means of production. . . . The market creates the illusion of unlimited absorptive capacity.'[74] Department II paid inflated prices for means of production during the expansion; but capitalists in Department I paid the same wages as their counterparts in Department II. As a result, the commodities produced in II could not be sold, due to the relatively low wages in I. Disproportionalities and the 'problem of markets' could be seen as 'two sides of a single phenomenon', the joint consequence of which was to discourage investments and precipitate the crisis. Whereas Hilferding had seen the adjustment process breaking down due to the immobility of fixed capital, Gertsenshtein inverted the argument: 'It is not a redistribution of *capital* between branches of industry that is needed . . . but a redistribution of *income* between the capitalists and the working class.'[75] Trying to reconcile the two opposing traditions of Marxist thought, Gertsenshtein soon found himself in political difficulties. What was the redistribution of income, inquired his critics, but a Social Democratic measure to alleviate crises? Gertsenshtein had offered what one reviewer called 'a typical Social Democratic presentation of the question'.[76] The

---

[73] Ibid., p. 79.

[74] Gertsenshtein, 'Osnovnye Elementy Teorii Krizisov', *Mirovoe Khozyaistvo i Mirovaya Politika*, no. 1 (January 1930), p. 65.

[75] Ibid., p. 73.

[76] A. Breitman, ' "Sinteticheskaya Teoriya Krizisov" Gertsenshteina', *Problemy Ekonomiki*, no. 4–5 (April-May 1931), p. 116.

'synthetic theory of crises' was the work of 'a typical eclectic-revisionist'.[77]

In a book entitled *Towards a Theory of the Capitalist Market* (1929) S. Guberman joined with Spektator and Maksakovsky in denouncing the Luxemburgist theory of chronic underconsumption. A lack of effective demand, he argued, could not serve as 'the direct cause of the crisis'.[78] But Guberman's most original contribution came when he considered the question of how monopolistic institutions might transform the pattern of the classical cycle and therewith the long-run trend of development. Not a Trotskyist himself, he picked up Trotsky's earlier theme (in the debate with Kondrat'ev) and carried it further than any other economist prior to Preobrazhensky's path-breaking study of the monopolistic cycle in 1931.

For Guberman, the essential difference between the classical and the modern cycle lay in the fact that traditionally a crisis halted production in the weakest firms; with the formation of cartels, the most powerful enterprises were now the focus of contraction, restricting output in their efforts to maintain prices. By impairing recoveries and lengthening depressions, 'organized capitalism' caused the curve of development to decline. Successive recoveries were delayed by the high cost of means of production; and when a recovery did begin, it was cut short by an earlier and more pronounced differentiation of prices between the two Departments of industry. In these circumstances the general length of the cycle might remain the same, but the relative length of its separate phases would change. In 1921 Trotsky had told the Comintern Third Congress that 'in periods of capitalist decline the crises are . . . prolonged . . . while the booms are fleeting, superficial and speculative'. Guberman integrated Trotsky's prediction with the Hilferding tradition of concentrating on institutional change, uneven price movements, and inter-industrial disproportionalities. 'If crises were to be explained by overproduction as such', he commented, 'then there is no doubt that under the influence of regulated production the conjuncture would be considerably stabi-

[77] Ibid., p. 109.
[78] S. Guberman, *K Teorii Kapitalisticheskovo Rynka i Krizisov*, Moscow 1929, p. 127.

lized and crises would be successfully overcome [simply by restricting output]. To the extent that crises . . . arise in consequence of the uneven movement of prices for means of production and means of consumption . . . it is clear that this unevenness is reinforced in monopoly capitalism, not weakened.'[79]

The common bond that united most Soviet cycle theorists was their aversion to Luxemburgism and their general adherence to the Hilferding tradition. Where the Stalinists spoke of capitalism's 'general crisis', the cycle theorists pointed to disproportionate, or uneven growth. The criticisms these theorists encountered were symptomatic of the rising division between the Hilferding and Luxemburg traditions brought on by the debate over capitalist stabilization. A persistent complaint among reviewers was that the theory of disproportionalities ignored the problem of underconsumption. I. Tsalogor, for example, insisted that disproportionalities could not be the sole cause of crises: the real problem was that new investments raised the organic composition of capital, displaced living labour, and thereby lowered the share of the working class in national income.[80] Commenting on Spektator's work, A. Lyusin agreed with Varga that the postwar crisis had been caused by mass impoverishment. Spektator had not included the structural contradiction between production and consumption, and his writing, for that reason, was 'profoundly non-Marxist'.[81] B. Livshits registered a similar complaint against Guberman.[82] In the political conditions of the late 1920s, the cycle theorists were fated to satisfy neither Bukharinists nor Stalinists. Showing that Bukharin's view of 'state capitalism' was in fact a distortion of Hilferding's *Finance Capital*, they also ran afoul of the rival Stalinist position that the 'problem of markets' had become chronic.

Among a few economists working on the fringe of business-cycle theory the Stalinist view predominated. In *The Dynamic of Crises and the Position of the Proletariat* (1927) Mary Smit maintained that

[79] Ibid., p. 230.

[80] I. Tsalogov, 'K Ponimaniyu Marksovoi Teorii Krizisov', *Pod Znamenem Marksizma*, no. 2–3 (February-March 1929), p. 58.

[81] See Lyusin's comments in *Problemy Ekonomiki*, no. 3 (March 1929), p. 127.

[82] See the review by B.L. in *Mirovoe Khozyaistvo i Mirovaya Politika*, no. 8–9 (August-September 1929), p. 189 et passim.

the capitalist countries were experiencing 'an epoch of long impoverishment of the proletariat that is without precedent—a catastrophe the equivalent of which cannot be found even in the medieval invasions of the barbarians'.[83] The impending 'agony of a slow death' meant that the classical pattern of business cycles was giving way to a chronic crisis: The 'agonizing lines [of statistics] clearly speak of a change in the very form and tempo of cyclical . . . crises and the beginning of some kind of new epoch in the economic history of Europe, in which the very concept of crisis is being modified. This new wave of fluctuations is apparently the beginning of a new period in the development of capitalism's internal contradictions, and therefore excludes the possibility of projecting earlier generalizations [of the cycle] into the future.'[84]

In *The General Crisis of Capitalism in Light of the Views of Marx-Engels and Lenin* (1929), M. Gol'man came to a similar conclusion: *'the final more or less protracted crisis of the capitalist system as a whole'* was under way.[85] The intensified struggle for world markets proved that capitalism faced a *'chronic* crisis of overproduction'. The system was living its last days, and the several phases of the classical cycle had now been telescoped into two: the crisis and a 'flabby recovery'. In 1850 Engels had given a 'genius-like formulation' of the two-phased cycle, showing that 'crises will be separated by short periods of sluggish . . . recovery'.[86] In his 1884 introduction to Marx's *Poverty of Philosophy* Engels had remarked that 'chronic stagnation . . . with only insignificant fluctuations' would become the prevailing norm.[87] Evidence of this tendency could be found in the fact that the American cycle had recently been shortened 'from seven years even to four'.[88] On the strength of these arguments Gol'man predicted that a world economic crisis was about to begin either in America or Germany and 'would constitute a brilliant empirical confirmation of the genius-like theoretical prognosis of Engels'.[89] The implication of Gol'man's thesis for Bukharin was

[83] M.N. Smit, *Dinamika Krizisov i Polozhenie Proletariata*, Moscow 1927, p. 124.
[84] Ibid.
[85] M. Gol'man, *Vseobshchii Krizis Kapitalizma v Svete Vzglyadov Marksa-Engel'sa i Lenina*, Moscow 1929, p. 7.
[86] Ibid., p. 37.
[87] Ibid., p. 38.
[88] Ibid., p. 36.
[89] Ibid., p. 70.

obvious: the partial stabilization of capitalism was 'turning into its own opposite, into an instrument that *reinforces the technological, economic, social, and political crisis of capitalism, that is . . . the general crisis of capitalism*'.[90]

The brief revival of Soviet business-cycle theory at the end of the 1920s demonstrated both the potential and the tragedy of this branch of economic research. Although Marx's most creative writing had centred on the business cycle, Soviet economists had not reverted to the classical Marxist approach until it was already too late. By this time the Stalinists sought proof of their own preconceptions, not theoretical subtlety. To superficial observers it appeared that the cycle theorists had done no more than prove the obvious through a needlessly circuitous route: the end of capitalism was at hand, whether it be called an 'organic depression' (Guberman), the 'agony of a slow death' (Smit), or 'the final more or less protracted crisis of the capitalist system as a whole' (Gol'man). When the world economic crisis struck in 1929, the results of the retarded development of business-cycle theory would become apparent: confusion about the cause of the crisis and its outcome would prevail—until Stalin intervened with the doctrine of the depression 'of a special kind'. The one economist who attempted to use the American experience to promote further business-cycle research—Evgeny Preobrazhensky—would find himself condemned for applying the theory of disproportionate growth. That Soviet Marxists neglected and even actively discouraged studies of the business cycle was ironic enough. But an even greater irony was in store. More than any other economist, Varga was responsible for initiating the move towards Luxemburgism. Yet in 1930 he too would be criticized for his divided loyalties to Hilferding on the one hand and Luxemburg on the other. Varga's personal frustration in applying the analysis of *Finance Capital* further exemplified the ambiguity of Hilferding's legacy and helps to explain the origins of 'Varga's Law'.

5. 'Organized Capitalism': Varga's Confusion

Varga had evinced a cavalier attitude towards theoretical consistency ever since the early 1920s. Interpreting capitalism's long-

[90] Ibid., p. 51.

run prospects in terms of the 'problem of markets', he had also applied Hilferding's concepts to explain periodic crises. With reference to the first postwar crisis he had written: 'There can be seen a general tendency of "organized" capitalism to regulate the partial overproduction arising from the anarchy of production by a very simple means—by stopping production.'[91] The same theme recurred in 1923–4, when Varga commented on the ability of American capitalists to avoid either serious price reductions or widespread bankruptcies.[92] An abundance of money-capital in America and 'the extreme concentration of production, the extraordinarily advanced monopolistic agglomeration of capitalist enterprises', had permitted the American bourgeoisie to overcome the crisis 'mainly by the limitation of production'. Although these remarks ignored the question of disproportionalities between industries, treating output as if it were a homogeneous aggregate, they led to the conclusion that modern capitalism 'is not capable of preventing the crisis, but it is strong enough to avoid damaging consequences for the capitalists'.[93]

In 1927 Varga became more aware of the limitations of both capitalist organization and monetary policy. Now the issue was not whether the monetary authorities could prevent a crisis, but whether an excessive growth of the money supply could actually *cause* a crisis in production. In the summer and autumn of 1927 American monetary authorities took what many historians have considered the first step towards the stock-market crash. Interest rates were lowered in the hope of stimulating borrowing by consumers and investors. Varga sided with American critics who complained that increasing money-market liquidity would encourage speculation. Late in 1927 he wrote that 'the directors of the Federal Reserve Banks are following an extremely dangerous policy which . . . could lead to a very acute crisis'.[94] With a presidential election looming, the magnates of capital were putting new money

[91] Varga, 'Ekonomicheskoe Polozhenie Anglii', *Narodnoe Khozyaistvo* (November 1920), p. 78.

[92] Varga, *Plan Dauesa i Mirovoi Krizis 1924 Goda*, p. 17.

[93] Varga, 'Economics and Economic Policy in the First Half Year of 1924', *International Press Correspondence*, IV, no. 65 (11 September 1924), p. 703.

[94] Varga, 'Obzor Kon'yunktury po Stranam', *Mirovoe Khozyaistvo i Mirovaya Politika*, no. 10–11 (October-November 1927), p. 247.

into circulation to prolong stabilization and ensure a Republican victory. In April 1928 Varga quoted M.W. Alexander, head of the National Industrial Conference Board, warning of 'extravagant speculation'. According to the *New York Times*, almost the entire credit expansion had gone into brokers' loans and further share purchases. By the time the Federal Reserve began to raise the interest rate in June 1928, Varga had already decided that a stock-market crash was inevitable.[95]

The prospect of a financially induced crisis raised the question of whether the shock might spread from Wall Street to production. A number of economists believed that the effects on productive enterprises would be minimal: as Varga had indicated in the past, the capitalists would simply curtail output. Torn between 'organized capitalism' and the 'problem of markets', Varga was no longer so certain. American capitalists had clearly demonstrated that they could restrict the buildup of inventories, 'production being more speedily adapted to consumption'.[96] The ability to cut back on output meant that there was no longer any 'necessity of liquidating the surplus of commodities . . . by means of a sharp price drop . . . as in the crises of classical capitalism'.[97] No sooner had Varga dismissed the problem of demand instability, however, than he proceeded to confuse the issue by arguing that at best 'organized capital' could accomplish 'a one-sided adaptation to an anarchistic demand'. By halting production the capitalists would cause a 'wholesale discharge of workers', narrowing the market and causing a crisis. In effect, Varga was saying that 'organized capitalism' could regulate inventories but not demand. From this proposition he implicitly concluded that crises of *overproduction* could be avoided (Hilferding's influence), whereas crises of *underconsumption* were inevitable (Luxemburg's influence).

The need for this confusing distinction would never have arisen had Varga understood that for Hilferding—as for Marx—crises of

---

[95] Varga, 'Economics and Economic Policy in the First [should read Second] Quarter of 1928', *International Press Correspondence*, VIII, no. 45 (7 August 1928), p. 806.
[96] Varga, 'Economics and Economic Policy in the Third Quarter of 1929', *International Press Correspondence*, IX, no. 67 (5 December 1929), p. 1423.
[97] Ibid.

general overproduction resulted from partial *disproportionalities*. Marx had shown that inadequate demand was the 'final cause' of crises, but that the volume of demand did not vary independently, being determined by production and investment decisions. Lenin made the same point when he told the Narodniks that the relation between production and consumption must be put 'in its proper, subordinate place'; that it 'cannot explain crises'.[98] Whereas Marx and Lenin analysed the cycle in terms of the 'anarchy of production', Varga was now substituting 'an anarchistic demand'. His failure to appreciate the role of disproportionalities within production left no alternative. Either crises must arise from unforeseen variations in demand or else capitalism would become stabilized, just as Bukharin had predicted. This conclusion was starkly presented in Varga's comment that 'monopolization . . . might eliminate the lack of proportion between the individual branches of production as a cause of crises, but it could by no means remove the anomaly of the restricted consuming power of society in antagonistic conditions of [income] distribution'.[99]

Bukharin had launched the debate over 'state capitalism' by setting aside the problem of disproportionalities. The capitalist state, he assumed, might mediate between industries and thereby co-ordinate production. The negotiations leading to the European iron and steel cartel had been a prime case in point. However, Bukharin's interpretation of Hilferding involved at least one fundamental oversight: the capitalist state could not plan what it did not own. As Lenin had seen, it could not resolve the contradiction between 'the social character of production . . . and the private, individual mode of appropriation'. In other words, 'state capitalism' could not put an end to competition and the struggle between individual capitalists over the distribution of surplus-value.

Hilferding had been aware of this limitation, deciding that a 'universal cartel', or its equivalent in the form of a universal plan, ultimately required the expropriation of the finance-capitalist oligarchy as 'the last phase of the struggle between the bourgeoisie and the proletariat'. The difficulty was that Hilferding had wavered in this conclusion, adding that the 'seizure of six big Berlin banks

---

[98] Lenin, *Collected Works*, III, p. 168.
[99] Varga, 'Economics and Economic Policy in the Third Quarter of 1929', p. 1424.

would at once signify control over the principal branches of large-scale industry'. Soviet and Social Democratic writers alike took this qualification to mean that with the appearance of modern banking institutions the key to controlling the business cycle had been discovered. Through monetary (and fiscal) policy the most disturbing variations in aggregate demand could be overcome. In the very attempt to refute this argument, Varga was now laying the foundations of an ideological conundrum remarkably similar to Bukharin's. In their critique of Luxemburg, Dvolaitsky, Leikin, and others had already denied that 'an anarchistic demand' could be the cause of contemporary crises. The state, claimed Dvolaitsky, could borrow idle capital, place it in circulation, and artificially create a multiple expansion of demand. After the experiments of Hitler and Roosevelt, Varga too would eventually recognize the significance of 'artificial stimuli', coming to the view that the capitalist state really did command the ability to 'influence and modify the cyclical development of reproduction'. By omitting the concept of disproportionalities, Varga's reasoning could only end in a new variant of the theory of 'organized capitalism'.

The only Soviet economist to offer an unambiguous insight into the contradictions of American monetary policy in the late 1920s was N. Osinsky. In *My Heresies Concerning the United States of America* (1926) Osinsky warned that stabilization in America could be undermined by an excess of liquid capital. Americans were exhibiting a 'feverish-speculative attitude', and the national economy was 'falling into an extremely unstable condition'.[100] Late in 1927 Osinsky published another book, *Does an Economic Crisis Threaten America?* Two years before the Wall Street panic he catalogued the forces eroding American prosperity: sporadic intervals of stock-market uncertainty; the growth of consumer credit to finance purchases of automobiles, furniture, and appliances; land speculation; the relative weakness of industrial construction compared to public works; the gradual decline of industrial prices. In classical capitalism it had been mainly businessmen who were driven into bankruptcy. In the forthcoming crisis this situation would be reversed: up to 30 per cent of Americans would be locked

[100] N. Osinsky, *Moi Lzheucheniya o Soedinennykh Shtatakh Severnoi Ameriki*, Moscow 1926, p. 33.

by various forms of debts into payments they would be unable to meet. American consumers were 'living on time payments, their entire budget being devoted to repaying loans'.[101] So long as jobs were secure, the treadmill would continue and credit would expand the market artificially. By creating a 'significant, constant excess' of liquid funds, however, the Federal Reserve authorities were providing the 'impetus for the onset of a general crisis or a deep depression'.[102] The moment a pause occurred in the reproduction of capital, the inflated market would collapse through an implosion of consumer demand and a wave of personal bankruptcies.

Bukharin's projection of 'organized capitalism' and Osinsky's warnings of an impending catastrophe—these were the extremes within which Soviet discussions moved in the closing years of capitalist stabilization. All the great theoretical issues emanating from the works of Hilferding and Luxemburg had been canvassed: few answers had been found. The economists had been given their say, and now the practical men of the party apparatus were becoming impatient. At the party's Fifteenth Congress in December 1927, Stalin had already staked out his own position, telling Bukharin that 'the *general* and *fundamental* crisis of capitalism . . . is becoming deeper and is shaking the very foundations of the existence of world capitalism'.[103] While the economists debated abstract theory, Stalin devised his own conceptualization of what had occurred since 1917. The first period of revolutionary upsurge had been betrayed by the Social Democrats, whose theories of class harmony represented 'social fascism'. The second period of 'rotten stabilization' was now ending. The third period would be one of wars, revolutions, and economic collapse.

In his post as principal economic adviser of the Comintern, Varga had to accept the responsibility for elaborating the 'official' (i.e., Stalin's) point of view. An implicit directive had been issued to demonstrate that the 'problem of markets' would lead to the third period. Despite prevalent suspicions of Rosa Luxemburg, *The Accumulation of Capital* appeared to offer a ready-made solution.

[101] Osinsky, *Ugrozhaet li Amerike Ekonomicheskii Krizis?*, Moscow and Leningrad 1928, p. 13.
[102] Ibid., p. 67.
[103] Stalin, *Works*, X, p. 292.

An overt rehabilitation of Luxemburg was politically problematic, for Lenin's view of 'third-party' theories of imperialism was well known. On the other hand, Luxemburg's claim that the accumulation of capital automatically created a crisis of realization conformed perfectly to Stalin's thesis that the end of stabilization must follow from the restoration of prewar levels of output. Bukharin's forecasts depended on the assertion that investments in new technology would enable the capitalist countries to expand their internal markets. Convinced that Bukharin had misunderstood the significance of mass impoverishment and the anarchy of demand, Varga now undertook to dispute the theory of internal market creation by refurbishing Luxemburg's thesis and presenting it as 'Varga's Law'.

5
Neo-Luxemburgism and the 'Hilferding Tinge'

In *The Accumulation of Capital* Rosa Luxemburg had criticized Marx's reproduction schemes for concentrating exclusively on disproportionalities as the cause of crises. The schemes, she argued, allowed for crises 'only because of a lack of proportion within production, because of a defective social control over the productive process. [They] preclude, however, the deep and fundamental antagonism between the capacity to consume and the capacity to produce in capitalist society, a conflict resulting from the very accumulation of capital which . . . spurs capital on to a continual extension of the [external] market.'[1] Luxemburg believed there was a clear contradiction between Marx's discussion of reproduction in *Capital* Volume 2 and his references to the 'limits of consumption' in Volume 3. There Marx had declared: 'The final cause of all real crises always remains the poverty and restricted consumption of the masses as opposed to the drive of capitalist production to develop the productive forces as though only the absolute consuming power of society constituted their limit.'[2]

How could the 'limits of consumption' be the cause of crises when Marx simultaneously argued that the reproduction of capital inaugurated a process of market creation? Bukharin had recalled Marx's answer in his own critique of Luxemburg, showing that a growth of industrial output required new expenditures on *constant* capital (machinery, materials), which in turn called for further expenditures on *variable* capital (wages to hire additional workers). 'The "limits of consumption"', Bukharin wrote, 'are expanded by

[1] Luxemburg, *The Accumulation of Capital*, pp. 346–7.
[2] Marx, *Capital* Volume 3, pp. 472–3.

production itself.'[3] The scale of investment depended on profit opportunities, and employment would rise so long as the capitalists saw an advantage in expanding operations. The 'limits of consumption' would cease to expand, and become a genuine *constraint* on production, when wages rose high enough to jeopardize the rate of profit, thereby discouraging new investment. Thus Marx had observed that working-class consuming power was 'limited' because labourers were hired 'only as long as they can be profitably employed by the capitalist class'.[4]

Luxemburg contended that in the absence of 'third parties' the accumulation of capital inevitably entailed a realization crisis; Bukharin and other adherents to the Hilferding tradition argued precisely the opposite—that the process of accumulation and investment invariably broadened capitalism's internal market. The only conceivable salvation of Luxemburg's approach might have been to argue that each successive round of investment tended towards self-negation by creating *technological unemployment*. In fact, Marx believed that the 'absolute' volume of employment would tend to grow despite technological change, albeit at a slower rate than expenditures on plant, machinery, and materials. In Marx's words: 'With the growth of the total capital, its variable constituent, the labour incorporated in it, does admittedly increase, but in a constantly diminishing proportion.'[5] Luxemburg had understood this section of Marx's argument perfectly, telling Tugan-Baranovsky that his assumption of 'an absolute decrease of the variable capital is in striking contrast to reality. Variable capital is in point of fact a growing quantity in all capitalist countries; only in relation to the even more rapid growth of constant capital can it be said to decrease.'[6]

As of 1928 Varga began trying to pry open the door Luxemburg had slammed shut on Tugan-Baranovsky. 'Varga's Law' stated that in 'pure' capitalism, accumulation automatically caused an absolute decline in the number of productive workers, and therewith a chronic realization crisis. The 'law' embraced the Luxemburgist

---

[3] Luxemburg and Bukharin, *Imperialism and the Accumulation of Capital*, p. 204.
[4] Marx, *Capital* Volume 3, p. 472.
[5] Marx, *Capital* Volume 1, pp. 781–82.
[6] Luxemburg, *The Accumulation of Capital*, p. 336.

thesis that accumulation destroyed rather than created a market. But it was also neo-Luxemburgist—and this must be emphasized—in the sense that Varga believed Luxemburg had been right for the wrong reasons. She had failed to clinch her thesis because she agreed with Marx that employment would tend to grow despite technological change and industrial 'rationalization'. Since 1926 Varga had been moving to the belief that industrial reorganization reflected a chronic excess of productive capacity in industry, the corollary of which had to be chronic unemployment. The final round in the debate over capitalist stabilization turned on the conflict between Bukharin's interpretation of Hilferding and Varga's neo-Luxemburgist reformulation of the theory of chronic crisis.

1. Industrial Rationalization and 'Varga's Law'

Varga's understanding of the business cycle had little in common with that of the theorists of the Hilferding tradition. Whereas these writers accepted Lenin's view that the volume of consumption was 'subordinate' to production, Varga saw a chronic tendency towards a contradiction between the productive forces and social 'consuming power'. Competition compelled the capitalists 'always to apply the latest means of production . . . to raise the organic composition of capital, to expand the total productive power beyond the consuming power of society'.[7] Quoting Marx on the 'final cause of all real crises', Varga wrote at the end of 1927: 'The formation of monopolies and rationalization means . . . a decrease in the proportion of variable capital [or wages] to the yearly value of products, i.e., a decrease of the working-class share, or a still sharper operation of the "final cause".'[8] In *Capital* Volume 1 Marx had explained that the workers' share *must* decline with the rise of the organic composition, for a greater portion of the social product would necessarily go to the replacement of constant capital. 'There can be no greater error', Marx protested, 'than the one repeated after Adam Smith by Ricardo and all subsequent political economists, namely

[7] E. Varga, *Problemy Mirovovo Khozyaistva i Mirovoi Politiki*, Moscow 1929, p. 30.

[8] Varga, *The Decline of Capitalism*, London 1928, p. 9.

the view that "the portion of revenue so said to be added to capital, is [totally] consumed by productive labourers".[9] The further industrialization advanced, the greater would be the portion of the capitalists' revenue spent on equipment and materials. Varga's interpretation of this problem amounted to the assertion that crises occurred because workers were not paid sufficient wages to consume the mounting output of machines.

In the spring of 1928 Varga's gravitation towards Luxemburg became more pronounced with an article on 'The Crisis of Capitalist Rationalization'. Data from America indicated that for the first time in history the number of productive workers (those creating surplus-value) had declined during a period of industrial expansion. Between 1919 and 1926 employment in agriculture, industry, mining, and railway transportation had fallen by 8 per cent.[10] Varga thought the statistics proved that 'the postwar development of capitalism in the USA fully corresponds to the Marxist theory of the development of "pure" capitalism. An absolute reduction in the number of workers takes place together with a rapid . . . increase in the volume of commodities produced per worker.'[11] The rate of labour displacement in some branches of production had exceeded the rate of absorption in others because no new markets were available: American farmers had ceased to be 'third parties' and were now engaged almost exclusively in commercial agriculture. Reverting to the views Bessonov had expressed in 1923, Varga maintained that only the *process* of rural stratification creates a market; thereafter the working class must shrink in numbers and become 'absolutely' impoverished. At earlier stages in the growth of capitalism the effects of technological change had been offset:

'[Variable capital] became relatively smaller, but it also grew [in absolute terms] thanks to the rapid increase of the total capital. This was possible, above all, because . . . handicrafts, once a part of the peasant economy, were detached from the latter and replaced by factory production. At the same time, the use of machinery in agriculture increased, that is, use of the products of large-scale

[9] Marx, *Capital* Volume 1, p. 736.
[10] Varga, *Problemy Mirovovo Khozyaistva*, p. 49.
[11] Ibid., p. 50.

industry. . . . Labour power, freed . . . from agriculture . . . found employment thanks to the extension of industrial production. . . . The process of . . . converting peasants into agrarian capitalists has been completed in the USA. The further expansion of industry along these lines is impossible.'[12]

Use of new technology had brought with it 'a massive displacement of workers by machines' and 'a drop in the sum total of industrial wages'. Without renewed access to 'third-party' markets, the depletion of working-class incomes could not be made good. The relationship between this line of thought and Luxemburg's *Accumulation of Capital* was so obvious as to require acknowledgement: 'The actual development of the USA is approaching the condition of "pure" capitalism, and in this regard the question arises—or more correctly, could be raised by the supporters of Rosa Luxemburg's theory—as to whether obstacles now emerge to the further accumulation and realization of surplus-value.'[13]

In theory, Varga assured his readers, surplus-value could be realized; in practice it could not. Despite the achievements of monopolies in the regulation of production, competition forced the continuous adoption of new means of production and aggravated the contradiction between output and sales. The only possible way to mitigate the chronic crisis of the capitalist system was to transfer income from capitalists to workers. 'But only Social Democrats can seriously believe that the capitalists will raise wages in order to find buyers for their surplus commodities. This would be senseless, for it would mean that the capitalist class as a whole would voluntarily grant the working class a part of the surplus-value.'[14] In *The Accumulation of Capital* Luxemburg had already pointed out that 'maintenance of an ever-larger army of workers [cannot] be the ultimate purpose of the continuous accumulation of capital'.[15]

Varga was less discreet than other economists in his reference to Luxemburg, but he was not the first to speculate on the consequences of technological unemployment. The debate with Bukharin about the effects of changes in industrial organization had

[12] Ibid., pp. 52–3.
[13] Ibid., p. 54.
[14] Ibid., pp. 57–8.
[15] Luxemburg, *The Accumulation of Capital*, p. 334.

been continuing since 1926. In that year M. Batuev had written of a rising 'relative overpopulation' in Europe due to productivity gains that necessitated either unemployment or overproduction.[16] Two years later Batuev broadened the scope of his original article to include the 'Europeanization of America'. Attributing the 'crises' of 1924 and 1927 to 'a condition of chronic and growing unemployment', he declared that America was afflicted with 'an enormous, under-utilized productive apparatus'.[17] The fact that expanded reproduction had not resumed following the previous two crises demonstrated that the 'normal pulsation' of healthy capitalism had ceased.[18] Where Batuev differed from Varga was in his more prudent choice of references. Marx appeared to be a more convincing authority than Luxemburg, and Batuev found the following remark in *Capital*: 'A development of the productive forces which would diminish the absolute number of labourers, i.e., enable the entire nation to accomplish its total production in a shorter time span, would cause a revolution because it would put the bulk of the population out of the running. This is another manifestation of the specific barrier to capitalist production.'[19]

A third writer who came to a similar point of view independently was Modest Rubinshtein. In *The Contradictions of American Capitalism* (written in 1928 and published in 1929) Rubinshtein declared that American unemployment was 'totally unique in the entire history of the capitalist world'.[20] In every branch of industry labour conditions were deteriorating because of the advance of technology. The latest information from the Federal Reserve confirmed the emergence of a chronic reserve army: in 1928 American industry provided jobs for 87.9 per cent of the number of workers who had been employed in 1919. Another government source, taking 1923 as the base year, placed the figure at 84.2 per

---

[16] M. Batuev, 'Besrabotitsa i Otnositel'noe Perenaselenie v Evropeiskom Khozyaistve', *Sotsialisticheskoe Khozyaistvo*, no. 6 (1926), pp. 49–50.

[17] Batuev, 'Priroda Poslevoennoi Amerikanskoi Kon'yunktury', *Sotsialisticheskoe Khozyaistvo*, no. 2 (1928), p. 96.

[18] Ibid., p. 101.

[19] Batuev, 'Besrabotitsa i Otnositel'noe Perenaselenie . . .', p. 45; cf. Marx, *Capital* Volume 3, p. 258.

[20] Modest Rubinshtein, *Protivorechiya Amerikanskovo Kapitalizma*, Moscow 1929, p. 130.

cent.[21] Displacement of labour and skills had left the 'minimum health and decency budget' of the Department of Labour beyond the reach of most working-class families.[22] Concentrated in factory towns, American workers lived in 'barracks, dirtier and more repulsive than cattle sheds'.[23] In order to control its 'serfs', trustified capital maintained private armies and manipulated both the police and the courts, arresting or lynching trade-union organizers.[24] One American newspaper had even admitted that 'thousands of women and children' were starving because of a miners' strike in Pennsylvania. 'Industrial slavery' and 'police terror' had become the mainstays of 'a despotic tyranny reminiscent of Tsarist Siberia'.[25] Social Democrats believed in an American 'economic miracle', a 'workers' paradise', and 'an organized, crisis-free development of capitalism'. Rubinshtein thought the unprecedented ruthlessness of American exploitation must be attributed to the 'rapidly growing lack of correspondence between the productive apparatus and effective demand'.[26]

For the past decade Soviet Marxists had been attempting in a variety of ways to demonstrate the impossibility of a normal business cycle in modern conditions. To prove the existence of a chronic crisis was to sustain the hope of systemic breakdown and keep alive the prospect of further revolutions. All Soviet economists shared these political commitments, but many were becoming alarmed at the tendency to encourage revolutionary expectations by compromising Marxist theory. In the case of the 'rationalization crisis' the break with Marx's *Capital* was too palpable to be ignored. Criticism of the new views of Varga, Batuev, and Rubinshtein began with Spektator, who clung to the view (shared by Varga only two years previously) that labour intensification in modern capitalism was far more important than technological advance. While the existence of unemployment could not be denied, its cause was not at all novel: the level of investment activity was simply too low to maintain full employment. Correcting Varga's interpretation of

[21] Ibid., p. 118.
[22] Ibid., pp. 74–6.
[23] Ibid., p. 25.
[24] Ibid.
[25] Ibid., p. 143.
[26] Ibid., pp. 8–9.

Capital, Spektator demonstrated that Marx had expected a 'relative' decline in variable capital to be accompanied by an 'absolute' increase in the number of productive workers.[27] Varga's remarks about 'pure' capitalism were nothing but a throwback to the 'absurd idea' of Tugan-Baranovsky that capitalism might continue to develop even in the face of a secular contraction of the work force. Bukhartsev gave Varga credit for publicizing the American data but also took him to task for confusing 'relative' and 'absolute' labour redundancy.[28] E.S. Gorfinkel' complained that Marx 'never and in no place spoke of the inevitability of an absolute fall in the number of workers employed by industry in conditions of "pure" capitalism'.[29] There was no difference, in his opinion, between Varga's position and Luxemburg's.[30] P. Shubin remarked that Varga's error resulted from his attempt to 'correct' and 'supplement' Marx. The new theory involved 'an extraordinary overestimation of the role of technological progress' and was founded on the 'Luxemburgist theory of realization'.[31] Through his 'vulgar overestimation' of technology Varga had forgotten that rationalization consisted primarily in the intensification of labour and not in the use of new equipment that would raise labour productivity.[32] Indicating that Varga had gone beyond the bounds of discretion, Shubin warned that 'opportunism has many faces'.[33]

Probably the most perceptive contribution to this debate (and many others) came from Osinsky. In an address to the Communist Academy in April 1928, Osinsky cautioned Varga against premature conclusions: 'with Russian haste, people are already beginning to construct yet another theory—of the absolute reduction in the labour-power employed by American industry.'[34] The new theory

[27] Spektator, 'K Probleme Besrabotitsy v Kapitalisticheskikh Stranakh', *Planovoe Khozyaistvo*, no. 7 (July 1928), pp. 198–9.

[28] Bukhartsev, 'Posle Stabilizatsii', *Bol'shevik*, no. 21–2 (30 November 1928), pp. 133–5 *et seq.*

[29] E.S. Gorfinkel', 'Problemy Besrabotitsy v Epokhe Monopolisticheskovo Kapitalizma', *Ekonomicheskoe Obozrenie*, no. 8 (August 1929), p. 91.

[30] Ibid., p. 100.

[31] P. Shubin, 'Kapitalisticheskaya Ratsionalizatsiya i Zhiznennyi Uroven' Proletariata', *Bol'shevik*, no. 18 (30 September 1929), p. 97.

[32] Ibid., p. 104.

[33] Ibid., p. 110.

[34] Osinsky, 'Ekonomicheskaya Depressiya v Soed. Shtatakh', *Mirovoe Khozyaistvo i Mirovaya Politika*, no. 7 (July 1928), p. 14.

suggested a 'permanent crisis' and flew in the face of reality: to deny the existence of expanded reproduction in America was nonsense. After the coming crisis, predicted Osinsky, 'the American economy will pass through still another cycle of reproduction, and in this cycle *the present records will be surpassed*. Not in every branch, I do not go that far, but in several branches this will occur.'[35]

Alone among Soviet economists Osinsky appreciated the absurdity to which present discussions were leading: while some authors marvelled at the 'technological revolution' in America others denied any growth whatever, seeing only stagnation. Osinsky believed much of the confusion could be resolved if account were taken of the true nature of investment planning. Expanded reproduction required 'technical reserves' exactly as it depended on a reserve of disposable labour-power.[36] Noting that 20 per cent of American industrial capacity was not in use, Batuev had rushed to infer that America was in the grip of a chronic crisis. A more sobre appraisal would take into account the need to anticipate future demand in current construction. To tailor a new plant to existing demand was to guarantee inefficiency and high-cost production at a later date. Had he been more blunt, Osinsky might have added that the fixation of some of his colleagues on 'excess capacity' also reflected the lack of reserves in the Soviet economy, a factor that contributed to the grain strike but was nevertheless foolishly hailed as a triumph of economic planning.

A more obvious problem with the theory of the rationalization crisis was the tendency of its proponents to overlook the distribution of 'consuming power' in the sphere of commodity circulation. Varga himself noted that from 1919 to 1926 close to 4 million new jobs had been created in the 'non-productive' sectors of the American economy, in commerce, the public service, the motor and hotel trades, and so on.[37] Yet when urging that a contradiction between production and consumption was inevitable, Varga riveted his attention on industrial wages. Marx had called distribution expenses the *faux frais* of capitalist reproduction; but he did not suggest that they could be ignored in assessing disposable income.

[35] Ibid., p. 15.
[36] Ibid., p. 13.
[37] Varga, *The Decline of Capitalism* (1928), p. 23.

The sale and servicing of a commodity was 'non-productive', although it did shorten the turnover period of industrial capital and thereby helped to sustain or increase industrial profits. Varga should have been more conscious of this fact: his own calculations showed that the rate of surplus-value in America was rising steadily, notwithstanding the decline in the number of workers who could strictly be categorized as 'productive'.[38]

'Varga's Law' and the theory of the rationalization crisis must be seen as an effort to escape from the Hilferding tradition and to terminate the debate about capitalist stabilization. The dispute with Bukharin had dragged on too long: nerves were becoming frayed, and that encouraged serious errors of judgement. In preparation for the Sixth Congress of the Comintern, scheduled to meet in the summer of 1928, Varga published an extensive report on 'the decline of capitalism after stabilization'. The theme of the work was that 'Capitalism never was and never can be stable'.[39] Social Democratic reformists expected 'a new long-enduring boom', forgetting that postwar capitalism was historically unique: 'It is a different capitalism. It is no longer a "dying" capitalism but one already in the process of mortification.'[40] Bukharin, chairing the Congress, exasperated both his political adversaries and his economic critics by adopting exactly the position Varga had contemptuously attributed to European Socialists.

2. The Sixth Congress of the Comintern

Facing imminent defeat in his quarrel with Stalin, Bukharin shadow-boxed with his foe and attempted to convince foreign delegates there was no immediate war threat and therefore no justification for 'administrative measures' against Soviet peasants. In Bukharin's view the 'third period' had become 'the period of capitalist reconstruction'. In Soviet discourse, 'reconstruction' denoted the industrial renovation that had been under way in the domestic economy since 1926. Bukharin used the term in the same sense when speaking of the capitalist economies: 'This period of

[38] Ibid., p. 29.
[39] Ibid., p. 8.
[40] Ibid., p. 7.

reconstruction of capitalism "coincides" with the period of reconstruction in the USSR [and includes] . . . the establishment of a new technological basis.'[41] Bukharin later told the delegates that the 'third period' thesis had been 'discussed' within the Soviet party and 'amended to make it more precise'. The real import of the amendment was its inclusion of Stalin's insistence on the inevitability of war.[42] Reading the newly-drafted thesis into the record, Bukharin interpreted it to suit his own purpose: 'by taking note of a third period we emphasize that the stabilization of capitalism cannot disappear from the world economy in the course of a single day. And this must be emphasized. It is precisely on these grounds that our delegation supports the postulate of the third period.'[43]

To illustrate capitalism's longevity Bukharin once again surveyed an array of new inventions and industrial processes in the West, including the electrification of industry, new ways of producing synthetic fuels, the manufacture of artificial silk, use of light metals such as aluminium, the spread of automobile transportation in America, and the revolutionizing of factories with assembly-line forms of organization. Seven years earlier Trotsky had told a similar gathering that the curve of development had turned irrevocably downwards. Now Bukharin announced that recent innovations 'convincingly' demonstrated the opposite: 'the curve of development of the capitalist economy, both from the quantitative and the qualitative point of view, marks definite progress'.[44]

'State capitalism' was the superstructural counterpart of this 'technological revolution'.[45] Mindful of recent discussions, Bukharin distinguished between the newest state-capitalist forms and those of 'war capitalism', or what Social Democrats 'had the impudence to describe . . . as "war socialism" '. During the war cartels had been comandeered by the state; now they were being 'linked up with and grafted onto public organs', sometimes through

[41] Bukharin, 'The International Situation and the Tasks of the Comintern', *International Press Correspondence*, VIII, no.41 (30 July 1928), p. 726.

[42] See Stalin, *Works*, XI, p. 207–8.

[43] Bukharin, 'Reply to the Discussion', *International Press Correspondence*, VIII, no. 49 (13 August 1928), p. 865.

[44] Bukharin, 'The International Situation . . .', p. 726.

[45] Ibid., p. 727.

state ownership but more frequently by capturing the state 'from below'. The prevailing tendency was 'along the line of the bourgeoisie of all categories becoming transformed into receivers of dividends, notwithstanding various antagonisms, frictions, etc.'[46] 'Certain comrades' were still expressing doubt about state capitalism. Bukharin recommended that they read the work of Lapinsky—on the 'Napoleonic state'—and consider the fact that on Wall Street Herbert Hoover was known as 'the director general of American business'. 'The fact that Hoover is described as Director General of Trusts is in itself a striking political expression of the process of grafting which is taking place between the capitalist trust organizations and the capitalist political and state organizations.'[47]

For Bukharin the only serious threat to the long-run stability of state capitalism lay in the risk of war between organized national trusts: 'wars will inevitably be accompanied by revolutions'.[48] Internal difficulties were of little concern, for the state 'regulates the process of production'. In this respect the capitalist and the proletarian states were identical: in both cases 'the "secondary" (the superstructure) regulates the "primary" (the basis), and there is nothing terrible about it'.[49] The further state capitalism advanced, the less likely would crises become: 'Under [full] state capitalism . . . crises would be impossible, although the "share" of the workers may steadily decline. This diminishing share would be taken into account in the plan.'[50] The advance of state capitalism could not be denied simply out of prejudice against Rudolf Hilferding. When a number of delegates protested against the inclusion of Hilferding's ideas in the new Comintern Programme, Bukharin rejected the claim that he had given the document a 'Social Democratic "Hilferding tinge"'. 'It does not follow', he retorted, 'that because Hilferding speaks of finance capital, nothing he says about it is true. . . . Lenin's opinion of Hilferding's *Finance Capital* is . . . well-known.'[51] When the critics persisted, Bukharin announced

[46] Bukharin, 'Reply to the Debate on the Programme Question', *International Press Correspondence*, VIII, no. 59 (4 September 1928), p. 1036.

[47] Bukharin, 'The International Situation . . .', p. 727.

[48] Bukharin, 'Reply to the Discussion', p. 868.

[49] Bukharin, 'Report on the Programme of the Communist International', *International Press Correspondence*, VIII, no. 56 (27 August 1928), p. 986.

[50] Ibid.

[51] Ibid., p. 985.

that he was willing 'to come to the defence of "poor" Hilferding'
and 'to take the "prewar" Hilferding under my protection'.[52] In
Imperialism Lenin had described monopoly capitalism as moribund
and parasitic: 'One of the shortcomings of the Marxist Hilferding',
he had commented, 'is that on this point he has taken a step
backwards from the non-Marxist Hobson.'[53] To the demand that
the new Programme deal more exhaustively with parasitism and
decay, Bukharin replied:

'There is a tendency in our ranks to overestimate the so-called
parasitic aspect of capitalism. . . . In my opinion . . . it is wrong to
assert that the tendency of the parasitic degeneration of capitalism is
universally supreme and that it determines everything. If this were
so it would mean that the productive forces of capitalism have
already ceased to develop. As a matter of fact they are developing
and rather rapidly. It is by no means out of the question that in
certain countries . . . the productive forces of capitalism will grow
with extraordinary rapidity. We are passing through a peculiar
phase of capitalism in which science is linked up with technology
more closely than ever before, when technological invention
assumes grandiose proportions, when science is passing through a
remarkable period of development.'[54]

Stalin and Varga had contended that the colonial revolution and
industrial rationalization were undermining the labour aristocracy.
Bukharin answered that new technology would permit an extension
of exports, the receipt of new super-profits, and the creation of a
new working-class aristocracy. The reformist labour organizations
would be integrated all the more closely with employers' organizations and the organs of the imperialist state.[55] As far as Varga's
latest discoveries were concerned, Bukharin declared that the whole
theory of the rationalization crisis and the 'absolute' growth of
unemployment was simply 'the Luxemburg theory' in a new guise:
'this problem is not as simple as some comrades think'. The political
significance of unemployment 'in the period of an upward trend of
development' was not the same as it might be if there were no

[52] Bukharin, 'Reply to the Debate . . .', pp. 1034–5.
[53] Lenin, *Selected Works*, I, p. 790.
[54] Bukharin, 'Reply to the Debate . . .', pp. 1036–7.
[55] Bukharin, 'The International Situation . . .', p. 731.

prospect of re-employment: 'I absolutely disagree with the argument advanced here by many comrades to the effect that the internal possibilities of American capitalism have been "exhausted". They have not yet been exhausted and . . . I am on principle opposed to this point of view. It is wrong both in theory and practice . . . it is a reiteration of Rosa Luxemburg's theory.'[56]

Dramatizing the division within the Soviet party, Bukharin added a further provocation by asserting that stabilization should no longer be thought of as 'relative': such a definition 'no longer corresponds to the present situation'. The United States was 'marching ahead'; German capitalism was developing 'rather rapidly'; 'old usurer France' was becoming 'a substantial industrial country'; and even Britain was augmenting her productive forces in the fields of chemistry and electronics. To recognize these facts was not to indulge in 'pessimism'—as Stalinists charged—but merely to avoid being stupid: 'We must draw a distinction between optimism and stupidity. These are two different things. If we do not wish to be stupid we must take the facts as they are. This is the first obligatory prerequisite for all non-stupid tactics.'[57] If a real crisis of capitalism did exist, it was in relations between state-capitalist trusts, in the international arena: 'We must not picture the crisis of capitalism and of the capitalist system as a steady decline in almost all capitalist countries or even in a majority of countries. . . . The crisis of capitalism lies . . . in the world economy [as a whole].'[58]

In Bukharin's judgement, 'Varga's Law' represented nothing more than a Luxemburgist effort to re-enact the whole dispute with Trotsky over internal and external conditions. By denying the possibility of internal market-creation Varga was vindicating Stalin's claim that the 'third period' would be one of wars and revolutions. Notwithstanding the taunting reference to 'stupidity', Varga answered Bukharin's charges in a matter-of-fact tone. Increases in the productivity and intensity of labour, he told the delegates, had resulted in 'the rise of a new kind of unemployment, what I call structural unemployment, which is economically different from the industrial reserve army we used to know in the

[56] Bukharin 'Reply to the Discussion', p. 871.
[57] Bukharin, 'The International Situation . . .', p. 728.
[58] Ibid.

past'.[59] After listing unemployment data from several countries Varga asked:

'What does this development signify? . . . It means that technological progress, the progress in the productivity and intensity of labour, has surpassed the capacity of the market. Before the war it happened that owing to technological progress some workers were temporarily thrown out of work, but owing to the expansion of the capitalist market the unemployed invariably found work again. . . . The consequences revealed themselves in India, in China, on the periphery, where unemployment [caused by imports from the developed countries] was associated with the starvation and death of millions. Today we find that the expansion of the market no longer suffices to provide work again for those who have previously been thrown out of work in the imperialist countries.'[60]

Apart from America, structural unemployment was most apparent in Britain, where the number of workers in industry and transport had declined by 6 per cent between 1923 and 1928, while the index of production rose by 7.6 per cent.[61] Neither the American nor the British market offered any further prospect of expansion. As Varga remarked: 'the former impetus to the expansion of the capitalist market, that of the passing of the agriculturalist from natural economy to commodity economy, is coming to an end in America, while in England, I believe, it has already ended'. Only one conclusion could follow: 'the struggle for markets is going to become more and more acute in the near future'.[62]

The exchange between Bukharin and Varga paraded the division within the Soviet leadership for Communists from all countries to see. To the politically sensitive it was obvious that Varga had come forth as the spokesman of a new 'official' point of view. The eclipse of Bukharin was reflected in the new Programme, finally adopted in September. The passage dealing with unemployment implicitly incorporated the neo-Luxemburgist theory that the reserve army must grow absolutely and become a chronic affliction in conditions

---

[59] See Varga's comments in *International Press Correspondence*, VIII, no. 46 (25 July 1928), p. 817.

[60] Ibid., p. 818.

[61] Varga, *The Decline of Capitalism* (1928), p. 22.

[62] Varga in *International Press Correspondence*, VIII, no. 46 (25 July 1928), p. 818.

of 'pure' capitalism: 'The breakup of the world economy into a capitalist and a socialist sector, the shrinking of markets and . . . [the] technological progress and rationalization of industry, the reverse side of which is the closing down and liquidation of numerous enterprises, the restriction of production, and the ruthless and destructive exploitation of labour, leads to chronic unemployment on a scale never before experienced. The absolute deterioration of the conditions of the working class becomes a fact even in certain highly-developed countries.'[63]

To Bukharin's exposition of finance-capitalist organization (in the preliminary draft) the final version of the Programme added that 'although capitalist organizations grow out of free competition, they do not eliminate the latter, but exist over and alongside of it, and thereby give rise to a number of very acute, intense antagonisms, frictions and conflicts'.[64] The inclusion of this explicitly Leninist formulation in the Programme both demonstrated Varga's success and provided the first hint of its limitations. Stalinists were perfectly happy to give Varga free rein in discrediting Bukharin; they were not, however, prepared to countenance an overt rehabilitation of Luxemburg. Having been instrumental in sealing Bukharin's fate, Varga must have been amazed when menacing questions soon began to be asked about his own.

3. 'Varga's Law' as 'Bourgeois Contamination'

Besso Lominadze, a Comintern functionary who had been active on Stalin's behalf in China during 1927, brought the matter of 'Varga's Law' to official attention when he told Varga that there was no need to revise Marx: 'Capitalism develops and declines under the same laws that Marx laid down, and we do not have to think out any new laws.'[65] While the new 'law' provided the only plausible justification yet given for Stalin's talk of the 'third period', there was one difficulty: Varga had based his discussion on the premise of a

[63] 'The Programme of the Communist International', *International Press Correspondence*, VIII, no. 92 (31 December 1928), p. 1754.

[64] Ibid., p. 1751.

[65] See Lominadze's comments in *International Press Correspondence*, VIII, no. 53 (23 August 1928), p. 934.

'technological revolution' in the West—and after the summer of 1928 an 'overestimation' of technology came to be identified as one element of Bukharin's 'Right Deviation'. By accepting Bukharin's slogan of a 'technological revolution' and inverting it to signify technological unemployment, Varga and his co-thinkers had generated the suspicion that they too might be ideologically contaminated.

A. Leont'ev, long a prominent critic of 'organized capitalism', pinpointed the problem when reviewing a new edition of one of Rubinshtein's books. Leont'ev did not dispute the rapidity of technological advance: after all, Stalin had recently declared that 'technology is not only progressing but is racing forward'.[66] However, Leont'ev made the further observation that Rubinshtein had committed a fundamental error, equating recent innovations with those of the first industrial revolution, which had laid the material foundations for a new social organization. Did Rubinshtein really believe, asked Leont'ev, that the second industrial revolution would have a similar effect, creating the basis for 'organized capitalism'? 'The analogy between current technological changes and those of the previous industrial revolution', Leont'ev explained, 'is needed by Social Democrats to justify their thesis of a new phase in the development of capitalism—their thesis of organized capitalism and economic democracy'.[67] If Rubinshtein wished to avoid confusion he would remove such 'incidental' defects from any future edition of his work.

Leont'ev's Stalinist rebuke was matched by an equally hostile Bukharinist criticism originating with S. Wurm. Varga was trapped in the crossfire between the two factions, and his career fell under a question mark for the first time. In the summer of 1929 the tenth plenary meeting of the ECCI was scheduled to draw up a balance of events since the Sixth Congress. In February Wurm published an article on 'The General Law of Capitalist Accumulation', which substantiated the complaint that Varga was revising Marx. Closely paraphrasing *Capital*, Wurm showed first that growth of the reserve army was a necessary prelude to a new wave of investment, and second that new accumulation customarily reabsorbed labour and

[66] See Leont'ev's review in *Problemy Ekonomiki*, no. 1 (January 1929), p. 168.
[67] Ibid., p. 169.

even added to the total number of employed workers. Machines did displace men, but they also created new jobs in branches manufacturing the means of production. Technological unemployment was neither unique nor chronic: in both *Capital* and *Theories of Surplus-Value* Marx had allowed for exceptional cases wherein individual industries might experience an absolute reduction of employment.[68] Recognizing these isolated exceptions, Marx had nevertheless argued that the prevailing tendency throughout industry as a whole was to expand employment opportunities. If a rise in the organic composition of capital eventually did have a negative impact upon total employment, it would only occur *after* the entire industrial plant had been renovated, and then only if technological progress came to a sudden halt. In the meantime, the most likely outcome, as Marx had foreseen, was an absolute increase in employment, albeit at a declining rate of growth.[69] Even if all Varga's arguments were sound, they would still not prove his point, for they dealt exclusively with the domestic American economy. And how was it possible to exclude America, the most powerful country in the world, from any foreign market she chose to penetrate?

To this sort of interrogation Varga had no answer except to refer to the statistics. At the end of March 1929, he published new data from the Federal Reserve. From 1924 to 1928 the number of factory workers had fallen by 5.2 per cent, compared to an increase in output of 16 per cent.[70] In May Varga reported to a commission of the ECCI making preparations for the plenary meeting in July. His chief complaint about the decisions of the previous congress was that they had not given sufficient emphasis to the growth of organic (or structural) unemployment. The latest data confirmed the existence of 'gigantic, organic unemployment' in both Britain and America. As for Wurm's article, Varga told the ECCI that Marx had distinguished between the historical-concrete nature of unemployment and the purely theoretical. In Marx's day it was a historical

[68] S. Wurm, 'Rezervnaya Armiya', *Kommunisticheskii Internatsional*, no. 8 (22 February 1929), p. 30.

[69] Ibid., p. 32.

[70] Varga, 'Desyat' Let Krizisa Kapitalizma', *Bol'shevik*, no. 6 (30 March 1929), p. 28.

fact that the work force did grow despite the rising organic composition of capital: 'But Marx never spoke of this as a purely theoretical thesis or suggested that matters must always develop in this way.'[71] On the contrary, Batuev had already found a quotation proving that Marx expected absolute unemployment to be the signal for proletarian revolution: 'that which is now occurring', promised Varga, 'is chronic, expanding, organically developing mass unemployment; it is an element of the crisis of capitalism and of the revolution in exactly the way Marx suggests'.[72] The crisis brought on by new technology confirmed Marx's analysis of the contradictions of 'pure' capitalism.

At the same meeting Wurm once again challenged Varga, this time by the more polemical route of recounting Lenin's conflict with the Narodniks. Long before Luxemburg's *Accumulation of Capital*, Lenin had argued that 'from an abstract-theoretical point of view the destruction of small-scale producers . . . signifies the creation, not the curtailment of the internal market'.[73] Productive consumption might expand more rapidly than personal consumption, but Lenin held that the two were inextricably connected: 'Thus the growth of the internal capitalist market [wrote Lenin] is to a certain extent "independent" of the growth of personal consumption, being due mainly to productive consumption. But it would be a mistake to understand this "independence" to mean the complete separation of productive from personal consumption: the first can and must grow more rapidly than the second . . . although it is obvious that in the final analysis productive consumption always remains connected to personal consumption.'[74]

Taking the form of new investments, productive consumption *created* personal consumption. Varga's error resulted from his acceptance of 'Rosa Luxemburg's theory of accumulation' and his neglect of the law of uneven development.[75] As his trump card, Wurm now produced figures even more recent than those used by

[71] See Varga's edited report in *Kommunisticheskii Internatsional*, no. 18 (7 May 1929), p. 40.
[72] Ibid.
[73] See Wurm's reply to Varga in *Kommunisticheskii Internatsional*, no. 21 (29 May 1929), p. 42.
[74] Ibid., p. 43.
[75] Ibid., p. 42.

Varga. From March 1928 to March 1929, the number of industrial workers in America had actually *grown* by 8.71 per cent.[76] Wurm's case appeared to be incontestable. Varga had found a 'law' of 'pure' capitalism where nothing really existed but the growing unevenness of a distorted American business cycle. The supposed 'law' was suspect from beginning to end. On the one hand, Varga thought industrial rationalization induced the capitalists to curtail production, in which case capitalism was organized and potentially crisis-free. On the other hand, the rationalization crisis was attributed to the absence of 'third parties', an argument based on Luxemburg's position and 'a false interpretation of the views of Marx'.[77] Did Varga subscribe to Hilferding's deviation or Luxemburg's? Was he a rightist or an ultra-leftist? An important clue came in the factional struggles within the Workers' (Communist) Party of America.

At the Sixth Congress in 1928 Jay Lovestone had endorsed Bukharin's viewpoint, claiming that 'American capitalism is still on the ascendant'.[78] A steady rise in the real income of American workers proved that America was an 'exception' to the general crisis of the capitalist system. Varga had argued that the income of the working class as a whole declined—through structural unemployment—while that of employed individuals grew. Lovestone turned this remark to his own advantage, saying that 'Comrade Varga is correct when he states that the American standard of living is not going down. The fact of the matter is that real income has been increasing by 7 per cent each year. What the opposition [that is, the American Stalinist faction] confuses is real wages with the rate of exploitation [or the growth of labour intensity].'[79] In the spring of 1929, on direct orders from the ECCI, the American party removed Lovestone from the leadership. In June Lovestone was expelled for denying the leftward movement of the masses and for predicting a rise in real wages, a 'second industrial revolution', and a 'new wave of prosperity'.[80]

[76] Ibid., p. 40.

[77] Ibid., p. 41.

[78] See Lovestone's comments in *International Press Correspondence*, VIII, no. 53 (23 August 1928), p. 934.

[79] Ibid., p. 935.

[80] I. Zekk, ' "Amerikanskoe Protsvetanie" i Pravaya Opasnost', *Kommunisticheskii Internatsional*, no. 13 (29 March 1929), p. 33.

When the tenth plenum of the ECCI met in July 1929, Otto Kuusinen (one of Stalin's cronies) presided in place of Bukharin. Fulminating against 'stabilization-communists', Kuusinen decided that Varga was implicated in the Lovestone affair and the 'Right Deviation'. The deviants had adopted the slogan of a 'second industrial revolution' and had vastly overestimated the quantitative aspects of technological change. Radio, aircraft, and other new inventions were scientifically significant, but until they became objects of mass production they would remain 'of relatively small economic importance'.[81] Citing Lenin's comments on monopolistic parasitism, Kuusinen announced that the 'capitalist mode of production is *no longer wide enough* for the development of the productive forces of labour'. If production had risen in America, it was due to the greater intensity of labour and an upward leap in the rate of exploitation.

Kuusinen admitted that in his work for the Comintern Congress of 1928 Varga had given 'due prominence to the intensification of labour in capitalist rationalization'. Nevertheless, Varga's belief in rising real wages had prevented him from understanding that 'capitalist rationalization brings with it an absolute worsening of the position of the working class'. By defining 'real wage' as money income in relation to the level of prices, Varga had used the term in what Kuusinen called 'the narrowest sense'. Marx, in contrast, thought that even with a rising real wage the workers' income would fall below the value of labour-power (its replacement cost), 'if the increased wear and tear of labour-power . . . is not compensated'.[82] The purpose of this convoluted argument was to demonstrate that the worker's well-being would decline because he would expend more energy through industrial speed-ups than he could replace with his income. This original error on Varga's part had then led to another in the form of the new 'law', which ignored the revolutionary sentiment of the masses, underestimated the political struggle of the workers, and implied an automatic—but gradual—decay of capitalism. Varga would be prudent, admonished

[81] Kuusinen, 'The International Situation and the Tasks of the Communist International', *International Press Correspondence*, IX, no. 40 (20 August 1929), p. 838.

[82] Ibid., p. 839.

Kuusinen, to learn from the errors of Luxemburg and cleanse himself through self-criticism:

'. . . it is particularly important to give through our propaganda a clear picture of . . . the contradictions of capitalism. This is the point on which we must concentrate our sharpest criticism. . . . Even our self-criticism must be wide awake in this regard, to prevent us from making even the least concession to a tendency which might land us in the belief in a gradual "decay" of capitalism. A precautionary example is the mistake made by such a great revolutionary as Comrade Rosa Luxemburg, who in her desire to construct a simple, purely economic law of the collapse of capitalism, was diverted into the wrong channel. I do not know if I am mistaken when I assume that the "tendency of the decreasing number of workers" brought forward by Comrade Varga (which he connects with the process of the final conversion of peasants into farmers and with . . . the industrialization of the colonies) contains the germ of a new theory of the gradual decay of capitalism. The desire to find a consistent, unequivocal and terse economic motivation for the inevitable collapse of capitalism is a perfectly legitimate desire. . . . [But] why should we want new laws concerning the collapse of capitalism when Marx has formulated this matter consistently and clearly?'[83]

The real rationale for Kuusinen's rambling indictment was to warn Varga that he was unwittingly providing theoretical support to adherents of the 'Right Deviation'. Adopting his finest professorial demeanour, Varga appeared blissfully unaware of the political difficulties he faced and demanded his right to free speech: 'If I should become convinced that something new has taken place in the international situation . . . which does not exactly tally with the picture so far considered correct by the Comintern, I shall always submit such conviction to the Comintern, even if I should run the risk of being accused . . . of opportunistic transgressions. To my mind it is the greatest opportunism to keep silent because of a fear of clashing with the prevailing line of thought. This is the most dangerous kind of opportunism, unworthy of a Communist.'[84]

[83] Ibid., p. 842.
[84] See Varga's comments in *International Press Correspondence*, IX, no. 48 (11 September 1929), p. 1020.

As if rebuking an errant student, Varga told Kuusinen that one might be right or wrong in assessing the significance of technology, 'but the fact itself of technological progress being estimated too low or too high is neither a Left nor a Right deviation. The Right Deviation begins only when someone overestimates the consequences of technological change for the stabilization of capitalism.'[85]

To link an improved standard of living with a rising real wage was only to use the two concepts 'as calculated in the statistics of the entire world'.[86] To suggest that living standards had not been rising in Germany, America, and Britain was to adopt a position 'which is not true'. Varga reluctantly agreed to accept Kuusinen's false terminology if the party insisted. But the result would be to invite ridicule: 'When a Communist worker says in discussion with a Social Democratic worker that the standard of living has been lowered, the Social Democratic worker will say to him: That is not so, just look at the statistics. Then the Communist worker must say to the Social Democrat: If you please, we mean by standard of living something different from what you do.'[87] With respect to the new law Varga attempted to be conciliatory: 'I am far too modest a person to author a law. . . . I never spoke of a law. I merely spoke of a tendency.'[88]

Expected to debase himself and serve as an example to others, Varga had not played his part according to the 'official' rules. In the first of many appearances as a leading participant in Comintern affairs, Molotov observed that by failing to recant his errors Varga was playing, 'so to speak, a reactionary role' and soon would not 'find himself in a Communist position'.[89] Kuusinen fumed over the fact that Varga continued to speak 'against the thesis of the decline in the standard of living of the working class'.[90] Why, he demanded,

[85] Varga's reply to Kuusinen in *International Press Correspondence*, IX, no. 41 (21 August 1929), p. 867.

[86] Ibid., p. 865.

[87] Ibid., p. 866.

[88] Ibid.

[89] Molotov, 'The Comintern and the New Revolutionary Upsurge', *International Press Correspondence*, IX, no. 49 (12 September 1929), p. 1045.

[90] Kuusinen, 'Concluding Speech', *International Press Correspondence*, IX, no. 53 (25 September 1929), p. 1144.

had Varga suddenly become so modest? Only recently he had thought that mass unemployment was 'the inevitable result . . . of the inner contradictions of capitalism'. To verify his discovery Varga had at one point called upon the American economist Rexford Tugwell (later a member of Roosevelt's 'brain trust'). Such a reference left no doubt in Kuusinen's mind that the so-called 'law' was a 'bourgeois baby' wrapped up 'in the napkin of "Marxian" phraseology'. Bourgeois statistics were deliberately designed to obscure the class struggle and had led Varga astray. The ideological contamination of such a prominent authority illustrated the need for new political standards in economic research:

'Naturally, we have to make use of bourgeois statistics. Marx and Lenin also made use of them. . . . [However] great care must be taken. . . . Especially he who has to have intercourse with bourgeois economic circles as a professional matter, like Comrade Varga, should know that he always runs the risk of being contaminated with ideological filth and vermin. Only supreme Marxian discrimination, such as Lenin possessed, can serve as an absolute guarantee against contamination by the filth of bourgeois economics. . . . None of us has an absolute guarantee of keeping pure from the vermin of bourgeois economics if he does not take the most careful measures of Marxian hygiene. Comrade Varga is a conscientious investigator, he is conscientious with all his facts, but his method is not always unobjectionable and his conclusions are not always pure. I therefore reiterate: when having intercourse with the filthy society of bourgeois economists the most rigid, scientific Marxian hygiene is indispensable. One should particularly take care to keep one's head clean.'[91]

Staged for manifestly political reasons, Kuusinen's attack on Varga created a sensation, but there were no lasting consequences. For the next decade the theoretical outlook summarized in 'Varga's Law' became the hallmark of Stalinism. Whenever Varga encountered difficulties, the charge of 'Luxemburgism' would surface anew, but after the tenth plenum of the ECCI few economists would dispute the definition of the 'third period' in terms of chronic unemployment and chronically excessive industrial capacity. For the sake of ideological appearances Varga would have to become

[91] Ibid., p. 1146.

more tactful, utilizing Luxemburg's approach without being so explicit concerning its origins. With that proviso, the economists would be left for the most part to discipline their own ranks and find their own way. The American economic crash late in 1929 distracted attention from Varga's minor transgressions, and by 1933 he was once more firmly entrenched as Stalin's most dependable confidant and adviser on international economic affairs. A more immediate factor helping to rescue Varga in the summer of 1929 was a bizarre political blunder on Bukharin's part.

4. Bukharin on 'Organized Economic Disorder'

In April 1929, Bukharin had been relieved of editorial responsibility for *Pravda*. At the end of May and again at the end of June, however, *Pravda* published two astounding articles in which he appeared to retract his previous view of state-capitalist organization. Whether the articles were approved because they were taken to constitute self-criticism, or whether Bukharin was simply being afforded the rope with which to hang himself is not clear. Whatever the case, Bukharin made use of a pretended criticism of Social Democrats to liken the Stalinist bureaucracy to the Leviathan State. The first essay, 'Certain Problems of Contemporary Capitalism in the Eyes of Bourgeois Theoreticians', dealt with the incongruity between capitalism's technological virtuosity and its mounting philosophy of despair.[92] Bourgeois economists had finally realized that the end of an era was at hand, that 'monopoly consumes "free competition" ' and replaces it with a state-capitalist oligarchy of bureaucrats and millionaires. To illustrate this new awareness Bukharin quoted the German economist Schmalenbach, who spoke of 'chained capitalism', Keynes, who had written of 'the end of *laissez faire*', and Sombart, who believed that 'high capitalism' had been superseded by 'late capitalism' or a 'new feudalism'.

Returning to a familiar thesis, Bukharin argued that 'the old methods of spontaneous regulation through the market' had passed into history. Yet in place of 'organized capitalism' he now held that the market economy had given way to a new set of contradictions.

[92] *Pravda*, 26 May 1929.

'Careerism' had triumphed over initiative, and the 'bureaucracy' had become a new stratum of 'parasites'. True, the process of social degeneration was concealed by a number of euphemisms: 'irrational spontaneity' had been replaced by what was called 'rational organization', the theory of the market by 'the "science" of organization'. In fact, the new science was window-dressing for arbitrary power. An 'enormous apparatus' of social control was being created: 'The concerns and trusts . . . represent a most complex human machine. But this same machine controls the people. The "apparatus" to a large degree dominates over the people.' With 'quivering delight' Social Democrats were hailing this monstrosity as 'the most "socialistic" form of socialism'. They were overlooking the fact that capitalism was creating 'a "semi-planned" but at the same time bureaucratic type of economy' in which class contradictions must continue to flourish.

Although speaking of *capitalism's* 'apparatus', Bukharin clearly hinted that the problem of an inhuman bureaucracy had been inherited in Soviet Russia along with the means of industrial production created under the old regime. In the name of 'rational organization' the Stalinists were building a 'new oligarchy'. By comparing the stifling inefficiency of bureaucracy to the vitality of a market economy, moreover, the article took a swipe at Stalinist 'planning'. Within the Politburo Bukharin had fought Stalin over pricing policy, urging that the state regulate prices, but in response to peasant needs. Taking the position that 'primitive socialist accumulation' had become unavoidable, Stalin replied that Bukharin wanted 'to abolish the role of the state as regulator of the market'.[93] The appeal for flexible prices proved that Bukharin was 'firmly held captive by petty-bourgeois elemental forces'.[94] At a joint meeting of the party's Central Committee and Central Control Commission—and to Bukharin's face—Stalin read aloud that section of Lenin's Testament questioning Bukharin's grasp of dialectics.[95] As a futile protest Bukharin used the article on contemporary capitalism to show the 'putrid' character of Stalinism, to warn of a new class struggle with the peasants, and to

[93] Stalin, *Works*, XII, p. 47.
[94] Ibid., p. 51.
[95] Ibid., p. 73.

denounce the use of administrative measures in both industry and agriculture.

The second article, 'The Theory of Organized Economic Disorder', ostensibly discussed Hermann Bente's book *Organisierte Unwirtschaftlichkeit* (1929).[96] Here Bukharin was even less subtle, attacking the non-productive expenses of a bureaucratic economy and the tendency of organizational 'means' to become 'an end in themselves'. Producing 'mountains of reports', bureaucrats were said to respect only authority and 'published theses'. 'Bureaucratic-centralist' regulation degenerated into a 'fetishism of forms', a 'fanaticism for order', and a 'fear of responsibility'. The 'problem of leadership'—Stalin's by implication—had emerged as *'the central problem'*. Mass pressure was needed to substitute for the 'knout' of competition. Otherwise bureaucrats would persecute creative people for the disorder inherent in monopoly itself. 'The Soviet reader will be struck', concluded Bukharin, 'by the formal similarity between certain organizational problems posed by Bente . . . and those problems that are on the order of the day and are being resolved by Soviet practice.' The most outstanding similarity the reader was advised to consider was 'the problem of the apparatus' in both capitalist and socialist societies.

Assuming the two articles were as transparent to *Pravda's* editors as Bukharin expected they would be to his readers, one can only infer that they were published for the deliberate purpose of allowing their author to say too much. Time and again both essays took the existence of state-capitalist monopolies to be an established fact. One such passage served as a veritable *précis* of all the key points over which Bukharin had disagreed with Lenin: 'Problems of the market, of price, of competition and crises increasingly become problems of the *world* economy, being replaced within the "country" by the problem of organization. . . . Even the problem of all problems, the so-called "social question", the problem of relations between classes and of the class struggle, is a problem intimately connected with the position of one or another capitalist country on the *world* market.'[97]

Such a definitive statement of the 'Right Deviation' was exactly

[96] *Pravda*, 30 June 1929
[97] Ibid.

what Stalin and his supporters needed. At the ECCI plenum of July 1929 Kuusinen protested that Bukharin was contaminated by the same filth as Varga: the capitalist law of value had become 'the idol' that Bukharin worshipped.[98] Heinz Neumann, a Stalinist representative from the German party, added that Bukharin's indifference to class struggle in the capitalist countries was 'bound to lead to the one-sided orientation according to which the revolution can only be victorious in the event of war'.[99] The Bukharinist theory of 'ultra-monopoly' omitted 'the fundamental contradiction between the increased productive capacity of industry and the limited capacity of the market . . . this very market problem constitutes one of the basic principles of our revolutionary policy in the third period.'[100]

In the late summer and autumn of 1929 the Soviet press waged a relentless campaign against the Right Deviation. A resolution passed by the Comintern plenum revealed that even before the Sixth Congress in 1928 'Comrade Bukharin showed signs of disagreement with the general political line'. These 'signs' had subsequently matured into a 'Right-Deviation platform' based on conciliation of rich peasants and denial of the 'ever-growing shakiness of capitalist stabilization'. The touchstone of all Bukharin's errors was the 'anti-Marxist "theory" of the weakening of the internal contradictions of capitalism'. The article on 'Organized Economic Disorder' demonstrated that 'far from repudiating his anti-Marxist "theory" . . . [Bukharin] is persisting in his errors and deepening them'.[101] The Comintern clearly had no option but to 'relieve' its former leader of all his political duties.

In the periodical press the campaign began at the end of August 1929 with an editorial in *Kommunisticheskii Internatsional*. The origin of the Right Deviation was recounted as follows. 'As early as the Sixth Congress of the Comintern there appeared an embryonic outline of that monstrous overestimation of capitalist stabilization

---

[98] Kuusinen, 'Concluding Speech', p. 1153.

[99] See Neumann's comments in *International Press Correspondence*, IX, no. 51 (17 September 1929), p. 1080.

[100] Ibid., p. 1081.

[101] 'Resolution of the X Plenum of the ECCI on Comrade Bukharin', *International Press Correspondence*, IX, no. 45 (30 August 1929), p. 965.

which [Bukharin] has given in his latest works. In his first draft of the theses on the world situation . . . he attempted to reduce the "third period" mainly to the *growth* of the capitalist economy, slurring over the elements that are *undermining* capitalist stabilization.'[102]

Responding obediently to the 'official' cue, Bukhartsev attacked Bukharin's 'Menshevik appraisal' of the 'third period' and examined the process whereby the 'left' positions taken by Bukharin in the early years had blossomed into 'right opportunism'.[103] In one breath the rightists denied that the problem of markets had become 'the basic problem of contemporary capitalism'; in the next they defended the role of 'market spontaneity' in the Soviet Union—a splendid example of duplicity whereby capitalism was supposed to be planned while socialism required a market! Aleksandr Kon claimed that Bukharin's deviation was essentially methodological and resulted from the habit of 'thinking in terms of extremes' and analysing phenomena in their 'chemically pure' form to the exclusion of concrete dialectics.[104] Bessonov joined in the refrain: Bukharin fetishized organizational forms and abstracted from class contradictions.

In October 1929 Varga's Institute of World Economics and World Politics gathered an impressive array of economists to denounce the theory of 'organized capitalism' and perform an ideological *post mortem*. E. Khmel'nitskaya reviewed her earlier arguments in the article of 1927 and quoted Lenin, writing that the 'theoretical essence of the mistakes of Comrade Bukharin is that he replaces the dialectical relationship between politics and economics (which Marxism teaches us) with eclecticism.'[105] This 'mechanistic, non-dialectical approach' caused Bukharin to forget that 'internal contradictions spill over into the sphere of external relations' and

[102] 'Teoreticheskie Vyvody tov. Bukharina i Politicheskii Vyvod Kommunisticheskovo Internatsionala', *Kommunisticheskii Internatsional*, no. 34–5 (31 August 1929), p. 10.

[103] Bukhartsev, 'Teoreticheskie Oruzhenosty Opportunizma', *Bol'shevik*, no. 16 (31 August 1929), p. 26 *et passim*.

[104] Aleksandr Kon, 'Neskol'ko Zamechanii o Teorii "Organizovannovo" Kapitalizma', *Problemy Ekonomiki*, no. 9 (September 1929), pp. 49–50.

[105] '*Organizovannyi Kapitalizm*'—*Diskussiya v Komakademii*, 2nd ed, Moscow 1930, p. 94.

interact with the 'external contradictoriness' of the world economy.[106] I. Itkina similarly remarked that the anarchy of the world market 'grows out of the profound internal contradictions of capitalism . . . out of the contradiction between production and consumption. . . . The internal and external contradictions are linked together and condition one another'.[107] Not a single contradiction could exist in the world economy, according to I. Markov, without having an impact on 'national' economies: 'Comrade Bukharin's distinction between "organized" national economies and an anarchic world economy is purely artificial.'[108] Markov grasped an important truth when he noted that the debate over capitalism's prospects had in part been a projection of domestic politics: 'To the extent that the stabilization of capitalism is growing stronger and the advent of the world revolution is being postponed, the "salvation" of the USSR must lie with its organized internal forces. And how should these forces be organized? From Bukharin's viewpoint it is clear that we must not under any circumstances clash even with a section of the peasantry. On the contrary, the class struggle must . . . be limited and replaced by class peace. . . . It follows that we must not force the construction of *kolkhozy* and *sovkhozy* [collective and state farms], we must increase the production of consumer goods and integrate this with a general plan that emphasizes the accelerated development of light industry'.[109]

Claiming that industrial rationalization had been converted into a 'holy war' against the standard of living of the working class, Rubinshtein also mentioned the connection between internal and external problems: 'Comrade Bukharin's article on "The Theory of Organized Economic Disorder" is not simply an exposition of a theory belonging to Bente, whom nobody knows or is interested in. . . . The "striking formal similarity with our problems" . . . is in Comrade Bukharin's exposition far from being either formal or a coincidence. Describing the bureaucratic ossification of monopoly and of the abstract "apparatus as a whole", Comrade Bukharin has

[106] Ibid., p. 97.
[107] Ibid., p. 133
[108] Ibid., p. 149.
[109] Ibid., p. 151.

in mind not "late capitalism" but the Soviet economy . . . our planned economy, centralization [and] the wager on large-scale production in agriculture.'[110]

Having rediscovered the relation between the internal and external contradictions of capitalist society, and even the effect this interaction might exert upon Soviet politics, the economists did not presume to go further and inquire how economic contradictions within the Soviet Union might be affected by the Stalinist programme of self-imposed isolation. That task fell to Trotsky, who would argue in exile that the human tragedy of the Five-Year Plan resembled the earlier process of capitalism's 'levelling out in reverse': shortages and disruptions that the Stalinists blamed on 'wrecking' and 'sabotage' were really self-created bottlenecks and disproportions, which could not be removed without recourse to the world market. 'National Socialism', declared Trotsky, had more to do with the ideas of Hitler than with those of Marx and Lenin. [111]

In the early 1930s the Stalinists would equate the fall of Bukharin with a return to the 'Leninist stage of political economy', mechanically repeating the law of uneven development on every conceivable occasion. It is worth remembering, however, that this was Leninism with a unique Luxemburgist twist. Regaining his former authority, Varga would argue that the law of unevenness really signified a chronic tendency whereby 'the purchasing power of the broad masses lags behind the productive capacity of society'.[112] In Varga's mind Leninism had come to mean that capitalist monopolies might 'eliminate the disproportion between separate branches of production, but . . . could never abolish the contradiction between the limited consuming power of the masses and the productive capacity of society given the antagonistic relations of distribution'.[113]

When the ECCI passed final judgement on Bukharin in February 1930, the resolution complied with Varga's interpretation and attributed the economic catastrophe in America—the ultimate

[110] Ibid., pp. 122–23.
[111] Trotsky, 'Sovetskoe Khozyaistvo v Opasnosti!', *Byulleten' Oppozitsii*, no. 31 (November 1932), p. 5.
[112] *'Organizovannyi Kapitalizm'*, p. 7.
[113] Ibid., p. 10.

refutation of 'organized capitalism'—to 'the contradiction between the growth of the productive forces and the narrowed markets' at a time when all capitalist countries faced 'a lengthening of periods of depression, which assume a chronic character'.[114] The 'strengthening of capitalist rationalization' and the 'extraordinary intensification of labour' (as suggested by 'Varga's Law') had become responsible for 'chronic unemployment'.[115] Turning away at last from Bukharin's theory of a moving equilibrium, Soviet economists were now in the process of leaping backwards to a theory of markets associated originally with Kautsky and Luxemburg. The boundaries of legitimate theoretical discussion had been politically circumscribed; the central problem of Soviet economic debates through the past decade remained unanswered. The 1930s began with the same problem as the 1920s; that is, the need to establish some definite relation between the classical business cycle and the long-awaited terminal crash of the capitalist system.

[114] See the resolution in *Mirovoi Ekonomicheskii Krizis (Kollektivnaya Rabota Instituta Mirovovo Khozyaistva i Mirovoi Politiki)*, Moscow 1930, p. 325.
[115] Ibid., p. 327.

6
Confusion in 1929–1930

The collapse of share prices in America in October 1929 tore the ground from under Bukharin's feet and made further debate about 'organized capitalism' pointless. In November 1930 Bukharin confessed to his 'right-wing deviations', urged a persistent struggle in all Communist parties against the 'right-wing danger', and condemned the 'anti-communist, anti-proletarian' activities of Jay Lovestone and other American supporters. The *Pravda* articles of May and June 1929, he now admitted, had gone beyond the formulations of Engels and Lenin and were written 'in the spirit of the bourgeois theory of organized capitalism'.[1] Eight years later Bukharin would pay with his life for his attempt to thwart Stalin. But the 'unmasking' of Bukharin did not yet signal the end of the Hilferding tradition in Soviet political economy. That would come in 1931—in so far as the end of a theoretical tradition can be pinpointed—with the denunciation of Trotsky's former colleague Evgeny Preobrazhensky. During the early months of 1930 the initial Soviet response to the American crisis continued to draw upon Hilferding's ideas, and nowhere was this tendency more apparent than in the writings of Varga.

To suspicions of a lingering 'Hilferding tinge' the events of 1929–30 added a new debate about the length of the business cycle under conditions of monopoly capitalism. A number of Soviet economists believed that the cycle had been shortened from nine to three or three and a half years, a view frequently linked to Engels's predictions of cyclical abnormality. A more immediate influence

[1] Bukharin, 'Declaration to the CC of the CPSU', *International Press Correspondence*, X, no. 54 (27 November 1930), p. 1120.

bolstering the theory of the abbreviated cycle could be found in the writings of the American economist W.C. Mitchell. According to Soviet interpretations of Mitchell (whose work was translated into Russian on Gertsenshtein's initiative), the American economy had experienced no fewer than four cycles since 1919, ending success- ively in 1921, 1924, 1927, and 1930.[2] In every previous case the crisis had been followed by a rapid recovery. Indeed, in Mitchell's view the term 'crisis' had become purely descriptive, denoting the intensity of an economic fluctuation but by no means a necessary phase of the normal cycle. The most acute changes in economic activity were gradually being 'subordinated to a certain degree of control'. Panics were becoming less common, crises giving way to 'recessions'. Six months before the Wall Street débâcle Mitchell and several other prominent figures published *Recent Economic Changes in the United States*, which summarized the findings of a semi-governmental committee headed by Herbert Hoover. The report enthused over the prospect of a 'New Era' of endless prosperity, foreseeing few obstacles to the maintenance of the 'economic balance' and 'dynamic equilibrium of recent years'.[3] The spectacular failure of this prediction immediately raised serious questions about the ideological orthodoxy of Soviet economists who might be associated with Mitchell's 'apologetic' theories.

The theory of the abbreviated cycle appeared most plausible to those writers who expected the American economy to undergo a brief but necessary purgative. It was not difficult to find evidence to support this interpretation. Unlike classical crises, that of 1929 saw no prior accumulation of inventories. Speculation appeared to be limited to the stock market, where share prices had soared into the world of make-believe. Between March 1925 and September 1929 the 'Annalist' index had climbed by more than 350 per cent.[4] Brokers' loans rose from $3,000 million in 1926 to more than

[2] See Varga, 'Economics and Economic Policy in the Second Quarter of 1929', *International Press Correspondence*, VIII, no. 43 (28 August 1929), p. 928.
[3] See G. Mekhanik, 'Mitchell i evo Kritik t. Gertsenshtein', *Mirovoe Khozyaistvo i Mirovaya Politika*, no. 4 (April 1931), p. 38.
[4] Varga, 'Mezhdunarodnyi Birzhevoi Krakh—Predvestnik Nadvigayushchevosya Ekonomicheskovo Krizisa', *Kommunisticheskii Internatsional*, no. 46–7 (22 Novem- ber 1929), p. 21.

$8,ooo million three years later.[5] Small savers bought shares for the sole purpose of reselling at a higher price, regardless of the dividends paid. In his economic survey for the third quarter of 1929, Varga commented that production indicators were inconsistent with stock-market performance: 'there is increasing indications that the business boom has passed its peak and that the deterioration of business in August and September is not merely seasonal but the beginning of a transition from boom to crisis'.[6] One of the most widely respected market analysts, Professor Irving Fisher, was quoted saying on 17 October that share prices would continue to rise. To this forecast Varga replied: 'Fisher sings the praises of increasing prosperity and the consistently growing possibility of profit. . . . Since it is an undeniable fact that the number of workers immediately engaged in creating value and surplus-value . . . is on the decline, it is incomprehensible whence a lasting increase of the profits of all enterprises, such as Fisher predicts, is to be derived . . . the surplus-value appropriated within the country . . . has a tendency to sink in consequence of the rapid accumulation of capital with a declining number of workers.'[7]

In a single week at the end of October, a total of $25,ooo million in 'fictitious values' were wiped out. From their peak quotations of 1929, General Electric shares fell by 38 per cent, General Motors by 51 per cent, International Harvester by 42 per cent, Chrysler by 71 per cent, Westinghouse by 50 per cent, United States Steel by 29 per cent, and RCA by 65 per cent.[8] Despite the panic on the exchange, however, American politicians and business leaders expressed confidence that the disturbance would not spread to production. The effect of the crash on both consumer and investor confidence was vastly underestimated. In December the chairman of Bethlehem Steel remarked: 'Never before has American business been so firmly entrenched for prosperity as it is today.' The president of the National Association of Manufacturers commented: 'I can observe little on the horizon today to give us undue

[5] Varga, 'Economics and Economic Policy in the Fourth Quarter of 1929', *International Press Correspondence*, X, no. 8 (20 Feburary 1930), p. 128.

[6] Varga, 'Economics and Economic Policy in the Third Quarter of 1929', *International Press Correspondence*, IX, no. 67 (5 December 1929), p. 1438.

[7] Ibid., p. 1439.

[8] Varga, 'Mezhdunarodnyi Birzhevoi Krakh . . .', p. 18.

or great concern.' The vice-president of National City Bank of New York agreed: 'Conditions are more favourable for permanent prosperity than they have been in the past year.' The most common perception was that apart from stock-market speculation, the economy was fundamentally sound. The setback to speculators was even a healthy development: a mild 'recession' would restore sobriety in capital markets and permit a solid recovery.

Although political conditions in the Soviet Union might have been conducive to radicalism, few economists were willing to predict imminent capitalist disaster. A glimpse into the range of current thinking came with a survey, published in mid-December 1929, by the newspaper *Torgovo-Promyshlennaya Gazeta*. The views of those interviewed varied widely. One respondent noted that it was too early to say whether America faced a 'crisis' (an extraordinary contraction of output) or a 'depression' (an interlude of stagnation). In either case, he claimed, there would be no worldwide crisis on the scale of 1920–21, for Europe had not experienced a cyclical expansion, without which there could be no classical crisis. L.A. Mendel'son believed that some branches of American industry would suffer a crisis, while in Europe the existing depression would deepen. I. Zvavich took the view of European business editors, who expected a return of speculative capital from New York to redress payments imbalances and permit a reduction in interest rates. Two other economists predicted a full-scale crisis in America, while Spektator added, 'it is entirely probable that the present crisis . . . at a maximum will last into the next autumn, assuming Hoover does not succeed as early as the spring in bringing about a temporary improvement'.[9] In a separate article Eventov cited the evidence offered in *Recent Economic Changes*. The available statistics suggested that the production cycle had been detached from price movements; output might decline, but there would be no significant change in prices, since monopolies would adjust operations to suit the market.[10] At the opposite extreme, L. Mad'yar disputed the 'bourgeois legend' that the catastrophe could

[9] See 'Ekonomicheskii Krizis v SASSh i Mirovoe Khozyaistvo', *Torgovo-Promyshlennaya Gazeta* (17 December 1929).
[10] L. Eventov, 'Legenda ob "Organizovannom" Kapitalizme', *Bol'shevik*, no. 21 (15 November 1929), p. 23.

be restricted to the stock market: 'We are dealing not just with a crisis on the exchange but with the beginning of a world economic crisis.'[11] The editors of *Bol'shevik*, wherein Mad'yar's article appeared, were less certain. In their own footnote they recommended that the question be accorded further discussion and analysis.

By far the most outstanding feature of the American crisis during the next several years was an unprecedented collapse of investments. As W. Arthur Lewis has written, 'net investment became negative in 1931, i.e., capital depreciation was not made good, fell to *minus* 5.8 billion dollars in 1932 (1929 prices) and did not again become positive until 1936. . . . The low level to which investment fell, and its failure to recover, is the most important feature of the slump, and the fact that 1922 to 1929 had seen such a high level of investment is without doubt an important reason why investment was so small in the 1930s.'[12] In Germany (the second principal victim of the crisis), as in America, fixed capital installed during the previous decade paralysed the normal mechanisms of economic revival. Germany had borrowed heavily from the United States during the years of industrial rationalization. When the influx of capital halted, the German government resorted to deliberate deflation in order to reduce costs and maintain the exports needed to acquit commercial and reparations obligations. Expecting that currency devaluation would awaken public fears of an inflation on the scale of 1923, German monetary authorities contributed to the social and political breakdown that brought Hitler to power. In the election of September 1930 Hitler led the Nazi Party from ninth position to the second-largest party in the Reichstag, precipitating the most serious political crisis since the fall of the monarchy. In Britain, where the industrial index declined much less dramatically, Oswald Mosley and sixteen other dissident Labour MPs published what Varga described as 'a fascist programme . . . of . . . organized capitalism'.[13] The longer the crisis lasted, the less predictable became its political consequences.

---

[11] L. Mad'yar, 'Birzhevoi Krakh v SASSh', *Bol'shevik*, no. 22 (30 November 1929), p. 65.

[12] W. Arthur Lewis, *Economic Survey 1919–39*, London 1949, p. 54.

[13] Varga, 'Economics and Economic Policy in the Fourth Quarter of 1930', *International Press Correspondence*, XI, no. 8 (24 February 1931), p. 161.

From America and Germany the disaster spread rapidly to countries supplying raw materials, a number of whom were off the gold standard by the end of 1930. World agricultural prices plunged, and new barriers to trade were erected everywhere, beginning with the Hawley-Smoot Tariff in the United States. In a manner reminiscent of the early 1920s, Varga reported that the decline of capitalism involved a 'tendency towards the division of the world into separate, increasingly isolated parts'.[14] As the international terms of trade turned against primary producers, so within each country large firms maintained prices more successfully than did agricultural or less organized industrial producers. In Germany prices of means of production fell by 2 per cent between August 1929 and August 1930, compared to a 10 per cent drop for industrial materials.[15] In America steel prices had fallen 20 per cent by 1932, compared with an 80 per cent decline in output. In both countries industrial prices were generally more stable than output. The results in terms of unemployment were predictable. By the end of 1930 German industrial output had dropped 25 per cent and unemployment was approaching 4 million. In America the fall in production was even greater, while unemployment stood between 6 and 9 million.

1. Varga's Renewed Difficulties With Hilferding

From his earliest remarks on the crisis, Varga still wove his own ideas together with those of Hilferding. One month after the collapse of share prices, he surveyed the wreckage on Wall Street and commented: 'The Communist admirers of the theory of "organized capitalism", of the theory of "a lessening of internal economic contradictions" (Comrade Bukharin), will be given pause by what is occurring on the American exchanges.'[16] But Varga was not yet ready to forecast an immediate crisis in production: 'disguised overproduction' would become manifest when small merchants and manufacturers had to dump commodities in order to

[14] Varga, 'Problemy Krizisa', *Mirovoe Khozyaistvo i Mirovaya Politika*, no. 2–3 (February-March 1931), p. 28.

[15] Varga, 'Economics and Economic Policy in the Third Quarter of 1930', *International Press Correspondence*, X, no. 56 (6 December 1930), p. 1149.

[16] Varga, 'Mezhdunarodnyi Birzhevoi Krakh . . .', p. 18.

pay their debts, but the bigger capitalists might regulate their inventories and postpone losses for several months.[17] On 17 December 1929 Varga addressed a special meeting of the Institute of World Economics and World Politics and presented a more detailed explanation of the causes of the contraction and why large capital might emerge with minimal losses. To begin with, the main victims of the fall in share prices were small businessmen, private savers, and would-be capitalists. These people had been forced to speculate because of monopolistic barriers to new investment in productive assets: 'the small capitalists are forced either to deposit their capital in savings-banks, or, if they want a higher return, to play on the exchange'. The prevalence of monopolistic firms in most branches of industry had made it virtually impossible to found new enterprises. 'I believe that the development of American capital to the highest stage of monopolization is the economic basis for stock-exchange speculation.'[18] In *Finance Capital* Hilferding had shown that the high profits of 'organized' industries reduced entrepreneurial income elsewhere and discouraged new productive investment; the effect of cartels was 'to impede the placement of new capital'.[19] Varga saw a similar mechanism at work in America, permitting the larger capitalists to take advantage of the crisis, expropriating small savers by buying up shares at bargain prices.

Notwithstanding his theory of the historically unique character of American unemployment during the late 1920s, Varga now believed that the crisis would be of a basically 'classical type'—but with several unique features. Its cause was classical inasmuch as it involved the inadequacy of working-class incomes: 'the internal cause of *all real crises* is the limit on social purchasing power in antagonistic conditions of distribution compared to the attempt of the capitalists to expand production without limit'.[20] But 'the monopolistic character of American capitalism and the fact that there are great surpluses of gold within the country changes the character of the crisis to a certain degree'. Given the intimate

[17] Ibid., p. 29.

[18] Varga, 'Krizis v SShA—Obshchii Ekonomicheskii Krizis', *Mirovoe Khozyaistvo i Mirovaya Politika*, no. 2 (February 1930), p. 8.

[19] Hilferding, *Das Finanzkapital*, p. 321.

[20] Varga, 'Krizis v SShA . . .', p. 5.

connections between the banks and large-scale industry, there was little probability of a 'classical' monetary and credit crisis. 'Everyone knows that Ford, General Motors, and United States Steel can be given credits, for they will not be bankrupted—and the same applies to the large banks.'[21] The stability of the American banking system would guarantee the solvency of large enterprises in which banking capital had been invested. As Gertsenshtein told the same meeting of the Institute, 'when the concentration of banking acquires enormous dimensions . . . the dependence of banks on the fate of one or another enterprise declines, and the collapse of the enterprise cannot so easily entail the collapse of the bank'.[22] Both Varga and Gertsenshtein were drawing upon Hilferding's account of how the effects of a crisis might be controlled. In *Finance Capital* Hilferding had argued that the concentration of banking capital would 'prevent a large, well-directed bank from becoming so dependent on one or a few enterprises . . . as to be dragged into failure with them'.[23]

At the end of January 1930, Varga published *The End of American Prosperity* and maintained his ambiguous position. Referring to a 'classical crisis of overproduction', he again remarked that there was no reason to expect that 'the course of the crisis will correspond, in every detail, to the classical type of which Marx wrote'.[24] By virtue of their monopolistic organization, large enterprises would weather the storm without serious difficulties: 'These enterprises are too closely integrated . . . with finance capital, and for that reason banking capital will go to any length to prevent their destruction.'[25] Small firms were already perishing and being absorbed by large competitors, who could avail themselves of the gold reserves and lending capacity of the banks. In the crisis of 1920–21 Varga had seen finance capital adopting the novel tactic of forcing the working class to bear the burden of cyclical contractions. A decade later he offered the same hypothesis: '. . . the basic

[21] Ibid., p. 8.

[22] Quoted in N. Il'yukhov, 'O Literature po Ekonomicheskomu Krizisu v SASSh', *Bol'shevik*, no. 11–12 (30 June 1930), p. 119.

[23] Hilferding, *Das Finanzkapital*, p. 396.

[24] Varga, *Konets Amerikanskovo Protsvetaniya*, Moscow and Leningrad 1930, p. 66.

[25] Ibid., p. 67.

difference in the pattern of a crisis under monopoly capitalism—by comparison with classical capitalism—lies . . . in the fact that *the burden of the crisis is largely transferred by the capitalists to the proletariat and the less well-to-do strata of the population.* In classical capitalism the disproportion between the productive and consuming power of society was resolved during a crisis primarily through a sharp drop in prices. . . . The capitalists took the loss. Under monopoly capitalism the capitalists can protect themselves from a fall in prices and erase the disproportion with the help of a sharp and prolonged decline in production. This means that *the burden of the crisis falls mainly upon the proletariat in the form of prolonged mass unemployment*; it also means that although small capitalists, merchants, and artisans must lower the prices of their commodities in order to facilitate sales and use the proceeds to meet their payments, the big capitalists either do not lower prices at all or do so much less significantly.'[26]

The current crisis, Varga argued, might see a more important drop in prices than during a typical monopolistic contraction, because the existing price index was still 40 per cent above its 1913 level, which more closely corresponded to the real 'value' of commodities. All the same, Varga expected the losses of monopoly capital to be relatively small. Moreover, the ability of monopolies to maintain prices would also impede the spread of the crisis to other countries. In classical capitalism crises had always spread from one country to another through price slashing and international dumping. By May 1930 events overtook this portion of Varga's analysis, obliging him to admit to an audience in Leningrad that he had erred: 'I believed the transition to an international crisis would take much longer than has proven to be the case. *The fact that the crisis phase has spread to the whole world in only half a year is due to the influence of the general crisis of capitalism.*'[27] Even at this date, however, Varga expected the American economy to enter the post-crisis phase of 'depression' by the autumn or winter of 1930, with Europe following in the spring or summer of 1931.[28]

[26] Ibid., p. 68.

[27] Varga, 'Mirovoi Krizis i evo Problemy', *Problemy Marksizma*, no. 4–6 (1930), p. 99.

[28] Ibid., p. 96.

In the most general terms Varga was saying that finance capital had little to fear from the crisis. On the other hand, he believed the same could not be said of the ensuing phase of depression. Here the effects of the 'general crisis' would make themselves obvious. Traditionally, crises had been overcome through 'the expansion of the capitalist market both within each country and in other countries not yet included within the capitalist orbit'.[29] 'Varga's Law' and monopolistic pricing prevented expansion of the internal market, and there were no virgin territories left to exploit. The curve of development must decline accordingly: 'The alternation of the phases of crisis, depression, expansion, a high conjuncture, and a new crisis—which was characteristic of progressive capitalism— no longer exists for large parts of the world economy; now periods of chronic depression and more acute phases of crisis follow one another.'[30] In many countries the outlook was one of 'chronic depression'. The capitalists would resist new investments because the existing market was inadequate; should they be tempted to renovate their fixed capital, they would exacerbate the problem of markets by adding to 'structural' unemployment. In all its essentials, Varga's analysis resembled the position he and Trotsky had taken in 1921–2. The novel factor accounting for both the cause of the crisis and the impossibility of another recovery was the tendency towards a permanent contraction in the number of productive workers. In April 1930 Varga expressed confidence that recent developments would 'put an end to the quarrel in our ranks . . . over "Varga's Law", as my opponents call it'.[31]

No sooner had Varga expressed the hope of a truce amongst economists than his critics began to pick his work apart. By describing the crisis as being simultaneously 'classical' and unique, he had attempted to give meaning to the concept of capitalism's systemic, or 'general', crisis. The crisis was 'classical' in the sense that it was caused by the contradiction between production and consumption; it was unique due to the presence of finance capital; the 'general crisis' would come into play by preventing a renewed

[29] *Mirovoi Ekonomicheskii Krizis—Kollektivnaya Rabota*, p. 9.
[30] Ibid.
[31] Varga, 'Economics and Economic Policy in the First Quarter of 1930', *International Press Correspondence*, X, no. 26 (4 June 1930), p. 463.

process of market expansion. Problems began when other economists queried the so-called classical element of Varga's explanation. At the meeting of Leningrad economists in May 1930, a number of participants demanded to know how Varga could see a 'classical' crisis when he had omitted the 'material basis' of the classical cycle, namely the uneven reproduction of fixed capital caused by differential variations in the rate of profit. As B. Livshits pointed out, Varga's account of underconsumption could not be reconciled with Marx's view that the share of the working class invariably rose on the eve of a crisis. 'The essence of the question', according to Livshits, was 'the decline in the norm of profit; every increase in wages represents . . . a fall in the norm of profit.'[32] Following this lead, another participant remarked that 'the limits of consumption are expanded by the force of the reproductive process, with the result that the contradiction [between production and consumption] finds its relative, temporary resolution in the . . . accumulation of productive capital'.[33] A third critic confirmed that for Marx 'fixed capital is the material basis of the cyclical movement of capitalism'. Varga's exposition was flawed by his adoption of 'the methodological basis of Luxemburgism'.[34] L. Kasharsky summarized the catalogue of complaints by saying that 'Comrade Varga directly attributes the cause of the crisis to the contradiction between production and consumption, or, in other words, to the narrowness of consumption resting on a capitalist basis. But amongst Marxists, it seems, there are few exceptions to the proper view that a crisis cannot be viewed as the direct result of this contradiction.' Varga's new position failed to include 'the conditions of the reproduction of capital', the problem Marx had treated as 'the most essential of all'.[35]

For the Leningrad economists, both 'classical' crises and that of 1929 were caused by a failure of investment activity. In contrast with the traditional Marxist view, Varga had taken the neo-Luxemburgist position that it was investment itself that caused the

[32] See Livshits's comments on Varga's report in *Problemy Marksizma*, no. 4–6 (1930), p. 100.
[33] Ibid., p. 101.
[34] Ibid., p. 103.
[35] Ibid., p. 107.

crisis by narrowing the market. This assertion now required Varga to confront a significant contradiction in his own thought. When challenging Bukharin he had argued that competition *compelled* the capitalists 'always to apply the latest means of production . . . to raise the organic composition of capital, to expand the total productive power beyond the consuming power of society'.[36] The theory of *compulsive* investment marked a further departure from the Marxist approach, leaving no room for a cycle governed by movements in the rate of profit. Varga therefore replied to his Leningrad critics this way:

'Comrade Livshits asserted that an expansion ends because the norm of profit declines. This is a . . . conception that contradicts Marxism but that can be found in Sombart, Cassel, and other bourgeois economists. When Marx speaks of the decline of the norm of profit, he relates it to the course of capitalist development in general—not to the separate phases of the industrial cycle. The thoughts developed by Comrade Livshits are characteristic of Hilferding and Cassel, not of Marx. This theory slurs over all the contradictions of capitalism; it is a purely apologetic theory and in fact it is untrue.'[37]

This remarkable denial of the role of the profit rate in generating the cycle served to underline the basic incoherence of Varga's outlook. The dilemma emerged clearly when Varga next told the meeting that 'the tendency towards a *chronic* disproportion between productive and consuming capacity' shortened periods of recovery. Why? Because 'if the capitalists know that their productive apparatus is under-utilized even at the high-point of the conjuncture, they will be less inclined to expand their productive apparatus. For this reason, crises and depressions turn out to be longer, expansions are shorter and less violent.'[38] Was investment so compulsive as to be indifferent to the rate of profit? If so, most economists would infer that a revival of investments must be followed by a 'classical' recovery. If, on the other hand, investment was not purely compulsive, then as Wurm had argued in 1928 it must follow that the capitalists could 'organize' themselves and

---

[36] Varga, *Problemy Mirovovo Khozyaistva i Mirovoi Politiki*, p. 30.

[37] Varga, 'Mirovoi Krizis i evo Problemy', p. 109.

[38] Ibid., p. 110.

refrain from aggravating the allegedly 'chronic' disproportion between production and consumption. Once again Varga's eccentric combination of Hilferding and Luxemburg appeared to involve a simultaneous right- and left-wing deviation, or a tendency to minimize the crisis in one breath and exaggerate it in the next. The inevitable consequence was to invite criticism from two directions.

One of those most inclined to minimize the crisis in the early weeks of 1930 was I.M. Pavlov, a leading analyst with the newspaper *Torgovo-Promyshlennaya Gazetta*. Reluctant to welcome a cataclysm prematurely, Pavlov thought the American economy was merely passing through a 'seasonal' downturn that would be even less severe than those of 1924 and 1927. Proof of this interpretation could be seen in the low rate of interest and the absence of bankruptcies. Varga had dismissed these critical indicators by referring to the unique attributes of finance capital. But surely, claimed Pavlov, that approach wildly exaggerated the power of financial institutions in the United States. If the Federal Reserve system were in fact able artificially to maintain a low interest rate, 'that would be very good for the Federal Reserve system and highly unsatisfactory for those comrades who only yesterday were justifiably criticizing the theory of organized capitalism'. Varga appeared to be comparing the role of finance capital to that of Soviet planning and was therefore treading 'a dangerous and slippery path'. The 'enthusiasm' of those who foresaw a full-scale crisis in America was 'perfectly normal and psychologically—but only psychologically—justified'. But as Pavlov pointed out, 'what we are least in need of is the replacement of a Marxist analysis . . . with psychological constructs'.[39]

While Pavlov condemned Varga for excessive haste, other economists found him guilty of hedging. In their view Hilferding's influence could only lead to an underestimation of the severity of the crisis. In a survey of the literature at the end of June 1930, N. Il'yukhov contended that Varga and Gertsenshtein were both unduly influenced by the organizational themes of *Finance Capital*. 'The attempt to show the impossibility in principle of monetary and credit crises under monopoly capitalism, an attempt that on the

[39] I.M. Pavlov, 'Krizis ili Depressiya?', *Torgovo-Promyshlennaya Gazeta* (29 December 1929).

whole depends on the views of Hilferding . . . associates its authors with those who support the theory of "organized capitalism".'[40] Varga's exposition of pricing policy was no less contradictory than his view of investments. One moment he predicted the growth of inventories (which presumably strained the money market by creating the need for interim financing); the next he affirmed that monopolists could protect themselves against a fall in prices by restricting output. 'Comrade Varga's view', declared Il'yukhov, 'leads to a complete denial of the law of prices that characterizes the capitalist mode of production. In point of fact, monopoly capitalism does not negate this law but merely modifies it.'[41]

L.A. Mendel'son likewise attacked Varga for his timidity and warned against diminishing the significance of the 'general crisis'. By following Hilferding too closely on price formation and monetary policy, Varga had come to the typical right-wing conclusion that crises would become less severe under monopoly capitalism.[42] At the same time, Varga was also persisting in his ultra-leftist error, which Kuusinen had correctly associated with Luxemburg. The new law, said Mendel'son, consisted of a 'rejection of the Leninist definition of imperialism' and its replacement by the doctrine of 'third parties',[43] or by 'the basic thesis of Rosa Luxemburg'.[44] The Luxemburgist theory then led to the Trotskyist conclusion that normal cycles would be replaced by 'stagnation', an argument that in turn implied that the United States must be an 'exception' to capitalism's 'general crisis'. How else could Varga account for the fact that the American crisis, notwithstanding capitalism's terminal illness, was 'classical' in nature? In Mendel'son's words: '. . . if the *absence* of [cyclical] expansions is typical of the epoch of the general crisis; and if, on the other hand, the USA had a *long* period of expansion [from 1921 to 1929, ending in a classical crisis], then how else can this be explained except by saying that the general crisis . . . applies only to Europe?'[45]

[40] Il'yukhov, 'O Literature . . .', p. 121.
[41] Ibid., p. 125.
[42] Lev Mendel'son, 'O Nekotorykh Problemakh Mirovovo Krizisa', *Bol'shevik*, no. 6 (31 March 1931), pp. 33–4 et passim.
[43] Ibid., p. 30.
[44] Ibid., p. 28.
[45] Ibid., p. 32.

From Mendel'son's point of view the only correct position was that actually there had not been a 'classical' cycle in America, only two narrowly-based recoveries that lapsed back into 'acute depression' in 1924 and again in 1927. 'The movement of the cycle cannot be understood if one limits oneself to the scheme of the classical cycle.'[46]

The final affront to Varga came when V. Motylev, himself a former Luxemburgist, systematically repeated all the charges levelled by Mendel'son. Varga's theory of the rationalization crisis had overestimated the degree of capital investment in the 1920s, thus enabling him to see a 'classical' cycle. In reality, the effect of the 'general crisis' had been to prevent a genuine reconstruction of industry.[47] The years 1924 and 1927 thus represented 'acute depressions' in America, and Varga was profoundly mistaken when he thought the crisis of 1929 was 'normal' and 'classical'. Had he not overestimated the extent of new capital expenditures, he would not have been forced to explain the events of 1929 in terms of the Luxemburgist theory of the exhaustion of 'third-party' demand: '*In the formulation of Comrade Varga, the uniqueness of the general crisis of capitalism as the stage of monopoly capitalism disappears. Methodologically,* Comrade Varga passes over to the Luxemburgist interpretation of the question. Rosa Luxemburg deduced . . . the inevitable crash of capitalism directly from conditions in the market. . . . When Comrade Varga sees "the decisive factor in the economics of capitalism's crisis" *directly* in the contradiction between production and consumption, he gives a methodological interpretation of the general crisis in the manner of Luxemburg, not of Lenin.'[48]

Motylev agreed with Mendel'son that the 'law of the absolute decline in the number of workers' was absurd. Only one fact was needed to explain the American crisis: the slowdown of investment due to the 'general crisis'. This was the unique element, not the damage-control mechanisms of finance capital. If the monopolies could not control prices—and even Varga had admitted there

---

[46] Ibid., p. 37.

[47] V. Motylev, 'Osnovnye Problemy Sovremennovo Mirovovo Krizisa', *Bol'shevik*, no. 4 (28 February 1931), p. 59.

[48] Ibid., p. 57.

would be a decline, because the current price index was so far above that of 1913—then it necessarily followed that they could not prevent a credit crisis either. The monopolists had fixed expenses just as small capitalists did, and they too would face bankruptcy once prices fell and revenues shrank. The credit crisis had been delayed only because of the low level of investment prior to the crisis, which glutted the money market with inexpensive loan-capital. Once these reserves were depleted, a credit crisis would follow immediately. Varga's theory of a 'classical' cycle and a 'normal' crisis implied what Motylev called 'an opportunistic appraisal' of future prospects: it 'would mean that capitalism in the USA, as well as in all the countries dependent on the USA, will experience [another] important expansion in the near future'.[49] Motylev believed that at best American capitalists could look forward to 'stabilization of the crisis' at some generally depressed level.[50]

To place this intricate web of charges in proper perspective it will help to recall the damage done Varga's credibility by his encounter with Kuusinen in 1929. On that occasion the theory of the 'technological revolution' had officially been declared anathema, on the grounds that modern capitalism was parasitic. As Kuusinen had asserted: 'The capitalist mode of production is *no longer wide enough for the development of the productive forces of labour*.'[51] In 1929 and again in February 1930, the ECCI had connected 'chronic' depression and the fall in working-class incomes with the 'extraordinary intensification of labour'. In other words, the 'official' view, contrary to Bukharin's thoughts on the matter, held that no significant investments had been made in the West during the late 1920s. Mendel'son, Motylev, and others understood this argument to mean that capitalism had become moribund and therefore incapable of a 'normal' or 'classical' cycle since the beginning of the 'general crisis'—officially traced to 1914. This interpretation ignored the real surge in investments that had in fact occurred in both America and Germany. At the same time, however, it did

[49] Ibid., p. 70.
[50] Ibid.
[51] Kuusinen, 'The International Situation . . .', *International Press Correspondence*, IX, no. 40 (20 August 1929), p. 838.

correctly—even if accidentally—identify the cause of the American crisis: the dramatic failure of investments beginning in 1929–30.

Varga's acceptance of Bukharin's 'technological revolution' enabled him to avoid his critics' tendency to exaggerate capitalism's moribund character. Instead he saw the crisis in 'classical' terms, meaning, among other things, that it had been preceded by the traditional wave of new capital construction (investments were compulsive). To Varga it seemed that fresh investments had then narrowed the market through labour displacement, thus bringing on the crisis. By subscribing to the neo-Luxemburgist thesis that investments *destroyed* the market, Varga departed from the analysis of the cycle given in *Capital*—and he also misread the facts. What was needed in America was not less investment *tout court*, but less investment in over-extended industries and more rapid expansion in the fields opened by new technology, something that would not occur until the approach of war at the end of the decade. In the early months of 1930 Varga's position inevitably provoked suspicion of a 'Right Deviation': to most observers a 'classical' crisis implied a classical recovery. Varga attempted to evade this implication by arguing that monopolistic practices would lead to protracted unemployment through cuts in production. But how, demanded his critics, could this organized restraint then be reconciled with the notion of compulsive investments, which in turn were said to be caused by the persistence of competition? Varga had no convincing answer. To make matters worse, the answer he did propose came straight from Hilferding (although Hilferding, as the Soviet cycle theorists had realized, actually argued that organized capitalism would make crises more serious and even entail the breakup of cartels). In view of this string of inconsistencies one can well imagine what was running through the minds of Varga's opponents: what kind of crisis was this, when at the very worst of times finance capital emerged virtually untouched?

That Varga should find himself in such confusion was due to his effort to adopt a centrist position and avoid a repetition of his earlier humiliation by Kuusinen. But the attempt to combine the 'classical' with the unique ultimately satisfied no one, and Varga would soon be forced to shift his emphasis, lending greater priority to the role of the 'general crisis'. The pressures working in this direction can be better appreciated if we consider in greater detail two other possible interpretations of what was happening in America, Eventov's and Mendel'son's. In the Soviet context, Eventov's position proved to be the most right-wing of all, a virtual caricature of Bukharin's theory of 'technological revolution', while Mendel'son anticipated Preobrazhensky's exposition of how monopoly capitalism impaired the recovery mechanism of the 'classical' cycle.

2. A Short Cycle or Monopolistic 'Rottenness'?

The bond between Eventov and Mendel'son was that both attached great importance to the years 1924 and 1927. Late in 1929 Eventov was one of the first to affirm that America faced a 'regular crisis' rather than a 'depression'.[52] Clarifying this assertion, he added that the new crisis would be similar to those of the mid-1920s and would represent 'one of the phases of the three-to-four-year cycle' that had distinguished the American economy since 1921. There had been frequent mention of an abbreviated cycle in the Soviet literature throughout the 1920s. When the calamity of 1929–30 dwarfed the 'recessions' of earlier years, most economists put aside the theory of the abbreviated cycle and tended to think of a more traditional pattern, with nine years separating the crises of 1920 and 1929. Eventov represented the exception to this tendency, describing three cycles since 1921, ending successively in 1924, 1927, and 1930. While other economists worried that mention of the abbreviated cycle would associate them with Mitchell and the research being done by American business schools, Eventov held that cyclical distortion was the most outstanding proof of the 'general crisis' and conformed entirely to the expectations of Marx.

In *Capital* Volume 1 Marx had provided some support for Eventov's interpretation. 'Until the present time', he wrote, 'the cycle generally embraces from 10 to 11 years. But we have no reason to suppose that this number is constant. On the contrary, the laws of capitalism . . . provide grounds for suggesting that this period is changing and that it is gradually being shortened.' In a letter of 18 June 1875, Marx also observed that the 'greater frequency of periodic general crises is really remarkable. I have always viewed

[52] See the discussion in *Problemy Ekonomiki*, no. 12 (December 1929), p. 147.

the length of the cycle not as being constant, but as contracting'.[53] Engels frequently spoke of the ten-year cycle being shortened and modified because of the chronic problem of markets. In *Capital* Volume 2, where Marx explained his own opinion more fully, he pointed instead to the acceleration of 'moral depreciation' or technological obsolescence:

'To the same extent as the value and durability of the fixed capital applied develops with the development of the capitalist mode of production, so also does the life of . . . industrial capital . . . say an average of ten years. If development of fixed capital extends this life, on the one hand, it is cut short on the other by the constant revolutionizing of the means of production, which also increases steadily with the development of the capitalist mode of production. This also leads to changes in the means of production; they constantly have to be replaced, because of their moral depreciation, long before they are physically exhausted. We can assume that, for the most important branches of large-scale industry, this life cycle is now on average a ten-year one.[54]

Eventov and Modest Rubinshtein both saw Marx's prediction vindicated in the American study *Recent Economic Changes in the United States*. Eight hundred of the largest American firms had been surveyed concerning their policy on amortization. Of those who responded 43.6 per cent expected new equipment to pay for itself within two years; 64.1 per cent set the interval at three years or less.[55] 'Merciless competition', observed Eventov, 'forces the capitalists in every manner to shorten the period of reproduction and to strive for the utmost speed in amortizing the capital they have invested'.[56] In *The World Economic Crisis*, published in the spring of 1930, Rubinshtein explained the same data as follows: 'contemporary construction and engineering technology significantly shortens the period required for the renovation of fixed capital. This is inevitably reflected on the one hand in the shorter length of

[53] Quoted in L. Y. Eventov and L.A. Mendel'son (eds.), *Krizis v Severo-Amerikanskikh Soedinennykh Shtatakh*, Moscow 1930, p. 11.

[54] Marx, *Capital* Volume 2, p. 264.

[55] Eventov and Mendel'son (eds.), *Krizis v Severo-Amerikanskikh Soedinennykh Shtatakh*, p. 13.

[56] Ibid., p. 11.

cycles and the greater frequency of crises, on the other in the permanent under-utilization of fixed capital . . . even in periods of expansion.'[57]

The fact that fixed-capital investments could be recovered only by transferring the value of equipment to new commodities meant that more rapid amortization created the potential for overproduction. Nevertheless, Eventov claimed that a buildup of commodity inventories had been prevented by increased advertising expenditures, the growth of an extensive commercial apparatus, and the creation of 'fictitious demand' in the form of consumer credit.[58] These measures had expanded the market until the advent of technological unemployment, or 'the tendency towards a decline in the number of those employed by productive capital', finally revealed the 'structural contradiction' between capacity and demand. At that point the capitalists again reduced output in an effort to maintain prices. In the absence of any prior accumulation of unsold goods, the abbreviated cycle appeared to involve a new form of overproduction limited exclusively to fixed capital: thus a 'sharp devaluation of existing capital' was to be expected instead of the traditional 'forced liquidation of commodity stocks'.[59] Moreover, since the new cycle was limited to America, there was no chance of 'a world economic crisis in the Marxist sense'. Every crisis represented 'an outbreak of contradictions that have accumulated in a previous phase of expansion', and in Europe no expansion had occurred.[60] As for the longevity of the American crisis, by the spring of 1930 Eventov was already predicting that coming months would see a transition to the stage of 'depression', apparently in preparation for a new expansion.[61]

The argument that three complete cycles had occurred since 1921 caused other economists to ask what had happened to the 'general crisis'? The 'crises' of 1924 and 1927, it seemed, had been resolved

[57] Rubinshtein, *Mirovoi Ekonomicheskii Krizis 1930 Goda*, Moscow and Leningrad 1930, p. 94.
[58] Eventov and Mendel'son (eds.), *Krizis v Severo-Amerikanskikh Soedinennykh Shtatakh*, p. 27.
[59] See the discussion in *Problemy Ekonomiki*, no. 12 (December 1929), p. 147.
[60] Ibid.
[61] Eventov and Mendel'son (eds.), *Problemy Mirovovo Khozyaistva*, Moscow 1930, p. 59.

'without any serious social or political consequences whatever',[62] the decline of capitalism having turned out to mean 'a technological revolution every two to three years'.[63] This was hardly what Marx and Engels had expected. As one of Eventov's opponents put it: 'Neither theoretical reflection nor empirical knowledge provides any basis for assuming short cycles during the period of capitalism's collapse taking the form of *long periods of prosperity* and short, superficial, *moderated crises.*'[64] Y. Gol'dshtein spotted a decisive theoretical weakness in Eventov's distinction between the over-production of fixed capital and overproduction of commodities.[65] According to Marx, 'capital consists of commodities, and therefore overproduction of capital implies overproduction of commo-dities'.[66] Marx's comments in *Theories of Surplus-Value* were particularly damaging: 'In general the phrase *overabundance of capital* as against *overproduction of commodities* is often merely a prevaricating expression, or [that kind of] thoughtlessness that admits the same phenomenon as present and necessary when it is called "A", but denies it when it is called "B".'[67] Eventov's separation of the two concepts could only result in a theory of 'organized capitalism' under which the capitalists could regulate competition and avoid flooding markets despite excess productive capacity. Although the theory of more frequent cycles appeared to be the antithesis of Bukharin's belief in 'state-capitalist' stability, Gol'dshtein argued that in effect it amounted to another variant of the same deviation.

Noting the similarity between Eventov's view of inventory control and his own, Varga hastened to distinguish his position by arguing that Eventov had been too categorical in appraising the prospect of price stability. The more stubbornly Eventov denied the probability of declining prices, the more perceptibly Varga revised his own outlook. Soon Varga was admitting that production

[62] Charles Brown, 'K Kharakteristike Amerikanskovo Krizisa', *Sotsialisticheskoe Khozyaistvo*, no. 1–2 (1930), p. 32.

[63] Ibid., p. 36.

[64] Ibid., p. 35.

[65] See Gol'dshtein's review in *Mirovoe Khozyaistvo i Mirovaya Politika*, no. 5 (May 1930), p. 160.

[66] Marx, *Capital* Volume 3, p. 251.

[67] Marx, *Theories of Surplus-Value*, p. 375.

could not be adjusted spontaneously to demand: 'Even with full knowledge of the market position it is not possible on the outbreak of a crisis immediately to adjust output to decreased demand, since the extent of the drop in consumption cannot be established in advance and restriction of output . . . ensues only when the utter impossibility of disposal is fully apparent. Thus there arise . . . unsaleable stocks of goods.'[68] At the Leningrad meeting of May 1930 Varga reflected on his 'interesting debate with Comrade Eventov' and again stressed that some fall in prices was inevitable: '*In general* one can say that under monopoly capitalism the drop in prices must be less than under industrial [i.e classical] capitalism, because the cartels will endeavour to keep prices high. But in the *present* crisis there must be a fall in prices.'[69] By the end of 1930, partly in consequence of his quarrel with Eventov, Varga would more willingly include inventory accumulation and falling prices among the elements of the 'general crisis'.

If Eventov's presence on the 'right' helped Varga resolve one issue, it simultaneously mystified another. For Eventov, crises were caused not merely by the 'technological revolution', but also by the combination of increased productive capacity and technological unemployment; in short, his position on this matter too was identical to Varga's. Yet at the same Leningrad meeting Varga used this issue to talk himself into another contradiction. Eventov, he declared, had turned everything 'upside down'. Arguing that more rapid technological advances *caused* more frequent crises, he had interpreted Marx 'too mechanistically'. Marx had said that the renewal of fixed capital was the 'material basis' of the industrial cycle. But Varga asserted that 'the material basis is not the same thing as a cause'.[70] What Marx really meant was that the length of the cycle depended on social relations, or the contradiction between labour and capital. Varga's purpose in making this distinction was to emphasize his own belief that crises resulted from underconsumption. The Leningrad economists had suggested that fresh investments in fixed capital created an internal market. By the end

[68] Varga, 'Economics and Economic Policy in the Fourth Quarter of 1929', *International Press Correspondence*, X, no. 8 (20 February 1930), pp. 150–51.

[69] Varga, 'Mirovoi Krizis i evo Problemy', p. 94.

[70] Ibid., p. 97.

of 1930 Varga would pull out all the stops and adopt the diametrically opposite view that any recovery in America had to begin in Department II.[71] A long history of Marxist cycle theory would suggest that it was now Varga who actually turned Marx 'upside down'.

A more traditional approach to the role of investments came in the writings of Mendel'son, who defined the 'general crisis' in terms of a secular decline in the rate of fixed-capital formation. Mendel'son and Eventov co-edited three volumes on the American crisis, and the evidence suggests that preoccupation with the events of 1924 and 1927 began with Mendel'son and was then transformed by Eventov into the theory of the three-year cycle. In Mendel'son's own opinion, 'normal' cycles were no longer possible (although initially he did not indicate that this conclusion also applied to 'normal' three-year cycles).[72] The weakness of investment activity could be measured by industrial growth rates. Over the years 1917–29 American manufacturing output had risen by an average of 2.8 per cent annually—a rate that looked respectable when compared to the European performance but suffered by comparison with the 4.5 per cent annual average prior to the war. The 'right renegades' had been mesmerized by the American 'exception' only because of their lack of perspective. America was gradually being 'Europeanized': the automobile, chemical, and electrical industries had lost the bloom of youth, and the most important output gains had come from labour intensification.[73] America's convergence towards the European norm proved that in the world economy as a whole 'levelling tendencies' were at work 'on a declining basis'.[74] Recognizing the capitalist tendency to discard morally obsolescent equipment prematurely, Mendel'son also saw a countervailing force in the contradiction 'between the *potential opportunities* for a growth of the productive forces . . . and the socio-economic possibilities'.[75] The over-ripe nature of capitalism was

[71] Varga, 'Razvitie i Perspektivy Mirovovo Ekonomicheskovo Krizisa', *Bol'shevik*, no. 23–4 (30 December 1930), p. 56; cf. Varga, 'Problemy Krizisa', *Mirovoe Khozyaistvo i Mirovaya Politika*, no. 2–3 (February-March 1931), p. 30.

[72] Eventov and Mendel'son (eds.), *Krizis v Severo-Amerikanskikh Soedinennykh Shtatakh*, p. 52.

[73] Ibid., pp. 70–71.

[74] Ibid., p. 66.

[75] Eventov and Mendel'son (eds.), *Problemy Mirovovo Khozyaistva*, p. 86.

revealed by the fact that 'the system as a whole, having lost its relative progressiveness, is becoming a colossal obstacle to utilization of the available productive forces and their further development. This condition testifies to the beginning of the end, and precisely for this reason rottenness is the typical feature of *moribund* capitalism'.[76] 'The delay of technological progress' had proven to be 'the only area in which the genuinely "organized" character of contemporary capitalism makes itself felt'.[77]

Inability to realize the 'technological revolution' had led to deformation of the classical cycle. Historically, an economic crisis cleared the way for renewed expansion. Technologically obsolescent equipment was routinely devalued and taken out of use. But the rise in the organic composition of capital had made such losses unthinkable to modern industrialists. When a giant metallurgical enterprise faced bankruptcy, it simply merged with a stronger competitor, hastening the concentration and centralization of capital. The old equipment was conserved and in some cases modernized, in anticipation of a time when it could once again be pressed into service. In this way monopolies acquired a *reserve* of productive capacity (excess capacity) without having to undertake new construction and without initiating a genuine economic recovery. Periods of 'flabby recovery' during the 1920s had thus been followed by relapses into 'depression' in 1924 and 1927. 'The basic tendency', Mendel'son concluded, 'is undeniably towards . . . a shortening of the cycle. But the shortening is often neutralized by the fact that when expansions are brief or absent they are offset by long crises and depressions. Crises and depressions come more frequently, their duration increases, . . . and the general length of the cycle becomes indefinite.'[78] By underlining the growth of industrial reserves as an obstacle to the 'technological revolution', Mendel'son distinguished his own views from those of Eventov and simultaneously implied that Varga was wrong to see a chronic shortage of markets as the cause of the crisis. Varga had it backwards: the truth was that the market problem grew out of institutional impediments to investment activity. As it turned out,

[76] Ibid., p. 79.
[77] Ibid., p. 95.
[78] Varga, Motylev and Mendel'son (eds.), *Problemy Mirovovo Krizisa Kapitalizma*, Moscow and Leningrad 1931, p. 124.

Stalin found Varga's notion of compulsive investments more to his liking than capitalist reserves, and in the spring of 1931 Mendel'son acknowledged responsibility for both his own and Eventov's errors. At the same time, however, Mendel'son could take satisfaction from the fact that Stalin held that the world crisis was far from 'classical'. That much was made clear in June 1930.

3. Stalin's Intervention

In his report to the Sixteenth Congress of the Soviet Communist Party Stalin's mood was jubilant. Two years before, Bukharin had lauded capitalist stabilization while the Soviet government agonized over the grain strike. Now the Five-Year Plan promised a revolutionary increase in Soviet production while the capitalist world was crumbling. Stalin invited the party to reflect on the vast scope of the change:

'Recall the state of affairs in the capitalist countries two and a half years ago. Growth of industrial production and trade in nearly all the capitalist countries. Growth of production of raw materials and food in nearly all the agrarian countries. A halo around the United States as the land of the most full-blooded capitalism. Triumphant hymns of "prosperity". Grovelling to the dollar. Panegyrics in honour of the new technology, in honour of capitalist rationalization. Proclamation of an era of the "recovery" of capitalism and of the unshakable firmness of capitalist stabilization. "Universal" noise and clamour about the "inevitable doom" of the Land of Soviets, about the "inevitable collapse" of the USSR. That was the state of affairs yesterday. And what is the picture today? Today there is an economic crisis in nearly all the industrial countries of capitalism. . . . And the "universal" clamour about the "inevitable doom" of the USSR is giving way to "universal" venomous hissing about the necessity of punishing "that country" that dares to develop its economy when crisis is reigning all around. Such is the picture today.'[79]

Celebrating the fact that 'Things have turned out exactly as the Bolsheviks said they would', Stalin defined the official nature of the current crisis: it was 'a crisis of *overproduction*'; it was the first '*world*

[79] Stalin, *Works*, XII, p. 242–3.

economic crisis' of the postwar period, involving both agrarian and industrial countries; and by developing 'unevenly' in various parts of the world it confirmed the Leninist theory of imperialism.[80] No one could any longer deny that the capitalist countries had embarked upon 'a *descending* curve of growth'.[81] Frantically proposing one scheme after another to 'mitigate', 'prevent' and 'eliminate' crises, the capitalist gentlemen had forgotten that 'there have been periodical crises during more than a hundred years, occurring every twelve, ten, eight or less years'.[82] Having pronounced the last word on the matter of the cycle's length, Stalin turned to its cause. To his credit, he sidestepped the technical issues and reverted to Lenin's formulation in the debate with the Narodniks. 'The basis of the crisis', he declared, 'lies in the contradiction between the social character of production and the capitalist form of appropriation.'[83] When it came to explaining the meaning of this contradiction, however, Stalin ignored the theory of disproportionalities and leaned towards Varga:

'An expression of this fundamental contradiction of capitalism is the contradiction between the colossal *growth* of capitalism's potentialities of production . . . and the relative *reduction* of the effective demand of the vast masses of the working people, whose standard of living the capitalists always try to keep at the *minimum* level. To be successful in competition and to squeeze out the utmost profit, the capitalists are compelled to develop their technical equipment, to introduce rationalization, to intensify the exploitation of the workers . . . all the capitalists are compelled, in one way or another, to take this path of furiously developing production potentialities. The home and the foreign market, however, . . . remain on a low level. Hence overproduction crises.'[84]

While supporting Varga in general terms, Stalin also obliquely criticized him by emphasizing that the current crisis was anything but 'classical': 'The present crisis cannot be regarded as a mere recurrence of the old crises. It is occurring and developing under

[80] Ibid., pp. 244–6.
[81] Ibid., p. 247.
[82] Ibid., p. 250.
[83] Ibid.
[84] Ibid., pp. 250–51.

certain new conditions. . . . It is complicated and deepened by a number of special causes.'[85] The special causes included monopolistic pricing (which would prolong the crisis, not save the monopolies) and above all the 'general crisis' of the capitalist system, which had 'intensified the decay of capitalism and upset its equilibrium'. The mere example of rapid industrial growth in the USSR was shaking capitalism to its foundations; the colonial revolution and native industries were undermining imperialism; and the industrial countries' chronically excess industrial capacity and a 'permanent army of unemployed' made for the 'most profound world economic crisis that has ever occurred'.[86]

Satisfied that the capitalist world was falling to pieces, Stalin expressed concern about an issue the economists had scarcely considered. It was common knowledge among Bolsheviks that imperialists resolved their economic difficulties through war. In 1920–1921 Lenin had been content to aid in the reconstruction of a postwar 'equilibrium' by opening Soviet markets and encouraging the capitalists to mine Russia's raw materials. An invasion of foreign investors was to be preferred to an assault by foreign armies. During the mid-1920s Stalin had abandoned Lenin's policies in favour of socialism in one country, or economic 'independence'. Now he invited other countries to expand their trade with the USSR and take advantage of a growing market. More would be heard of this proposal at the World Economic Conference of 1933. Stalin explained his change of attitude in these terms: '. . . every time the contradictions of capitalism become acute the bourgeoisie turns its gaze towards the USSR, wondering whether it would not be possible to solve this or that contradiction . . . or all the contradictions together, at the expense of the USSR, of that Land of Soviets, that citadel of revolution, which, by its very existence is revolutionizing the working class and the colonies.'[87] Had the Soviet Union been capable of buying a significant volume of foreign goods without relying on credit, Stalin's proposal might have been taken seriously. As it was, Western governments were facing collapse over the issue of how to finance relief to their own unemployed.

[85] Ibid., p. 252.
[86] Ibid., p. 254.
[87] Ibid., pp. 262–3.

Stalin's invervention in the debates of the economists was the first of several that would occur during the 1930s. Being merely a 'genius' and not an expert, Stalin insisted only on defining the limits of acceptable discourse, and thereafter left the economists to fill in the details. The 'office' would follow the economic literature, determine who was in 'error', and periodically invoke sanctions against careless editorial boards or writers. When contentious issues subsequently arose, particularly after 1932, individual economists would document their opinions by obsequious quotations from the *ex cathedra* pronouncements of the Leader. The eventual effect of this interaction was to steer economic inquiry away from imaginative investigations and towards small ideas and practical analyses. The 'office' continued to depend on the economists to assemble the information available in the Western press; and by their choice of meaningful data, the economic researchers influenced official thinking. The evidence referred to in virtually any official declaration could be traced to an earlier article by one or another economist, Varga more often than not. But from 1930 onwards the atmosphere of Soviet discussions changed. Henceforth the facts had to be packaged in 'orthodox' quotations.

The immediate consequences of Stalin's address to the Sixteenth Congress were to halt talk of short cycles, to grant retrospective legitimacy to 'Varga's law' (although Stalin did speak of a 'relative' reduction in working-class incomes), and to resolve the issue of where to seek the cause of the crisis. For all his shortcomings, Stalin had done his homework. By referring to the contradiction between social production and private appropriation (which, incidentally, he did not explicitly attribute to Lenin), he adopted a formulation broad enough to permit general acceptance. The cause of the cycle would thereafter be explained by quoting Lenin's 'most faithful student and comrade-in-arms', and then interpreted by reference to underconsumption and the 'general crisis'. For Varga personally, Stalin's report to the party congress made it clear that more emphasis on the 'general crisis' and less on the damage-control mechanisms of finance capital was required. Responding to these signals, Varga eventually provided an interpretation of the crisis that was generally accepted as at least quasi-official.

In his economic survey of the second quarter of 1930 Varga

charged that Eventov's theory of short cycles reflected 'the influence of American business research'. The disturbances of 1924
and 1927, he stated, had not been genuine crises but 'merely
relapses both in view of their relatively slight intensity and in view
of their short duration'.[88] As far as prices were concerned,
monopolies, customs duties, and taxes would postpone their
adjustment to values, but it was obvious that 'by the time the crisis
is over the general price level will have sunk very close to the prewar
level, as indeed it theoretically should'.[89] In his survey for the third
quarter Varga indicated the mechanism through which the law of
value would be enforced. Rudolf Hilferding had shown that high
fixed costs would lead to rising unit costs of production if the scale
of industrial operations were reduced.[90] Varga now made the same
point: 'So as to avoid the increase of production costs, by reason of
insufficient exploitation of productive capacity, many enterprises
carry on production on a larger scale than would correspond to the
actual demand. In many cases it is impossible for technical reasons
to reduce production below a certain minimum. Either a certain
quantity must be produced or the works must be shut down.
Therefore we witness the remarkable fact that despite the pronounced drop in . . . prices, output is continued on a practically
undiminished scale.'[91] The technological superiority of the monopolies tended to generate its own negation: instead of preventing
bankruptcies, violations of the law of value brought them closer by
provoking an unplanned growth of inventories. This failure of
monopolistic price controls called for a new forecast. Whereas
Varga had originally expected the advent of the post-crisis stage of
'depression' in the autumn or winter of 1930, he now believed there
would be no improvement for another year, and even allowed for
the possibility that 1931 might see a catastrophe even greater than
that of 1930.[92]

In December 1930 Varga published in *Bol'shevik* an article

[88] Varga, 'Economics and Economic Policy in the Second Quarter of 1930',
International Press Correspondence, X, no. 39 (28 August 1930), p. 802.

[89] Ibid., p. 803.

[90] Hilferding, *Das Finanzkapital*, pp. 403-4.

[91] Varga, 'Economics and Economic Policy in the Third Quarter of 1930',
International Press Correspondence, X, no. 56 (6 December 1930), p. 1149.

[92] Ibid., p. 1156.

entitled 'The Development and Prospects of the World Economic Crisis'. Although his editors still claimed to detect 'debatable and incorrect positions', Varga took care to emphasize that this crisis was without precedent in its universality, length, and unevenness. The decline in prices, particularly for raw materials, exceeded that of all previous crises.[93] Redressing the defects of his original analysis, Varga wrote: 'It is necessary to emphasize that the strongly-developed monopolistic character of contemporary capitalism cannot prevent the drop in prices. True, monopolistic organizations attempt to maintain prices at their former levels. . . . This circumstance helps to prolong the crisis. Nevertheless, the majority of monopolistic organizations have been forced to lower their prices.'[94] Finance capital was also proving less stable in money markets than Varga had originally supposed. Balance of payments difficulties were driving up German interest rates and leading to more frequent bankruptcies. 'All these facts conclusively disprove the bourgeois theory of the decisive role of loan capital during a period of crisis.'[95]

On the most crucial question of the origin of the crisis Varga made it perfectly obvious that he had studied Stalin's speech: 'the basis of the general crisis of capitalism is the extreme sharpening of the contradiction between the social character of production and the capitalist form of appropriation . . . the expression of which is . . . *the contradiction between the producing and consuming power of capitalist society . . .* [which] *. . . in the period of the general crisis . . . tends to become chronic.*'[96] The 'economic essence' of the 'general crisis' was 'monopolistic rottenness'.[97] The competitive struggle compelled capitalists to invest or perish, and each successive wave of rationalization added to 'chronic mass unemployment' and 'chronic latent overproduction of commodities'.[98] Varga also moved to bring his position on the new 'law' closer into line with Stalin's: 'The organic composition of capital rises, variable capital

[93] Varga, 'Razvitie i Perspektivy . . .', pp. 36–38.
[94] Ibid., p. 40.
[95] Ibid., p. 44.
[96] Ibid., pp. 44–5.
[97] Ibid., p. 45.
[98] Ibid.

declines relatively (in some countries it is also now declining absolutely).'[99] Eventov's distinction between redundant capital and the overproduction of commodities was said to reveal 'his complete misunderstanding of Marxist teachings'. Bukharin's theory of 'a constant moving equilibrium' was described as 'utterly incorrect'.[100] Finally, to his survey of the errors of others Varga added his own limited self-criticism: at the tenth plenum of the ECCI in 1929 Otto Kuusinen had been correct to reject his 'unclear and mistaken formulation' on the question of working-class living standards.[101]

Varga continued to backtrack at a meeting of the Institute of World Politics and World Economics in March 1931. He reiterated that the basic contradiction was between 'social production and private appropriation', or 'between the unlimited efforts of the capitalists to expand production and the restricted consuming power of capitalist society in antagonistic conditions of distribution'.[102] The process of capital accumulation had become 'identical with the constant emergence of relative overproduction': each rise in the organic composition of capital displaced living labour-power and shortened the interval between crises.[103] The 'economic' disproportion between productive and consuming power—not Eventov's 'technical' problem of accelerated obsolescence—was the factor that interrupted each cyclical expansion at an earlier stage and created the trend towards chronic crisis. Monopolistic 'rottenness' had two aspects: the inability to utilize productive capacity fully and the enforced idleness of the most essential productive force of all, human labour-power.[104] During earlier stages of capitalism the contradiction between production and consumption led to *periodic* crises; 'in the period of the general crisis it entails a tendency to become chronic. The limits of the capitalist market even in the phase of expansion are insufficient for the complete utilization of the productive apparatus . . . [or] for supplying work

[99] Ibid., p. 46.

[100] Ibid.

[101] Ibid.

[102] Varga, 'Problemy Krizisa', *Mirovoe Khozyaistvo i Mirovaya Politika*, no. 2–3 (February-March 1931), p. 5.

[103] Ibid.

[104] Ibid., pp. 16–17.

to the entire proletariat. . . . *Unused means of production and unused labour power—"An excess of capital together with an excess of population"* (Marx)—*is in our view the most important economic indicator of the general crisis of capitalism.*'[105]

In agriculture Varga saw the same problem as in industry: the rapid capitalization of farming during the 1920s, the displacement of workers by tractors and mechanized harvesters, and the resulting tendency towards chronic overproduction—all these symptoms of the 'general crisis' resulted from monopolistic barriers to fresh investment in manufacturing. The chronic agrarian crisis was a logical corollary of the chronic industrial crisis. Excess capacity in the one sphere automatically stimulated excess investment in the other. And labour displacement in both narrowed the market for agrarian as well as industrial commodities. Driven from the land, small farmers drifted to the cities and joined the ranks of the army of unemployed. The agrarian crisis not only interacted with and reinforced the industrial crisis, but also constituted an insurmountable impediment to a 'normal' industrial recovery. From consideration of agricultural matters Varga turned directly to his new 'law'.

Throughout 1930 he had continued to speak of the absence of 'third parties' in the leading industrial countries. In *The End of American Prosperity* (January 1930) he wrote: 'The hopes of the bourgeoisie that the crisis will be easily overcome and will be followed by a new expansion are unfounded. We live in the period of the decline of capitalism. The time when crises could be overcome by movement in an upward direction, i.e., by expanding the sphere of activity of the capitalist mode of production, has passed. The expansion of the internal capitalist market . . . by way of converting self-sufficient peasants into commodity producers and hired workers (this is the main method of creating and expanding the internal capitalist market) is now completed in such imperialist countries as the United States, England, and Germany; 80–90 per cent of the value of peasant production is already absorbed by the capitalist commodity turnover.'[106]

The quarterly economic survey that appeared in April 1930 explained chronic unemployment by noting that 'the transform-

[105] Ibid., p. 20.
[106] Varga, *Konets Amerikanskovo Protsvetaniya*, p. 87.

ation of the peasants into small agricultural commodity producers is at an end in the advanced capitalist countries, while the extension of the external market meets with ever-increasing difficulties in view of the industrialization of the colonies and the existence of the Soviet Union'.[107] At the Leningrad meeting of May 1930 Varga accounted for the falling curve of capitalist development by showing that '*capitalism in general and on the whole has reached the limits of the ... market*'.[108] And in his *Bol'shevik* article of December 1930 he quoted Lenin's *Development of Capitalism in Russia* to argue that the 'process' of converting peasants into commodity producers, hitherto the key to market creation and therefore to cyclical recoveries, was finally exhausted.[109]

However much his detractors might complain about 'Luxemburgism', Varga was convinced that the possibility of a cyclical recovery could be definitively foreclosed only by referring to the problem of 'third parties'. The whole thesis that new investments displaced labour and narrowed the market—a thesis Stalin himself had embraced—would collapse if an alternative market could be created at the expense of rural handicrafts. If this crisis was indeed unique, it had to be because the 'process' of conversion had ended. Was this a Luxemburgist position? Varga thought not. At the Institute's meeting in March 1931 he exclaimed that his interpretation had 'absolutely nothing in common with Rosa Luxemburg. On the contrary, Luxemburg, just like the Narodniks, saw the existence of "third parties" as a necessary condition for the realization of surplus-value, whereas we have in mind *the process of converting peasants into component elements of capitalist society, that is, the process of destroying their role as "third parties"*.'[110]

If we assume that Varga was not being deceitful (probably he was), then it necessarily follows that he had not read Luxemburg recently. In *The Accumulation of Capital* she argued that 'Capitalism must ... always and everywhere fight a battle of annihilation against every historical form of natural economy that it encounters.'[111] Once the non-capitalist hinterland became a con-

[107] Varga, 'Economics and Economic Policy in the First Quarter of 1930', p. 463.
[108] Varga, 'Mirovoi Krizis i evo Problemy', p. 92.
[109] Varga, 'Razvitie i Perspektivy . . .', p. 47.
[110] Varga, 'Problemy Krizisa', pp. 13–14.
[111] Luxemburg, *The Accumulation of Capital*, p. 369.

stituent part of the capitalist mode of production, according to Luxemburg, the search for new external markets and 'third parties' must resume until the ultimate elimination of non-capitalist societies and the onset of the consequent chronic realization crisis caused the outbreak of imperialist wars. For Luxemburg, as Bessonov quite rightly understood in 1923, the 'process' of conversion had a finite limit, whereas for Lenin it was merely the first step in the perfection of the social division of labour. Varga's view was Luxemburgist in the strict sense of the word. And it was only by reverting to Luxemburg and by strengthening this element of his thought that he could finally abandon the position that the current crisis had any important traditional features. After the spring of 1931 the charge of Luxemburgism was heard less frequently and Varga's account of the agrarian crisis and its implications for the industrial cycle met with little protest. The 'office' had accorded 'Varga's Law' *de facto* recognition. The issue was silently allowed to fall into abeyance. A more pressing concern was now emerging, as the economic crisis gave rise to the political problem of fascism.

4. The Problem of Fascism

Preoccupied with technical issues and their own esoteric disputes, Soviet economists had shown little interest in the political dimension of the 'general crisis'. To the extent that a common approach had emerged, it involved a tendency to equate fascism with efforts by the capitalist state to intervene in the market and create a regime of 'class peace'. A typical case was the assessment of Herbert Hoover's posturing in the autumn of 1929. 'For the first time in the history of capitalism', Varga claimed, 'an attempt was made to counteract the cyclical course of capitalist production with "planned" measures'.[112] In reality, Hoover's much-vaunted 'plan' was a piece of showmanship designed for the press. Holding meetings at the White House with industrialists, railway executives, heads of utilities, and representatives of labour and farm groups, the president managed to produce a spate of newspaper photographs and optimistic forecasts. The spokesmen of American capital undertook to continue and even increase investment expenditures,

[112] Varga, *Konets Amerikanskovo Protsvetaniya*, p. 55.

even promising that workers would not be dismissed nor wages reduced. In return, leaders of the American Federation of Labour promised to raise no new demands for wage increases. Publicizing his achievement, Hoover announced that the meetings would 'guarantee that for the duration of the present situation no conflict should arise to impair the continuity of work'. The newspapers seconded the president's announcement, proclaiming a 'Capital-Labour Pact' and 'civil peace between Capital and Labour'. Varga replied that the ideology of 'civil peace' was the hallmark of fascism. The Hoover 'plan' had no chance of practical success and was actually designed for quite a different purpose:

'The leaders of American monopoly capital know this very well. Their real goal, indeed, is not to overcome the crisis but *to create a central organ for the purpose of struggle with the revolutionary movement, to create a fascist nucleus uniting under a single leadership all the existing but hitherto uncoordinated fascist forces*: the American Federation of Labour, the "company unions" . . . the Pinkerton detectives, the armed factory police etc. . . . . The great economic board to be formed to implement Hoover's programme . . . is the form of this organization. The process of fascization is advancing in the USA.'[113]

G. Safarov reported the activities of the American president to *Bol'shevik* readers and quoted the *Chicago Tribune* that Hoover had assembled a virtual 'economic trust of the United States'. William Green and Matthew Woll, president and vice-president of the AFL, had collaborated with industry in forming a fascist 'trust' that would put Mussolini's efforts to shame. 'The handicraft fascism of the Italian parvenu Mussolini pales before the new American standard, before the fascism of American finance capital.'[114] Rubinshtein gave a similar account: 'It is perfectly understandable that the first stage of the crisis brings forth not only a growth of fascism in many countries but also a certain increase in the importance to capital of the reformist parties and trade unions . . . the entire apparatus of the reformist organizations will be committed totally to the assistance of the financial oligarchy. . . . The

[113] Ibid., pp. 61–2.
[114] G. Safarov, 'Krizis "Organizovannovo Kapitalizma" ', *Bol'shevik*, no. 1 (15 January 1930), p. 72.

leading reformist organizations are doing everything in their power to preserve "peace in industry". . . . The process of fascization of the reformist organizations will no doubt be given a new impetus by the development of the crisis.'[115]

At the Sixteenth Congress of the Soviet Communist Party in the summer of 1930 Molotov devoted much of his speech to fascism and warned that Social Democracy was 'hastening at a quickened pace along the road towards the merging of the Social Democratic and reformist trade-union apparatus with the bourgeois state in the process of fascization'. The minority Labour government of Ramsay MacDonald in Britain had become 'one of the most important aids in carrying out capitalist rationalization, [standing] for greater oppression of the working class and for wage cuts all along the line'. In Germany the coalition government headed by Social Democratic Chancellor Müller had been used to reduce wages through compulsory arbitration and to cut back social insurance benefits. Then it was cast aside by the bourgeoisie. But finance capital, Molotov affirmed, 'still continues to set a high value on the services of the Social Democrats. It is not for nothing that in Germany there are twenty-two Social Democratic heads of police.'[116]

When the Müller government fell over the issue of how to finance unemployment relief—the same issue that later split the British Labour Party and led to the National Government—Varga began to write of a mounting struggle within the ruling class over the distribution of a diminished volume of profit. The industrial bourgeoisie demanded lower food prices in the hope of forcing wages down; agrarian capitalists replied with a demand for higher tariffs; light industry complained of the pricing policies of cartels; and manufacturers in general held commercial capital responsible for high retail prices. The economic crisis threatened to grow over into a political crisis, because the 'share in profits of the separate bourgeois strata depends on the economic policy of the state (with respect to tariffs, taxes, and cartels). Hence the uninterrupted friction between different strata of the ruling class over how to

[115] Rubinshtein, *Mirovoi Ekonomicheskii Krizis 1930 Goda*, pp. 114–15.
[116] Molotov, 'Report of the Activities of the Delegation of the CPSU in the ECCI', *International Press Correspondence*, X, no. 34 (25 July 1930), p. 651.

manage economic policy'.[117] The struggle over surplus-value would result in 'a crisis of the whole bourgeois political-organizational system'. In January 1931 Varga predicted that Germany would soon see an 'all-round crisis of the state'.[118]

One of the tantalizing puzzles of the early 1930s has always been why the European Communist parties, and especially in Germany, mounted such ineffective resistance to the rise of the radical right. From 1930 until Hitler's appointment as chancellor in 1933, Leon Trotsky repeatedly implored the Comintern and Social Democrats to form a united front and thereby keep the fascists isolated from the centres of power. As Irving Howe has recently commented: 'Had Trotsky's advice been followed . . . the world might have been spared some of the horrors of our century; at the very least, the German working class would have gone down in battle rather than allowing the Nazi thugs to take power without resistance. But Trotsky was not heeded.'[119] Why was the call for a united front so blithely ignored? On one level the answer is obvious: the Social Democrats had a powerful class base and a long tradition of turning out the vote; the Nazis, in contrast, recruited from the *lumpenproletariat* and the dispossessed petty bourgeoisie, a class that was considered incapable of political discipline or stable class consciousness. The Social Democrats commanded proven staying power and might freeze the Communists out of office; the Nazis, so the argument ran, would destroy their own credibility and help to create the conditions for a proletarian revolution. In that respect Hitler was the lesser evil and his victory could be construed, at least by Stalinists, as a step towards communism.

The discussions of Soviet economists indicate, however, that there was a second aspect to this question. For more than a decade before Hitler's first electoral success in 1930, Soviet Marxists had been fretting over the prospect of 'organized capitalism'. Now it seemed that Bukharinism just might be vindicated. How many times had Bukharin argued that the objective tendency of finance capital was to overcome class divisions, to subordinate the workers

---

[117] Varga, 'Ekonomicheskii Krizis Pererastaet v Krizis Obshchenatsional'nyi', *Kommunisticheskii Internatsional*, no. 32 (20 November 1930), p. 24.

[118] Varga, 'Economics and Economic Policy in the Fourth Quarter of 1930', p. 155.

[119] Irving Howe, *Leon Trotsky*, New York 1978, p. 142.

to the state, and to allow capital to make its appearance as a 'unified force'? In a regime of state capitalism Bukharin had expected the political authorities to serve as the mediating agents of finance capital, to supervise the distribution of surplus-value, and to implement what Bukharin had called 'the collective will of the consolidated bourgeoisie as a whole'.[120] If there was even a remote possibility that capitalism might surmount the crisis, Soviet economists felt, then it must lie in the direction of 'organized capitalism'. And who had invented 'organized capitalism' if not Rudolf Hilferding and the German Socialists? The natural conclusion was that Social Democracy was a far greater threat to the revolution than was Hitler. The Nazis were a counterfeit of Social Democracy, a vulgar reproduction of a far more potent political force. Claiming that there were no substantial programmatic differences between Social Democracy and fascism, the Comintern held that Socialists were in fact 'social fascists'. The Socialists disguised their subservience to capital by prattling about the 'social state' and 'economic democracy'; the Nazis did the same, only much less cleverly, by donning the ideological cloak of medievalism.

In a report to the ECCI in the spring of 1931 Dmitri Manuilsky portrayed the two parties as the Tweedle Dee and Tweedle Dum of finance capital. During the period of capitalist rationalization, Social Democracy had become 'the party of trusts and cartels. This was the period of their increased fascization.'[121] By 'fascization' Manuilsky meant the same as Varga; that is, the integration of Social Democratic parliamentarians and trade unionists into the state apparatus of 'decaying capitalism'. The 'social state' was the equivalent of fascism because it would use the trade unions to control the workers in the interest of capital in exactly the same way as Mussolini's corporate state. 'The worker can obtain employment only through the trade union, unemployment benefits are given through the trade-union office, the system of social insurance is closely bound up with the trade-union apparatus. The Social Democrats have entrenched themselves in all public institutions.' 'Tens of thousands' of Social Democrats were employed in the state

---

[120] Bukharin, *Imperialism and World Economy*, London 1972, p. 128.
[121] Manuilsky, 'The Deepening of the Economic Crisis', *International Press Correspondence*, XI, no. 30 (10 June 1931), p. 553.

bureaucracy, including the police, and had become 'the most faithful watchdogs of the capitalist system. . . . The conclusion . . . is that the Social Democrats . . . utilize the whole apparatus of the capitalist state in order to increase their pressure on the working class', the most conspicuous example being 'so-called compulsory arbitration' in wage disputes.[122]

In 1931 the Communist Party organization in Prussia appalled anti-fascist forces throughout Europe by conniving with the Nazis to bring down a Social Democratic provincial government. Manuilsky's address provided the rationalization for these tactics: what better way to aggravate the capitalist crisis than to help Tweedle Dee overthrow Tweedle Dum? In the most detailed analysis of fascism to date Manuilsky argued this way:

'Fascism is not a belated historical miscarriage of the Middle Ages; it is a product of monopoly capitalism based on the concentration and centralization of capital, the growth of trusts and cartels, which leads to the tremendous centralization of the whole apparatus for the oppression of the masses and the inclusion in it of the political parties, the apparatus of Social Democracy, of the reformist trade unions, of the co-operative societies, etc. The reason why its ideological forms bear [a] freakish character is that it is the political superstructure of *decaying* capitalism. But this retrograde ideology is interwoven with all the ideological attributes of bourgeois democracy of the epoch of monopoly capitalism, with the theory of "organized capitalism", of "industrial democracy", "peace in industry", the theory of "state capitalism as a new era in social relationships", the theory of the "non-class state", etc. Fascism . . . did not invent these ideas; it borrowed them ready-made from Social Democracy and clothed them in medieval formulae. And this community of ideas is the best evidence of the kinship between fascism and social fascism.'[123]

In the 'official' view of the Communist International, fascism had come to mean 'organized capitalism', or a tactic of capitalist self-defence common to all parties except those subservient to Moscow. The facile identification of Social Democrats with Nazis arose from the premise that the Communist parties were the sole legitimate

[122] Ibid., p. 554.
[123] Ibid., pp. 548–9.

political organizations of the working class. Such thinking would dominate Comintern discussions until the mid-1930s, when Hitler succeeded in creating a system of militarized 'state capitalism' and frightened Moscow into belatedly accepting Trotsky's strategy of the united front in support of Leon Blum's government in France. In that instance the Comintern deliberately collaborated to create a regime of 'organized capitalism', expecting the French to become a dependable ally against Germany. The hostile reaction of French capital to Blum's experiments in 'economic democracy' caused the French economy to sink deeper into the depression and became one of several arguments in favour of the next about-face in Comintern policy—the alliance with Hitler in 1939. From Stalin's perspective it was eminently preferable that Hitler should seize his *Lebensraum* from the ungrateful French capitalists rather than march the Reichswehr into the Land of Soviets.

7
The Slutskina and
Preobrazhensky Affairs

By the spring of 1931 Soviet economists had backed themselves into a theoretical *cul-de-sac*. Imagining themselves the heirs of Marx and Lenin, they had abandoned the Marxist theory of the business cycle in favour of the notion of a chronic 'general crisis' from which no (spontaneous) recovery was possible. Whatever meaning was attributed to the 'general crisis'—whether it involved a chronic failure of investments or chronically inadequate markets in conditions of 'pure' capitalism—the links between Soviet political economy and the work of Marx or Lenin had grown tenuous indeed. Within two years both Stalin and Varga would realize that they had seriously misjudged capitalism's cyclical resilience. The 'chronic' crisis would give way first to a depression 'of a special kind' and later to an expansion 'of a special kind'. Had Varga been aware that the 'pure' capitalism of the reproduction schemes was merely an abstract analytical device, he might have better understood the process of market creation and anticipated the cyclical recovery of the 1930s.

The theoretical problems experienced by Soviet economists after 1929 resulted from the failure of Soviet cycle theory. This branch of economic research had been crippled by the political dispute with Bukharin and the decision that the Hilferding tradition necessarily culminated in the Right Deviation. Lenin had taken a more sensible view, differentiating between the real Hilferding and the *ersatz* version constructed by Bukharin. *Finance Capital* had won Lenin's respect for its dialectical tension and open-endedness; the theory of 'third parties' provoked his enmity because it substituted a closed system for the complexities of real capitalism. When Soviet

Marxists religiously repeated the slogan of the 'general crisis', they traded theoretical imagination for political conformity.

The concept of the 'general crisis' was a reformulation of Engels's oft-quoted prediction that the ten-year business cycle would give way to 'a more chronic, long drawn-out alternation between a relatively short and slight business improvement and a relatively long, indecisive depression'. Even in the late nineteenth century, according to Engels, capitalism had begun to 'outgrow the control of the laws of the capitalist mode of commodity exchange'. Trusts and cartels were endeavouring to 'regulate production, and thus prices and profits'. Hilferding and Lenin were more cautious than Engels, believing that the laws of capitalism might be *modified* by the interaction between monopoly and competition (crises would become more acute in non-trustified sectors and would ultimately bring down the monopolies themselves), but also asserting that the laws studied by Marx could not be outgrown without a change of property relations and unified economic planning. So long as social production was privately appropriated, investments could not be planned, and production would continue to follow its anarchic pattern. Hilferding's *Finance Capital* and Lenin's *Imperialism*, each in its own way, provided a model of how the economic laws explained in *Capital* could be applied to modern phenomena.

The threat of fascism in the 1930s made it necessary to relate Marx's laws to the emerging role of the modern state. Lenin had always maintained that an understanding of the state must begin with the dialectical interaction between politics and economics. In 1917 he had written that 'state-monopoly capitalism is a complete *material* preparation for socialism' and 'the *penultimate* rung on the ladder of history' rising to socialism.[1] The 1930s brought a second round of pervasive state intervention and again raised many of the issues Lenin and Bukharin had debated concerning the years 1914–18. Having emphasized the tenacity of competition (as opposed to 'organized capitalism') in their polemics with Bukharin, Soviet economists were ill-equipped to foresee or explain the end of *laissez-faire*, entrepreneurial capitalism. While they identified fascism with 'organized capitalism', they simultaneously claimed that 'organized capitalism' was a figment of Bukharin's imagi-

[1] Lenin, *Selected Works*, II, p. 287.

nation. By implication fascism did not and could not exist. This conclusion may have been comforting, but it proved unrealistic. By the end of the decade it would come as a revelation to Varga and his associates that the capitalist state actually did possess a significant capacity for interfering with the business cycle.

In 1931 Evgeny Preobrazhensky published *The Decline of Capitalism*, the last expression of the Hilferding tradition in Soviet thought. The book's intention was to build upon the ideas of Hilferding and Lenin so as to ascertain more clearly how the modification of economic laws would alter the pattern of cyclical fluctuations. As a leading spokesman of the Trotskyist Opposition, Preobrazhensky had been expelled from the party in 1927 and exiled to Siberia for his work on domestic economic policy. When Stalin told Bukharin that the law of value must be suppressed within the Soviet Union in the interest of 'primitive socialist accumulation', Preobrazhensky left the Opposition and rejoined the party. In the hope of avoiding further political difficulties he concentrated his attention on the affairs of the capitalist countries. *The Decline of Capitalism* sought to predict the outcome of the crisis of 1929 by interpreting the available facts in the light of the law of value. Methodologically, the work stood squarely in the classical Marxist tradition; politically it was an affront to Stalin. Preobrazhensky's fatal indiscretion was to suggest that the progress of Marxist theory required more than quotations from the Leader.

The year 1931 saw the most dramatic political interference thus far in almost every field of Soviet academic life.[2] In economics this intervention led to the decision that Preobrazhensky's use of the theory of disproportionalities was anti-Marxist. But Preobrazhensky was by no means the only economist to fall victim to the personality cult during that year. S.D. Slutskina, a little-known writer of no lasting theoretical significance, suffered the same fate. Early in the year she published *The Basic Laws of the Development of Imperialism*, subtitled 'The Law of Uneven Development and the

[2] For an assessment of the causes of political intervention and its general effect on scholarly research, see John Barber, 'Stalin's Letter to the Editors of *Proletarskaya Revolyutsiya*', *Soviet Studies*, XXVIII, no. 1 (January 1976), pp. 21–41; see also Barber's 'The Establishment of Intellectual Orthodoxy in the USSR, 1928–34', *Past and Present*, no. 83 (May 1979), pp. 141–64.

Decay of Capitalism'. Thematically related to Preobrazhensky's work, Slutskina's book contained a grievous political error: she quoted Rudolf Hilferding on the law of value and did not pay adequate attention to Stalin's role in the 'Leninist stage' of political economy. The Slutskina incident served as the prologue to the Preobrazhensky affair and offered Stalinists the opportunity to reprimand severely the 'rotten liberals' who continued to stray beyond the guidelines of 'official' thought. The joint effect of the two incidents was so traumatic for the economic community that the economists thereafter prudently scrutinized official documents before—and often in place of—thinking. After 1931 Soviet writers would disagree with one another within the bounds of discourse established by Stalin and Varga, but rarely would they overstep them.

1. The Slutskina Incident

Slutskina's book appeared innocent enough at first glance. Confusion had been rife in Soviet economic circles since the autumn of 1929, and her work was designed to summarize, in textbook form, the conclusions reached to date. On the crucial issue of the day Slutskina was scrupulously precise. The cause of crises was 'the contradiction between the social [character of] production and private appropriation'.[3] Using the same terminology as Varga, Slutskina wrote: '*The contradiction between production and consumption, between the unlimited character of production . . . and the limited scope of consumption . . . is the central focus of all the contradictions of capitalism.*'[4] The conditions of realization in capitalist society were circumscribed by 'antagonistic relations of distribution', the principal expression of which was the displacement of living labour-power by machines. Thus the 'share of the working class in national income' was declining, and in 'several countries' there had been 'a fall of real wages' and 'the absolute impoverishment of the proletarian masses'.[5] Pursuing received opinion in all its intricacies, Slutskina

[3] S.D. Slutskina, *Osnovnye Zakonomernosti Razvitiya Imperializma*, Moscow and Leningrad 1931, p. 12.
[4] Ibid., p. 20.
[5] Ibid., p. 144.

faithfully coupled her description of technological unemployment with the contradictory observation that 'capitalism cannot resolve the problem of the technological revolution'.[6] To overestimate the installation of new technology was a Bukharinist error; to underestimate it was to subscribe to the Trotskyist theory of 'stagnation' (a reference to Trotsky's address to the Comintern Third Congress in 1921). The correct view was that capitalism entailed an 'extraordinary unevenness' in the development of the productive forces: 'By negating competition, monopolies negate the stimulus to develop technology. But at the same time, monopolies, which exist side by side with competition, bring to life new technological improvements.'[7]

As if these observations were not themselves sufficiently tortuous, Slutskina added another layer of confusion when she explained just what she meant by unevenness. By adopting Hilferding's account of how the price system governed relations between industries, she offered a disproportionality theory of crises and thus directly contradicted her comments elsewhere about the centrality of the incongruity between production and consumption. The only plausible interpretation of this inconsistency is that she was not fully aware of the differences between the two approaches. In classical capitalism, she explained, crises had been caused by uneven movements in prices and the rate of profit and were resolved by corresponding reallocations of the social capital. The continuous movement of capital from one branch of production to another created a 'levelling' tendency whereby the rate of profit was again equalized at the social average. This process of 'levelling', or of overcoming cyclical unevenness, had been interrupted by the rise in the organic composition of capital and its subsequent immobilization: 'Fastened in its fixed component . . . in the form of durable machines, buildings, blast furnaces, coal mines . . . turbo-generators, and so forth, capital must retain its existing form over a number of years and is not able, with its previous facility, to flow from one capitalist stream into another; it loses its "nomadic" character in the pursuit of a higher norm of profit.'[8]

[6] Ibid., p. 67.
[7] Ibid., p. 58.
[8] Ibid., p. 6.

To illustrate the phenomenon of immobilization Slutskina returned to Hilferding. *Finance Capital* had demonstrated that cartels were formed to protect and increase the rate of profit on existing fixed capital. In Hilferding's words: 'Cartelization signifies in the first place a change in the rate of profit. This change is accomplished at the expense of the rate of profit in other capitalist industries. The equalization of the rate of profit to the same level cannot be accomplished by means of a redistribution of capital . . . cartelization means that the competition of capital for spheres of investment is impaired.' Expanding Hilferding's thesis, Slutskina continued: 'The further the process of cartelization advances, . . . the greater are the limitations imposed upon the law of value and the law of the average norm of profit. One norm of profit exists for the large, cartelized branches of industry, another for the small, unorganized branches of industry. *The inequality of profits on the basis of the process of cartelization . . . produces a growing unevenness of development of the separate branches of capitalism.*'[9]

Hilferding had argued that excessive capital accumulation in the organized branches would accentuate disproportionalities and crises. Slutskina took the same view. An 'over-accumulation of capital' by cartels was the source of excess industrial capacity, and the existence of redundant fixed capital was the distinguishing feature of monopolistic 'rottenness'.

To judge from this account, the problem of unevenness could be analysed quite satisfactorily without reference to Lenin's *Imperialism*, let alone Stalin's 'contribution' to the further development of Leninism. The awkward fact was that Stalin considered himself the party's leading authority on unevenness. In the struggle with Trotsky he had insisted that the law of uneven development was the justification for socialism in one country. The reader will recall that Trotsky and Lenin had originally disagreed over the proximity of international revolution. Lenin had allowed for the victory of socialism in a few countries, possibly even in one country, whereas Trotsky thought the level of development throughout Europe was more or less uniform and would lead to an international socialist republic or a United States of Europe. When Stalin revived this issue in the mid-1920s, Trotsky replied that unevenness in the

[9] Ibid., p. 8; cf. Hilferding, *Das Finanzkapital*, p. 316.

tempo of economic growth had increased (America had overtaken Europe and the colonies were industrializing), while the *level* of development, through this same process, was subject to certain 'equalizing tendencies'.[10] Reducing the discussion to banalities, Stalin then retorted that levelling was 'one of the conditions for the increasing unevenness of development in the period of imperialism'.[11] This widely-acclaimed nonsense, in Stalin's mind at least, qualified him as Lenin's leading disciple. Economists with even a modicum of political sense either steered clear of 'tempos', 'levels', and their relation to unevenness, or buttressed their remarks with copious quotations from the Leader. In citing Hilferding instead, Slutskina committed a political outrage. Her innocent survey of the relation between monopolistic prices and decay took on the appearance of a political statement—possibly even from a Trotskyist perspective.

To this original *naïveté* Slutskina added several other instances of indiscretion. Lenin had spoken of the co-existence of monopoly and competition. Slutskina understood Lenin to mean that a new law was involved: 'This dialectical co-existence of contradictory tendencies gives a synthesis, which is the law of motion of monopolistic capitalism.'[12] After the incident with Varga, the 'office' was not interested in new 'laws', still less one that could be confused with a synthesis, whatever that meant. Further difficulties arose when Slutskina claimed that the 'possibility' of a crisis became a reality with the development of the credit cycle.[13] Later she wrote: 'In the epoch of imperialism, control over credit relations lies fully in the hands of the state. . . . In the epoch of imperialism, we see complete state control over loans and debts.'[14] Was this a theory of 'organized capitalism' or a reversion to the ideology of Kondrat'ev, Pervushin, and the bourgeois *kreditniki?* The reader was left to speculate. A hostile reviewer might easily find grounds for suspicion in Slutskina's further comment that ' "regulation" by way of credit can, through a change in the interest rate, exert one or another influence on the conjuncture.'[15]

[10] *Pravda* (14 December 1926).
[11] Stalin, *Works*, IX, p. 110.
[12] Slutskina, *Osnovnye Zakonomernosti*, p. 8.
[13] Ibid., pp. 13–14.
[14] Ibid., p. 83.
[15] Ibid., p. 135.

Slutskina's disjointed and careless arguments arose from her endeavour to popularize recent discussions without offering a clear theoretical perspective of her own. Thus she duly rebuked Hilferding for the theory of 'organized capitalism', Bukharin for that of 'pure imperialism', and Trotsky for the theory of 'equalization' or levelling. Stalin was recognized as an authority on unevenness and the necessity of 'the full construction of socialism in a single country'.[16] The book was neither a theoretical nor political provocation in any calculated sense; it was merely the work of a second-rank author with little political awareness. The editors responsible for its publication by Gosplan, the state planning agency, justifiably wrote in the foreword, 'Not all the problems touched on by Comrade Slutskina are worked out to the same degree.' In particular, the editors saw the need for an 'expanded critique of anti-Leninist theories of imperialism'.

I. Markov, the first writer to review Slutskina's work, endorsed these editorial concerns. In the journal *Problemy Ekonomiki* he congratulated Slutskina for demonstrating the decisive force of the law of uneven development 'on the basis of the works of Lenin-Stalin'.[17] But he also noted: 'The uncritical use by Comrade Slutskina of quotations from Hilferding might give cause for the charge that she has slipped into Hilferding's point of view.'[18] The work was careless in its treatment of the 'credit theory of crises', and its discussion of the law of value was simply 'incorrect'. Monopoly prices did not constitute a limitation on the law of value: they were merely 'a modified form of the law of value in the epoch of monopoly capitalism'.[19] Notwithstanding these criticisms, Markov thought Slutskina's oversights minor and felt they could be rectified by 'collective, comradely criticism'. On the whole, the book was a 'valuable' contribution to the Marxist theory of imperialism and would give 'a further impetus to creative work on those problems that the author has worked out either incompletely or mistakenly.'[20]

Other commentators saw a need for much more than 'comradely'

---

[16] Ibid., p. 140.
[17] See Markov's review in *Problemy Ekonomiki*, no. 7–8 (July–August 1931), p. 138.
[18] Ibid., p. 141.
[19] Ibid., p. 143.
[20] Ibid., p. 144.

criticism. In the journal of Varga's Institute another reviewer complained of Slutskina's 'weak attempt' to criticize the Trotskyists and the Rightists who had waged 'merciless attacks' in the hope of contaminating 'the purity of Leninist theory'. Not only had Slutskina passed over Stalin's contribution to the theory of unevenness; even more horrendous was her borrowing from the Trotskyist Preobrazhensky in her treatment of the law of value. In *The New Economics*, his major publication of the 1920s, Preobrazhensky had described how monopolies attempted to manipulate the law of value in the interest of capital accumulation. 'The idea of a "limitation on the law of value" in the epoch of imperialism', according to this second critic, 'has been adopted by Slutskina from Comrade Preobrazhensky, the one-time theorist of Trotskyism. Lenin, giving a brilliant analysis of imperialism, always stressed the contrary view that the laws of imperialism are based on the general laws of the development of capitalism.'[21] To propose a 'limitation' of these laws was to associate oneself with 'deviations from Marxism-Leninism . . . in the direction of the theory of "organized capitalism" and the Trotskyists' theory of "stagnation".'[22] For these reasons, Slutskina's book could not 'under any circumstances be recommended as a text for the study of the Leninist theory of imperialism and the law of uneven development'.[23]

Slutskina's fortunes took a stunning turn for the worse late in October 1931. In a long and bitter denunciation of editorial 'liberalism', Stalin upbraided the journal *Proletarskaya Revolyutsiya* for publishing what he termed Trotskyist 'contraband' about the history of the Bolshevik party. Weary of intellectual debates, Stalin declared Trotskyism the advance guard of counter-revolution. 'That is why liberalism in the attitude towards Trotskyism . . . is block-headedness bordering on crime, on treason to the working class. That is why the attempts of certain "*littérateurs*" . . . to smuggle disguised Trotskyist rubbish into our literature must meet with a determined rebuff.'[24] Was it not obvious, demanded

[21] See the review by Amatuni in *Mirovoe Khozyaistvo i Mirovaya Politika*, no. 9 (September 1931), p. 99.
[22] Ibid.
[23] Ibid., p. 102.
[24] Stalin, *Works*, XIII, p. 102.

Stalin, that a Bolshevik editorial board had no business aiding the 'smuggling activities' of Trotskyists?

The sharp attack on *Proletarskaya Revolyutsiya* sent a perceptible shudder through the Soviet press. A number of journals missed an issue, reappearing with editorial self-criticisms and a catalogue of articles on 'contraband' and 'wrecking'. Gosplan hurriedly marshalled a party 'brigade' to hold Slutskina responsible for her 'revision' of the Leninist theory of imperialism. Repeating Stalin's warnings against 'Trotskyist rubbish', a triumvirate of party functionaries charged Slutskina with having effaced the difference between Hilferding and Lenin and with sharing the opinions of the 'counter-revolutionary renegade, Trotsky'. Clear evidence of Slutskina's incipient Trotskyism could be found in her treatment of equalization as a more important tendency than unevenness.[25] Slutskina had not grasped even the ABC of Marxism: she had not learned that equalization was both the result and further cause of unevenness, as Stalin had repeatedly explained. In her economic analysis she had adopted Hilferding's view that monopolies could regulate production and prices, themselves being consciously regulated by the monetary authorities. Other economists—the reference was clearly to Varga—were advised to beware of falling into a similar error: 'Not long ago in our literature several economists, starting with an analogous thesis concerning the "organized character" of credit relations in contemporary capitalism, drew the conclusion that the present economic crisis ... will not be accompanied by credit and monetary upheavals. Reality has put this "theory" to rout.'[26]

A similar collective denunciation appeared in *Problemy Ekonomiki*, the journal that had published Markov's original review. Slutskina was accused of adopting 'the positions of Hilferdingism and Trotskyism'. The entire party knew full well that Stalin had 'worked out and developed' Lenin's theory of unevenness in the struggle against 'counter-revolutionary Trotskyism and all opportunist theories of "organized" capitalism'.[27] Slutskina's Trotskyist

[25] Nik. Il'yukhov, M. Priduvalov, and Zhukovskaya, 'Protiv Revizii Leninskoi Teorii Imperializma', *Bol'shevik*, no. 21 (15 November 1931), pp. 89–90.

[26] Ibid., p. 94.

[27] F. Kyun, S. Sergeev, and N. Snezhko, 'Protiv Trotskistskovo Izvrascheniya Leninskovo Zakona Neravnomernovo Razvitiya Imperializma', *Problemy Ekonomiki*, no. 10–12 (October-December 1931), p. 144.

perspective, rooted in 'Hilferdingism', led to the theory of 'two regulators' and two 'sectors', a manifest perversion of Lenin's belief that imperialism did not escape the laws of pre-monopoly capitalism.

The party's leading theoretical journal, *Bol'shevik*, entered the fray with an article by B. Borilin, Bukharin's former antagonist. Surveying an entire panorama of deviations, Borilin pointed to the real message of the Slutskina affair: after nearly a decade and a half of Soviet power the time had come for Marxist economists to cleanse themselves of the influence of Hilferding, Trotsky, and the like and to begin developing the Leninist stage of political economy. The class struggle on the economic front had to be mercilessly intensified, the fighters for pure theory armed with the writings of Stalin:

'When we speak of the Leninist stage of economic theory we must also include the further development of Marxism-Leninism given in the works of Comrade Stalin, which represents a luxurious deposit in the theoretical treasure-house of Marxism-Leninism. Economists have almost completely neglected to consider the question of working out Comrade Stalin's role in the area of economic theory.'[28]

Slutskina had won the distinction of becoming the first victim of the cult of personality among economists concerned with international affairs. Stalin's heavy-handed intervention prompted a rash of confessions. In a letter to *Problemy Ekonomiki* Slutskina recanted her errors. 'I consider it my duty as a Bolshevik-Leninist', she wrote, 'to provide in my future work, on the basis of the works of Lenin, Stalin, and party decisions, an extensive critique of the whole system of counter-revolutionary Trotskyism and to wage a merciless struggle against every sort of opportunism and rotten liberalism.'[29] The promised critique was not long in coming. Early in 1932 Slutskina confessed in detail how she had been contaminated by 'Hilferdingism' and Trotskyism, two deviations that

[28] Borilin, 'Protiv Izkazhenii Marksistsko-Leninskoi Teorii na Ekonomicheskom Fronte', *Bol'shevik*, no. 23–24 (30 December 1931), p. 72.

[29] See the letter in *Problemy Ekonomiki*, no. 10–12 (October-December 1931), p. 160.

had been systematized in the writings of Evgeny Preobrazhensky.[30] Markov's self-criticism followed Slutskina's. While admitting to a lack of Bolshevik vigilance, the unfortunate reviewer protested that he could not be held personally responsible for Slutskina's revisionism. After all, it was not he, but Slutskina who had quoted Rudolf Hilferding—an act that 'in itself is inadmissible and intolerable in the works of Communists'.[31] Next, the editors of *Problemy Ekonomiki* avowed that they too had been guilty of 'rotten liberalism' and insufficient Bolshevik vigilance, as shown by their publication of Markov's review. In future they would wage 'a decisive struggle, with Bolshevik implacability, against all distortions of Marxism-Leninism on the front of economic theory'.[32] The result of the Slutskina affair was the transformation of economic theory into a fighting 'front' in the class struggle. From that time on, 'brigades' of critics would periodically be marshalled to attack both Trotskyist deviants and their 'rotten liberal' sympathizers. When Preobrazhensky's *Decline of Capitalism* appeared, the newly mobilized 'vigilantes' were anxious to redeem their tarnished reputations.

2. The Preobrazhensky Affair

With the single exception of Trotsky himself, Preobrazhensky had been the foremost theorist of the Left Opposition, and certainly its most gifted economist. He had been the most vigorous among Bukharin's critics on domestic issues in demanding that the Soviet government manipulate internal prices, turn the terms of trade against the peasants, and pursue a programme of 'primitive socialist accumulation'. By 1931 Preobrazhensky had become alarmed at the consequences of forced collectivization and began to reconsider his earlier opinions. In a manuscript submitted to *Problemy Ekonomiki* he argued that the pace of industrialization during the second five-

---

[30] Slutskina, 'K Teorii Monopol'noi Tseny', *Problemy Ekonomiki*, no. 2–3 (February-March 1932), pp. 92–123.

[31] See the letter in *Problemy Ekonomiki*, no. 10–12 (October-December 1931), p. 160.

[32] 'Ot Redaktsii', *Problemy Ekonomiki*, no. 10–12 (October-December 1931), p. 164.

year plan had to decelerate in order to allocate greater material incentives. The 'hypertrophy of tempos in the development of heavy industry' had to give way to a period of adjustment and widening of the existing bottlenecks. Otherwise a crisis of over-production would occur in Department I. Not surprisingly, the manuscript was never published. One critic who saw the work remarked that in Preobrazhensky's 'schemes we have a clearly contrabandist penetration of the Trotskyist "declining curve" [with respect to the domestic economy], a Trotskyist denial of the socialist character of our economy . . . of the fact that we have entered the period of socialism and that a planned economy guarantees crisis-free development'.[33]

In *The Decline of Capitalism* Preobrazhensky confirmed sus-picions of his ideological relapse by applying to the capitalist countries the concepts he had earlier developed in his study of Soviet industrialization. In particular he concentrated on the altered role of the law of value. In *The New Economics* the operation of the law of value had been shown to depend on free competition and the mobility of capital. 'When there is trustification or syndication . . . prices systematically deviate from value. . . . The equalizing of the rate of profit between the trustified branches of production is rendered almost impossible; they are transformed into closed worlds, into the feudal kingdoms of particular capitalist organizations.'[34] Like Bukharin, Preobrazhensky had found the most demonstrative case of the decline in the law of value in the German war economy. 'The regulation of the whole of capitalist production by the bourgeois state reached a degree unprecedented in the history of capitalism. Production . . . was transformed *de facto* into planned production in the most important branches. Free competition was abolished, and the working of the law of value in many respects was almost completely replaced by the planning principle of state capitalism.'[35] The institutions of state capitalism had been dismantled after the war, but the law of value had

[33] G. Roginsky (ed.), *Zakat Kapitalizma v Trotskistskom Zerkale*, Moscow 1932, pp. 57–58.

[34] E. Preobrazhensky, *The New Economics*, trans. by Brian Pearce, London 1965, p. 152.

[35] Ibid., p. 153.

nevertheless failed to regain its former role as the pre-eminent regulator of capitalist society. American monopolies had imposed their own value relationships on international markets, and in Europe there were initial indications that bourgeois democracy might give way to state intervention in the labour market by way of fascist dictatorships. The objective of such dictatorships would be to offset stagnation and to compete with American monopolies by driving wages below the cost of the reproduction of labour-power:

'In the period when free competition reigned . . . the period when capitalism was describing an upward curve, it could permit itself the luxury of buying organized labour-power on the basis of the law of value. . . . In the period of capitalist decline, however, with reduced reproduction and the growth of unproductive demand, it is obliged to introduce a new type of labour discipline, organized in a compulsory manner and subjected to the fascist state through the fascist [trade] unions. And this means restructuring the operation of the law of value on the labour market to the advantage of the exploiting class.'[36]

In 1931 Preobrazhensky extended this analysis to include an original theory that the 'structural peculiarities' of monopoly capitalism had imparted a new pattern to the classical business cycle. Repudiating the 'official' perception of the 'problem of markets', he argued that 'Marx was perfectly correct to consider consumption in capitalist society a function of production'.[37] To say that there was idle capacity because demand was insufficient was, as Marx had once remarked, a tautology rather than a theory. The real problem was why the accumulation of capital no longer *created* the required demand. In the past a cyclical recovery had always reabsorbed the army of unemployed and created a 'supplementary market' for both consumer and capital goods. 'The basic fact is that expanded reproduction, on its own . . . would resolve the problem of markets.'[38] Instead of explaining the failure of the recovery mechanism, Soviet economists were now relying on 'quotations from our teachers'.[39] Too often they satisfied themselves 'with a

---

[36] Ibid., p. 159.
[37] Preobrazhensky, *Zakat Kapitalizma*, Moscow and Leningrad 1931, p. 8.
[38] Ibid., p. 9.
[39] Ibid., p. 4.

simple repetition of the general Marxist position that crises are explained by the contradiction between the social character of production and the private character of appropriation . . . the whole problem consists precisely in revealing the economic content of this formula.'[40]

Defying the prescribed orthodoxy, Preobrazhensky declared that he would rely instead on the methodology of *Capital*. Marx had believed that the unevenness of the renewal of fixed capital was 'the most direct and immediate cause of crises' and the most decisive factor in shaping the cycle. 'Since Marx was familiar with such unevenness and used it to explain the periodicity of crises, the task is to construct schemes of reproduction and of the cycle that start with the laws of proportionality, established in *Capital* Volume 2, and with the unevenness of the renewal and expansion of fixed capital. Then the analysis of the capitalist cycle . . . will portray how a typical periodic general economic crisis matures . . . [and will indicate] that there is no contradiction between the second volume of *Capital* and the third [where Marx considered the limits on consumption].'[41] In effect Preobrazhensky proposed to renew the work of Soviet cycle theorists, that of Spektator in particular, for 'he and a few other economists underlined the exceptionally important role of the process of the reproduction of fixed capital both for the theory of reproduction and for the theory of crises'.[42]

Reviewing different types of disproportionalities, Preobrazhensky illustrated how in each case a balance was restored through the action of the law of value. Were overproduction to occur in Department II, the prices of consumer goods would fall. The wage fund of the capitalists in heavy industry would then purchase a larger volume of labour-power; the rate of profit in this sector would thus rise, and through this stimulus to expanded reproduction the price realignment would ultimately broaden the market for consumer goods. Conversely, the emergence of overproduction in Department I would encourage renewed activity in the manufacture of consumer goods by lowering the costs of fixed capital and materials. In neither case was there any need for the immediate

[40] Ibid., p. 81.
[41] Ibid., p. 82.
[42] Ibid., p. 38.

physical movement of capital between sectors, only for a change in relative prices. The process of price adjustment partially devalued fixed capital in some industries while enhancing its value in others. The inter-departmental transfer of capital would occur 'through the vehicle of prices'.[43] From this standpoint, the classical response to disproportionalities was even simpler than most other economists, including Slutskina, had supposed.

More important than these examples of partial disproportionality, however, was the case of general overproduction affecting both Departments of industry simultaneously. This type of crisis normally followed a wave of capital construction. A surge of demand for fixed capital caused a general increase in prices and set in motion the process previously discussed by Maksakovsky and the other cycle theorists. When analysing the function of the law of value, Maksakovsky had argued that price movements followed changes in the sphere of production with a time lag. Capitalists responded blindly to high market prices, having no foresight with respect to future demand. As Preobrazhensky observed, they tended 'to adjust to current demand as if it were permanent', the necessary consequence being redundant capacity.[44] Beginning in heavy industry, a crisis would then spread rapidly throughout the economy. Once prices for fixed capital began to fall, the surviving firms would undertake to re-equip so as to reduce production costs: 'It is this re-equipping in order to satisfy a curtailed demand at lower prices that creates an additional market during the period of depression and serves to bring about a turning point in the conjuncture.'[45] Since every cyclical crisis created both the basis of recovery and the preconditions for the next crisis, Preobrazhensky concluded that '*a single acute economic crisis, whatever its origin might be, is sufficient to cause all the subsequent economic crises to repeat themselves periodically*'.[46]

If the classical business cycle was self-regenerating, the next question concerned the role of foreign markets and 'third parties'. On this issue Preobrazhensky departed sharply from Varga and the

[43] Ibid., p. 29.
[44] Ibid., p. 23.
[45] Ibid., p. 24.
[46] Ibid., p. 81.

entire Luxemburgist approach. Lenin had told the Narodniks that capitalism created its own market but periodically required access to foreign trade as a safeguard against domestic disproportionalities. Preobrazhensky agreed emphatically, declaring that 'new markets and the integration of new spheres into the capitalist commodity turnover . . . [make] the capitalist system more elastic with respect to the dynamic of expanded reproduction; they [do] so mainly because they temporarily [ease] disproportions that [arise] within the capitalist section of the world economy.'[47] Abstracting from world trade, Marx had made the same point in *Capital*, writing that a planned economy would safeguard itself against disproportionalities and bottlenecks through a policy of 'continuous relative overproduction'. Preobrazhensky held that the significance of foreign trade could not be measured by the volume of sales. On the contrary, the real purpose of an *external* market was to prevent *domestic* disproportions from causing a multiple contraction of the *internal* market:

'The enhanced possibility of sales abroad must facilitate the disposal of residual commodities that otherwise could not be realized without a crisis. . . . Even if only a part of this residue is sold . . . it has an enormous importance for the entire system. This is true not because of the absolute magnitude of the new market, which in general is of little consequence . . . but because sales in the external market make it possible . . . to check the contraction of the productive apparatus. . . . The new market is not important in its own right, as Rosa Luxemburg mistakenly believed. What matters is that it makes it possible to get by with a far smaller narrowing of the market that capitalism has created internally.'[48] The fact that cyclical recoveries were possible even without access to 'third parties' was 'convincing evidence of how incorrect was Rosa Luxemburg's theory of reproduction in so far as she attempted to criticize Marx on this point'.[49]

If foreign trade was of only secondary consequence, any failure of capitalism's recovery mechanism had to be sought internally, in the altered institutional structure of modern capitalism and its effects

[47] Ibid., p. 15.
[48] Ibid., p. 77.
[49] Ibid., p. 110.

on the law of value. The negative repercussions of monopolies were numerous. To begin with, recoveries were impaired by organizational barriers to entry and by the rise in the organic composition of capital, the enormous cost of establishing a new enterprise.[50] Next came the tendency stressed by Hilferding: monopolies reacted to a crisis not so much by lowering prices and renewing their fixed capital as by restraining output. Whereas in earlier stages of capitalism the profit motive encouraged the expansion of production, monopolies worked in exactly the opposite direction: 'The quest for the greatest profit at the present time leads not to the expansion, but to a contraction of production.'[51] Determined to protect their existing assets, monopolies resisted the introduction of new technology. Bukharin had thought modern capitalism was capable of a 'technological revolution'; Preobrazhensky believed a 'thrombosis' of the productive forces far more likely.[52] In order to preserve the 'hundreds of millions' they had invested in their present equipment, monopolies would forego 'tens of billions' in new production that would have resulted from the classical process of market creation.[53] Like Mendel'son, Preobrazhensky also saw a tendency for mergers to replace bankruptcies. Classical crises destroyed inefficient firms; monopoly capitalism preserved them.[54] The weak lingered on as the productive 'reserve' of the strong, and the monopolistic cycle postponed new construction until technologically obsolescent equipment had been reactivated. In brief, 'the monopolistic structure of capitalism so curtails—or perhaps it would be more true to say, so distorts—the action of the law of value that this law is now unable to regulate the process of reproduction as it did in the epoch of free competition'.[55]

The most distinctive characteristic of monopoly capitalism, and the factor more responsible than any other for altering the rhythm of the business cycle, was the practice of maintaining productive 'reserves'. Although unable to regulate demand, monopolies were

[50] Ibid., p. 13.
[51] Ibid., p. 14.
[52] Ibid., p. 16.
[53] Ibid., p. 31.
[54] Ibid., p. 30.
[55] Ibid., p. 19.

obviously in a far better position to estimate the market than competitive enterprises.[56] The law of value no longer caused productive capacity to overshoot demand in the way suggested by Maksakovsky. Monopolists were more restrained in adding new equipment, and when they did so their chief concern was to forestall the threat of new competition. Since fixed capital must be amortized over a number of years, a degree of 'excess capacity' had always existed in industry. In response to an irregular shift of demand, even competitive enterprises were able to use their existing equipment more intensively. But monopolies were unique in that they deliberately *planned* their reserves and made preparations for unforeseen demand that might otherwise invite new competition. Thus an *entirely new phase* was added to the classical cycle—the phase of reserve building—and the period of new capital construction moved from the immediate aftermath of one crisis to the eve of the next. The end of the reserve-building phase not only triggered the inevitable crisis, but also eliminated the incentive to recover from crises in the traditional way. If capital construction were undertaken in response to the crisis, it would merely duplicate the investments just made. The general tendency of monopoly capitalism was therefore to experience 'a gradual loss of the mechanism of recovery from a crisis'.[57] Periods of construction became brief; crises and depressions tended to lengthen. In the long run the system would gravitate towards simply reproduction: 'In general and on the whole this will mean that the entire capitalist system . . . must enter into conditions in which the very form of the cyclical movement gradually dissolves . . . in which gradual economic development comes to a general halt, and the tendency towards simple reproduction increasingly emerges. For this reason, we can affirm that a general economic crisis under monopolism, if it does not lead to a world war or is not interrupted by a technological revolution, will inevitably become . . . a general social crisis of the entire historic system of capitalism.'[58]

Recoveries were still possible even given this long-run tendency because of the unevenness of development between rival countries

[56] Ibid., p. 28.
[57] Ibid., p. 64.
[58] Ibid., pp. 96–7.

in their struggle for world markets. Even if the capitalist system as a whole now faced a period of contraction, it remained possible for some countries to gain at the expense of others. 'Lenin at this point made a very valuable addition to the Marxist theory of reproduction.'[59] Preobrazhensky referred to Lenin, but his critics would later discover a remarkable affinity between his exposition of unevenness and Trotsky's theory of differentiated *tempos* during an epoch of levelling and stagnation. This is what Preobrazhensky wrote:

'In a crudely simplified form the matter might be presented this way. With a general slowing in the tempo of world economic growth, development comes to a general halt at some points and regression might even occur, as in England for example; in other countries relations bordering on simple reproduction are established . . .; and finally, in a third group of countries, such as France, South America, certain colonies, and especially the United States, the tempo of economic development is more rapid than the world average. Thanks to this unevenness . . . in tempos of movement, separate parts of the world entity might experience the conditions for a . . . recovery, passing over into an expansion. . . . The growth in world purchasing power . . . is divided unevenly between separate capitalist countries, with the consequence that at some points a rise in tempos occurs, a forward movement, at other points a cessation of movement. As a result, we get not simply a cyclical form of movement on the part of the whole, but movement in one part of an entity, accompanied by a slowdown or even regression in other parts.'[60]

Reproducing the theory of differentiated tempos with which Trotsky had confronted Stalin, Preobrazhensky must have been aware that he was courting disaster. Even if he were to escape the charge of having produced 'Trotskyist contraband', how could he avoid the accusation of the opposite deviation: Bukharinism? Not only had he disagreed with Stalin on the compulsiveness of investments; he had also argued that monopolies could plan their 'reserves' and insulate themselves against the effect of crises. Bukharin had thought of 'organized capitalism' in terms of

[59] Ibid., p. 55.
[60] Ibid., p. 56.

expanded reproduction; Preobrazhensky was now setting forth a similar view of monopolistic planning, with the sole difference that he expected simple reproduction. On one point at least he did attempt to protect himself by commenting that monopolies could neither exert complete control over prices nor predict changes in demand with perfect accuracy. That would require a single regulator in the form of a unified economic plan. Hilferding had been right to argue that when every monopoly regulates its own activities independently, 'the entire system turns out [in Preobrazhensky's words] to be in a condition of growing disorganization'. Disproportionalities remained inevitable, and the absence of an integrative plan constituted 'the basic structural contradiction of the economics of imperialism'.[61] The fact remained, however, that Preobrazhensky's scheme of monopolistic reproduction was closely patterned after Marx's work in *Capital* Volume 2. Marx had described the case of 'pure' capitalism; Preobrazhensky made an analogous abstraction and spoke of 'pure monopolism'.[62] And what, the Stalinists would inquire, was pure monopolism? Preobrazhensky had obviously forgotten the Leninist thesis that monopolies and competition co-exist.

Had Soviet economists been free to judge Preobrazhensky's work on theoretical rather than political grounds, they might have found it worthy of serious consideration. In its fidelity to the method of *Capital, The Decline of Capitalism* was without doubt one of the most impressive works ever to appear in Soviet Russia. Varga had failed in his attempt to distinguish between the 'classical' and 'unique' elements of the modern business cycle; Preobrazhensky proposed to resolve the dilemma by deeming the current economic crisis the first 'classical crisis of monopoly capitalism'.[63] More consistently than any of his contemporaries, he strove to analyse the interaction between the systemic crisis and the cyclical fluctuations, a problem that had been a source of anxiety since the time of Engels. According to Preobrazhensky, the systemic crisis had begun with the imperialist war: the war itself had been 'a crisis of *transition* from one tempo of economic development to another,

[61] Ibid., p. 34.
[62] Ibid., p. 43.
[63] Ibid., p. 49.

slower tempo. Perhaps it was this very factor that explained the fact that capitalism reacted to this transition with a truly exceptional *intensification* of the struggle to redivide the world, that is, with war.' The crisis of 1920–21 had been atypical because of postwar readjustments, leaving the years since 1921 to provide the data with which the new theory of the cycle could be illustrated.

In much of his study Preobrazhensky concentrated on the American economy, where extraneous effects left over from the war years were less important than in Europe. The rapid growth of American exports had caused a multiple expansion of the domestic market during the war and immediately afterwards. Yet as Preobrazhensky pointed out, after 1921 'the share of exports in the production of the United States as a percentage of the value of the total product returned to prewar proportions despite the large absolute growth of exports. This fact quite clearly indicates that the further expansion of the United States relied primarily on the growth of the internal market'.[64] How had this internal market continued to develop in the absence of its former stimulus from trade? The real income of workers and farmers had certainly risen, but 'the most important element . . . was the expansion of demand within industry itself, both for new fixed capital and for other means of production. When the United States had faced a rapid export expansion in the war period, this growing demand was met through the more intensive use of existing equipment. A further expansion of production [after 1921], however, required an enormous increase of fixed capital.'[65] Contrary to Varga's belief, neither personal consumption nor the conversion of 'third parties' into commodity producers had provided the impetus for recovery. Instead, expanded reproduction had begun in the manner suggested by Marx, the only difference being that a relative scarcity of the means of production in this case resulted from wartime neglect of the capital stock rather than from 'classical' bankruptcies. With the exception of the year 1924, the expansion then continued right up to 1927.

In a system of competitive capitalism the year 1927 would have been one of economic crisis. Why had a depression occurred instead? In Preobrazhensky's opinion the answer lay in the

[64] Ibid., p. 110.
[65] Ibid., p. 113.

monopolistic practice of reserve building. Large enterprises could protect themselves against potential competitors only when their productive reserve was large enough to cover any unexpected rise in demand. Discussing the events of 1927, Preobrazhensky wrote as follows:

'At this point there appeared the most interesting moment in the unfolding of the cycle in the United States, namely the transition of the whole system to a rapid increase of its fixed capital, to the level of reserves characteristic of monopolism. More advanced equipment was brought into use, and this, plus the widespread practice of selling on credit in the consumer market, not only dampened the depression that had begun in 1927, but also guaranteed a supplementary expansion for American industry that lasted for more than two additional years.'[66] Explaining the 'riddle' of 1927, Preobrazhensky believed he had answered the question posed by Eventov: the years 1927–30 were not a self-contained cycle but merely a monopolistic adjunct to the classical pattern.

But the feature that made Preobrazhensky's work so obviously superior to Varga's was its focus on the unevenness of reproduction as the 'material basis' of changes in the level of economic activity. Better than any other Marxist writing of its day, *The Decline of Capitalism* demonstrated the inherent flexibility of the tradition of cycle theory begun in *Capital*. At the same time, it clarified the functional role of 'excess' industrial capacity and potentially removed a major obstacle to further progress in Soviet theory. A monopolist typically responded to the high organic composition of capital by deliberately planning for redundant capacity. Were he to assume, for example, a 4 per cent annual increase in demand over a five-year period, he would plan on a reserve capacity of 22 per cent. Within a ten-year framework the reserve would rise to 48 per cent. Although familiar with these problems because of his experience with Soviet domestic planning, Preobrazhensky remained uncertain as to what the typical reserve allowance of a capitalist might be. Nevertheless, he did see that the existence of reserves would significantly complicate the prospects for cyclical recovery. His analysis indicated that before the 'material basis' for a new cycle could be created (through a resumption of investments) a lengthy period of capital consumption, or reserve depletion, might inter-

[66] Ibid., p. 114.

vene. The length of monopolistic crises, in other words, would vary directly with the size of reserves.

Monopolistic 'planning' impeded recoveries, but by applying Marx's reasoning Preobrazhensky also realized that the possibility of recovery could not be ruled out in advance. Marx had shown that expanded reproduction generated disproportions; economic contraction, Preobrazhensky argued, would do the same. At some point the most durable forms of fixed capital would face paralysis because the less durable were not being replaced. The inevitable resumption of replacement demand constituted the 'natural limit' to cyclical contraction, or as Marx would have said, the 'material basis' for a new turning point in the cycle.[67] Whether or not a genuine expansion would follow would be determined by the scale of fixed-capital renewal. The predictive value of this argument can be gauged by comparing the following remark with the Stalinist view that the 'general crisis' precluded any hope of recovery:

'The most interesting year from the point of view of overcoming the crisis, to judge by all the signs, will be 1932. It is precisely in . . . 1932, and even more so in 1933, that it must become totally clear whether the capitalist system has lost its mechanism of recovery from a crisis, the mechanism that was characteristic of the epoch of free competition, or whether it still retains some reserves in this respect.'[68]

Until this question was finally answered, Preobrazhensky expected the capitalists to adopt any means available to raise the rate of exploitation. The rise of fascism would be a necessary consequence of the economic crisis unless such a catastrophe were forestalled by proletarian revolution. The 'official' view held that fascism was the next logical stage in the development of bourgeois democracy. Preobrazhensky insisted on the enormity and novelty of the threat: 'There is now every reason to believe that fascism represents not merely one of the forms of mobilizing bourgeois forces in the struggle with the proletariat, but a general tendency of the capitalist system to replace the bourgeois-democratic form of state . . . with the fascist form of state.'[69] During capitalism's youth the bourgeoisie could afford the ideology of 'Manchesterism'. Despite

[67] Ibid., p. 134.
[68] Ibid., p. 135.
[69] Ibid., p. 141.

concessions to organized labour, the rise of surplus-value had been assured.[70] 'Bourgeois democracy in politics corresponded to the period of classical capitalism and free competition, to the period of extensive action by the law of value.'[71] By distorting the law of value, monopoly capitalism created the need for a new method of determining wages. Fascism 'becomes a new form of state when capital can no longer dominate labour and guarantee the required level of exploitation by the former methods'. With the approach of a 'general social crisis' the bourgeoisie was turning to fascization of the trade unions, or 'their conversion from an instrument of proletarian economic struggle . . . into organs of direct suppression of proletarian resistance, into functioning organs of capital, having as their immediate objective an increase in the norm of exploit-ation'.[72] Fascism was the typical political superstructure of state-monopoly capitalism, the necessary consequence of interference with the law of value, the most direct evidence of the historic decline of the capitalist mode of production.

The reaction to Preobrazhensky's arguments was not merely negative, but so primitive as to surpass understanding, had it not been for Stalin's remarks about 'Trotskyist contraband'. Various authors accused Preobrazhensky of following the deviations of Bukharin, Hilferding, Kondrat'ev, Tugan-Baranovsky, Luxem-burg, Trotsky, Kautsky, and Spektator. How one man could concur with so wide and diverse a range of deviants was never made clear. The first indication of what to expect came from one E. Gromov. At a meeting of the Institute of World Economics and World Politics in March 1931 Preobrazhensky gave a summary of *The Decline of Capitalism*, the book itself having yet to appear. Gromov pounced on the claim that the uneven reproduction of fixed capital was the key to understanding the cycle: 'This position . . . has led . . . to a number of serious errors, at the root of which [is] abstraction from class contradictions in the epoch of the general crisis of capitalism and reduction of the problem of the cycle's modification to the conditions of the turnover of fixed capital.'[73] To Gromov's recollec-

[70] Ibid., p. 142.
[71] Ibid., p. 143.
[72] Ibid., pp. 145–6.
[73] E. Gromov, 'Reviziya Marksa i Lenina pod Flagom Teoreticheskovo "Sintesa" ', *Mirovoe Khozyaistvo i Mirovaya Politika*, no. 4 (April 1931), p. 68.

tion 'Marx never, in any place, said that the basic cause of periodic crises could be the turnover and uneven renewal of fixed capital. . . . *Marx saw the basic, decisive cause of periodic crises . . . in the contradiction between the social character of production and the private, individual form of appropriation, and therefore in the very contradictions of the social process.*'[74]

The fact that Preobrazhensky's completed book became available after Stalin's denunciation of *Proletarskaya Revolyutsiya* made its fate a foregone conclusion. I. Dvorkin, an energetic pursuer of 'Trotskyists' and one of the work's first reviewers, declared that 'Preobrazhensky's book . . . is a Trotskyist book, and the theory of crises and imperialism that it develops is a Trotskyist theory, assembled on the basis of Trotskyist methodology'.[75] Endorsing the Trotskyist 'theory of absolute stagnation' and the Bukharin-Hilferding theory of 'organized capitalism', Preobrazhensky had denied the law of uneven development and proclaimed the end of the business cycle. 'Trotskyism', wrote Dvorkin, '. . . declares that in the period of imperialism unevenness does not increase but grows weaker. We get the same thing from Preobrazhensky concerning the replacement of fixed capital. . . . Counter-revolutionary Trotskyism, having become the leading detachment of the counter-revolutionary bourgeoisie, must be grateful to Preobrazhensky for such lofty armaments, for such theoretical assistance.'[76] As Dvorkin saw it, the methodology of Trotskyism was identical to that of Bukharinism: both depended on 'abstractions'. Working with the abstract concept of 'pure monopolism', Preobrazhensky had invented 'the law of increasing reserves' as a form of planning and had overlooked the well-known fact that crises arise 'from the contradiction between the social character of production and the private form of appropriation'.[77] The whole theory of the monopolistic cycle had what Dvorkin called a 'social-fascist essence'.[78] In brief, 'we have before us an anti-Marxist, anti-Leninist, Trotskyist

---

[74] Gromov, 'K Probleme Kapitalisticheskovo Tsikla v Epokhe Vzeobshchevo Krizisa', *Problemy Ekonomiki*, no. 9 (September 1931), p. 93.

[75] I. Dvorkin, 'Trotskistskaya Teoriya Krizisov i Imperializma', *Pod Znamenem Marksizma*, no. 11–12 (November-December 1931), p. 170.

[76] Ibid., p. 187.

[77] Dvorkin, 'Trotskistskaya Teoriya . . .', *Pod Znamenem Marksizma*, no. 1–2 (January-February 1932), p. 60.

[78] Ibid., p. 61.

theory in its most complete and developed form'.[79] It would appear that Dvorkin was unfamiliar with the introduction to *Capital* Volume 1, where Marx said it was the fate of the economist to rely on 'the power of abstraction' rather than controlled experiments.[80]

Anxious to redeem themselves after their involvement in the Slutskina affair, the editors of *Problemy Ekonomiki* found space for a second article by Gromov. Triumphantly satisfied with his earlier insight, Gromov now pronounced *The Decline of Capitalism* 'a clearly Trotskyist document' that subscribed to 'the Kautskyan theory of ultra-imperialism or . . . "organized capitalism" '. The notion that monopolies could create 'a planned reserve of fixed capital' was an abomination: 'it is impossible even to speak of such "reserves" [being] consciously established by "monopolism".'[81] In Preobrazhensky's hands the law of uneven development had been transformed into 'a law of planned capitalist development'.[82] So long as the private character of appropriation existed, the search for profit would involve competition: 'And this "co-existence" of monopoly and competition, as a constant illustration of the law of the "negation of the negation", is preserved right up to the revolutionary "negation" of capitalism.'[83]

Just how ludicrous the criticisms became was revealed by the rising consensus that Preobrazhensky was not only a Trotskyist, but a disguised Luxemburgist too. The 'office' could live with Varga's doctrine of 'third parties'; it could not tolerate the theory of an 'automatic' collapse. And what was the tendency towards simple reproduction, asked the critics, but a modification of Luxemburgist breakdown theory, which tended to 'demobilize the working class, fatalistically inviting it to wait for the moment that the capitalist "machine" grinds to a halt'?[84] Borilin expounded the 'official' view of Rosa Luxemburg in these terms. 'Rosa did not understand that the cause of the collapse lies in such "things" as anarchy and the class

[79] Ibid., p. 70.

[80] Marx, *Capital* Volume 1, p. 90.

[81] Gromov, 'Novye "Otkroveniya" E. Preobrazhenskovo v Svete Leninskoi Teorii Imperializma', *Problemy Ekonomiki*, no. 10–12 (October–December 1931), p. 66.

[82] Ibid., p. 70.

[83] Ibid., p. 63.

[84] M. Engibaryan, ' "Novaya" "Teoriya" E. Preobrazhenskovo, ili Kontrabanda Trotskizma', *Bol'shevik*, no. 23–24 (30 December 1931), p. 125.

contradictions of capitalism, and not at all in a mechanically approaching impossibility of expanded reproduction. She wanted to understand this, her revolutionary instinct pointed in this direction, but in her theory she could not do so. Her theory in fact denies the importance of class contradictions and anarchy.'[85] Apparently forgetting that the Comintern had traditionally considered Luxemburg's views 'ultra-leftist', Borilin praised the insight of Comrade Stalin, who 'in full agreement with Lenin, declares that Rosa's theory of imperialism . . . is a *semi-Menshevik* theory'.[86]

According to A. Zorky, it was Preobrazhensky's Luxemburgist 'fatalism' that led him to believe in the inevitability of fascist dictatorships. Leninism made no provision for 'a new form of state'. True, Lenin had expected the 'state machine' to grow in the epoch of imperialism. But Preobrazhensky believed that 'Monopolism has completely rebuilt capitalism, it has created new relations between classes, a new form of state. . . . Such a theory of fascism has nothing in common with a Marxist-Leninist analysis, with party positions on the question of fascism'.[87] The correct view was that fascism represented a natural outgrowth of bourgeois democracy through the process of fascization.[88] Preobrazhensky's 'left' thesis of fascism's inevitability would have the effect of 'orienting the Communist parties towards passivity'.[89] When Preobrazhensky endorsed Trotsky's view that Communists should act as a 'third force', supporting Social Democrats in the struggle against Hitler, his detractors replied that this strategy would cause the Comintern to follow 'at the tail end of Social Fascism' and thus constituted 'a Trotskyist revision of Leninism'.[90]

All these criticisms eventually led back to the central charge that Preobrazhensky's errors were methodological in origin, that he had, as V. Balkov maintained, omitted the class struggle and fetishized

[85] Borilin, 'Protiv Iskazhenii . . .', p. 62.
[86] Ibid., p. 64.
[87] A. Zorkii, 'Teoreticheskoe Obosnovanie Passivnosti i Khvostizma v Bor'be s Fashizmom', *Mirovoe Khozyaistvo i Mirovaya Politika*, no. 10–12 (October-December 1931), p. 90.
[88] Ibid., p. 96.
[89] Ibid., p. 94.
[90] Ibid., pp. 98–9.

the reproduction of fixed capital: 'The final and chief cause of crises', reiterated Balkov, 'is the contradiction between social production and private appropriation. This definition, which appears to Preobrazhensky to be a banal phrase, establishes the most profound watershed between a genuine Marxist-Leninist theory of crises and all anti-Marxist, anti-Leninist "variations". Synthesized in this definition is the totality of moments that necessarily lead to periodic crises.'[91] The theory of inter-industrial disproportionalities, in Balkov's appraisal, was nothing more than 'the official dogma of Social Fascism' and led directly to the theory of 'organized capitalism': 'All anti-Marxist *proportionalist* theories of crises, which slur over the basic contradiction . . . all these theories differ from one another only in details and in their external form.'[92] E. Gurvich took a similar view, declaring that 'Preobrazhensky has completely distorted the position of Marx and Lenin in saying that capitalist production creates its own markets.'[93] Comrade Stalin had demonstrated that the problem of markets, 'the main problem of capitalism', had become 'monstrously acute'.[94] Lapinsky added that if Preobrazhensky had not attempted to soar over the party like a 'meteor', he would have avoided the deviation of 'economism'.[95] Another author saw *The Decline of Capitalism* as 'a variant of the usual bourgeois theory of disproportionality'.[96] Still another spoke of the need to refute Preobrazhensky's 'new, Trotskyist "variant" of the bourgeois and Menshevik theory of disproportionalities'.[97] A careful study was required of 'the teachings of Marx-Lenin and of all the new additions to the arsenal of Marxist-Leninist science . . . made by Comrade Stalin'.[98] In future all economic research must begin with 'the analysis of the current crisis and its peculiarities given by Comrade Stalin to the Sixteenth Party Congress', an

[91] V. Balkov, 'Kapitalisticheskoe Vosproizvodstvo v Trotskistskom Osveshchenii', *Problemy Ekonomiki*, no. 6 (June 1932), p. 111.

[92] Ibid., p. 116.

[93] Roginsky (ed.), *Zakat Kapitalizma v Trotskistskom Zerkale*, p. 67.

[94] Ibid., pp. 68–9.

[95] *Problemy Mirovovo Krizisa—Diskussiya v Institute Mirovovo Khozyaistva i Mirovoi Politiki Komakademii*, Moscow 1932, p. 86 et seq.

[96] A. Breitman, 'Zakat Kapitalizma v Krivom Trotskistskom Zerkale', *Mirovoe Khozyaistvo i Mirovaya Politika*, no. 10–12 (October-December 1931), p. 80.

[97] Engibaryan, '"Novaya" "Teoriya" . . .', p. 82.

[98] *Problemy Mirovovo Krizisa—Diskussiya*, p. 47.

analysis that was 'extraordinary in its theoretical profundity, clarity, and political accuracy'.[99] Only in this way would it be possible to understand 'the Leninist stage in the development of the Marxist theory of realization and crises'.[100]

How can the substitution of such inanities for intelligent theoretical criticism be explained? The political conditions of 1931 were obviously the principal reason both for the orchestrated assault on Preobrazhensky and for the level of the discussion. None the less, Preobrazhensky's opponents betrayed such appalling ignorance of the classical Marxist texts as to make it difficult to believe they had ever read them. A new generation was now entering Varga's institute, one trained in the 1920s and to whom the prewar Marxist debates were already ancient history. If the newcomers knew virtually nothing of Lenin's writings, could they be expected to be familiar with *Capital*? If they really believed Stalin's speeches theoretically 'profound', could they be expected even to understand a book like *The Decline of Capitalism*? The writers who led the attack on Preobrazhensky were the non-entities who would populate the research 'brigades' of the 1930s and who perhaps really did consider theory a fighting 'front'. Had these people come to the fore in the years after 1931, there would be no purpose in pursuing this study any further. A history of Soviet theory would then better end with Preobrazhensky's last book. No other work of remotely comparable theoretical quality was produced after 1931. As it happened, however, Varga was gradually regaining the leadership of the economic community that he had lost in 1929. And despite his limitations, Varga tended to stand above the sort of vilification to which Preobrazhensky was subjected. Under his stewardship, Soviet economists would find themselves preoccupied for the balance of the 1930s with a problem to which all the debates we have considered thus far were in a sense the prologue: the various experiments in capitalist 'planning' brought on by the Great Depression. Theorists of the stature of Bukharin or Preobrazhensky would make no further appearances. But Adolf Hitler and Franklin Delano Roosevelt were in the wings, awaiting the opportunity to give the Stalinists some practical lessons in 'organized capitalism'.

[99] Ibid., pp. 47–48.
[100] Ibid., p. 57.

8
Hitler, Roosevelt, and Capitalist 'Planning'

Suppression of the Hilferding tradition in Soviet economic theory came at a critical juncture. By the end of 1932 symptoms of economic recovery could be detected in the West. From a Luxemburgist viewpoint no such improvement should have been possible: no new 'third parties' had presented themselves in such countries as Germany and America, and no expansive new markets had been discovered. The Luxemburgist approach, with its emphasis on a chronic crisis, had been suited to the political requirements of 1929–30. Until 1932–3 it even appeared compatible with the facts. After that, however, theory and reality moved in opposite directions. Once again Soviet economists had to begin revising the schedule of capitalist collapse, this time without the assistance that might have come from *Capital* and subsequent developments in the Marxist theory of the business cycle.

For Marx the cyclical pattern of its movement differentiated the capitalist system from every other mode of production in history. But Marx did not give a precise explanation of how the cyclical dynamic might change as capitalism approached its historical *dénouement*. At one point he compared the classical cycle to the movement of the heavenly bodies: 'Just as the heavenly bodies always repeat a certain movement, once they have been flung into it, so also does social production, once it is has been flung into this movement of alternate expansion and contraction.' More than any other single remark, this comparison exemplified the ambiguity of *Capital*. Preobrazhensky had attempted to rejuvenate Marxist theory by analysing modern phenomena exclusively in terms of cycle theory. But the prevailing trend among Marxists had become to replace cycle theory with one of two conflicting hypotheses:

either capitalism was becoming capable of organized prosperity, as Bukharin had argued, or the classical cycle had been supplanted by irregular fluctuations superimposed on a chronic crisis, as the Stalinists claimed.

The experience of the 1930s brought this dilemma into the sharpest possible focus. Affirming that the 'general crisis' was indeed chronic, Stalin and Varga found themselves in the unpleasant position of denying what became steadily more obvious. Early in 1934 the pretence could no longer be sustained. Capitalism, it was announced, had entered a new phase—a depression 'of a special kind'. To announce the new phase was much easier than to explain what it meant. Just what was 'special' about this depression? How did it differ from those discussed in *Capital*? Some economists thought the 'special' character of events after 1933 could be explained only by the rise to power of Hitler and Roosevelt, both of whom inaugurated a period of unprecedented state intervention and 'artificial' market creation. But this line of thought was politically dangerous: to pursue it might lead to the conclusion that 'fascism' provided a cure for economic crises, that the 'fascist' state could 'organize' capitalist society, much as Bukharin had believed. Recoiling from this danger, Varga maintained that the improvement had to be attributed to capitalism's 'internal forces'. Preobrazhensky had been wrong to contemplate failure of the traditional mechanism for overcoming crises.

In his haste Varga overlooked the fact that this position too had unfortunate corollaries. Preobrazhensky had shown that the capitalists traditionally surmounted crises not by *discovering*, but by *creating* new markets through the resumption of investments. How could the theory of internal market creation be reconciled with Stalin's view of the 'problem of markets'? If the recovery mechanism really did remain intact, then it would follow that there was actually nothing 'special' about this depression; on the contrary, there would be every reason to expect a new expansion to ensue, just as it always had in the past. Suspended between the conflicting exigencies of ideological orthodoxy and economic reality, Soviet economists grappled with one central issue for the balance of the 1930s: how to measure the importance of state intervention as opposed to capitalism's spontaneous cyclical forces.

1. The Monetary and Credit Crisis of 1931

The impulse to large-scale state intervention came from the direction Varga had least expected. One of the few matters on which he continued to agree with Hilferding was the impossibility of a monetary and credit crisis in the epoch of finance capital. In the spring of 1931 Varga still believed that finance capital would see to the credit needs of its 'own' enterprises, despite the decline in monopolistic prices. In the firms most directly threatened monopolistic mergers would occur—or 'disguised bankruptcies'—a process Preobrazhensky and Mendel'son had included in the practice of reserve building.[1] In *The Decline of Capitalism* Preobrazhensky had associated the delay in the credit crisis with a slowdown of productive investment and an accumulation of idle money-capital.[2] Varga made the same point in his economic survey for the first quarter of 1931: '*The absence of a credit crisis, the superabundance of loan capital, and the low rates of interest at the beginning of the crisis* . . . are . . . consequences of the general crisis and of the monopolistic degeneration of capitalism.'[3] Both Varga and Preobrazhensky endorsed Hilferding's view that the credit cycle was an epiphenomenon of production and could, in theory, be neutralized.[4] But Hilferding also pointed out that this argument held good only if restrictions on output did not go so far as to threaten the stability of trusts and cartels. At some point, the reduced scale of output would so increase unit costs of production as to clear the way for the intervention of new competitors. In Hilferding's words: Each 'new reduction in output means a further immobilization of capital with the same general expenses and thus a new increase in [per-unit] costs and therefore a further reduction in profit, even if high selling prices are maintained. These conditions lend support to outsiders: the latter can count on low distribution and labour costs, because all [other] prices have been reduced, and

[1] Varga, 'Problemy Krizisa', *Mirovoe Khozyaistvo i Mirovaya Politika*, no. 2–3 (February-March 1931), p. 25.

[2] Preobrazhensky, *Zakat Kapitalizma*, p. 124.

[3] Varga, 'Economics and Economic Policy in the First Quarter of 1931', *International Press Correspondence*, XI, no. 27 (23 May 1931), p. 495.

[4] Hilferding, *Das Finanzkapital*, pp. 395–400.

that is why they . . . begin to compete with the cartel. The cartel is unable to maintain prices any longer, and the decline in prices extends to the cartelized industry. The artificial interference is corrected, and the formation of prices obeys the [law of value] from which the cartels vainly endeavoured to extract themselves.'[5]

Failing to link Hilferding's theory of prices with the fate of the banks, Varga had overlooked another consideration as well: the manner in which currencies had been stabilized in the 1920s. America's control of much of the world's gold supply had caused most currencies to be re-established on a gold-exchange standard. Central banks maintained their reserves partly in gold, partly in claims on such convertible currencies as the dollar and the pound sterling. When relative interest rates changed, these claims could be withdrawn and moved. A change in political conditions could likewise transform movements of short-term deposits into an instrument of political blackmail. The fragility of the system was demonstrated in March 1931, when Germany and Austria declared their intention to move towards the *Anschluss* by way of a customs union. The French, as Varga reported, were 'most unpleasantly surprised'.[6] Withdrawing deposits from the Credit-Anstalt in Vienna, they helped to incite a wave of currency crises that swept Britain off the gold standard and ended with devaluation of the American dollar in 1933.

By demanding that the Austrians renounce the proposal for a customs union, the French were responsible for what Varga called 'a new stage in the economic crisis'. 'So long latent', the credit crisis had at last become a reality.[7] Although the Bank of England extended short-term credits to Austria, by May 1931 affiliates of the Credit-Anstalt in Prague, Warsaw, Belgrade, and other centres came under pressure. The panic then spread to Germany. In July the Danatbank, one of Germany's largest, stopped payments. Negotiations in London failed to satisfy French conditions for international assistance, and other European countries, their own assets locked into Germany, began to sell sterling to acquire gold.

[5] Ibid., pp. 403–4.
[6] Varga, 'Economics and Economic Policy in the First Quarter of 1931', p. 498.
[7] Varga, 'Economics and Economic Policy in the Second Quarter of 1931', *International Press Correspondence*, XI, no. 45 (25 August 1931), pp. 825–6.

On 21 September 1931 Britain abandoned the gold standard. Within a period of months the achievements of the Dawes Plan were undone and the stage was set for governments to undertake a new role in crisis management.

The choice was stark: the state had either to 'sanitize' financial institutions or risk the possibility of catastrophic deflation through an implosion of the entire credit structure. From sanitation of the banks it was but a step to more ambitious programmes of capitalist 'planning'. As public funds were placed at the disposal of German banks, wages were reduced by decree in an effort to protect exports. *Vorwärts*, a leading Social Democratic journal, hailed the rescue operation as a move in the direction of 'popular control' of the economy. Rudolf Hilferding called the emergency decrees 'a legislative achievement of great significance. The intrusion of the state . . . far exceeds anything that occurred during the war or the period of inflation'. Interest rates and even cartel prices were to be brought under government supervision. 'Only government action', declared Hilferding, could 'supply the preliminaries of economic recovery in Europe.'[8] 'A more bare-faced fraud', answered Varga, had 'never been attempted by the social fascists'.[9]

Once the German government began to act, Varga suddenly grasped the truth of what was happening. As an instrument of finance capital, the state had no course of action but to subordinate everything to the salvation of the banks. Forgetting about compulsive investments, Varga came to the obvious conclusion that the plunging sales of heavy industry had helped to undermine the banking system. So long as unsold inventories continued to mount in every branch of manufacturing, there could be no prospect of fixed-capital renewal. 'The present position on the labour market affords the capitalists an occasion to attempt a reduction of the costs of production not by means of an enhanced productivity of labour by improving the machinery, but by a reduction of wages and an intensification of labour. All these facts make it highly improbable that investment activity will increase speedily.'[10] In America heavy

[8] *The Journal of Commerce*, 13, 15, and 16 February 1932.

[9] Varga, 'Economics and Economic Policy in the Third Quarter of 1931', *International Press Correspondence*, XI, no. 61 (2 December 1931), p. 1103.

[10] Varga, 'Economics and Economic Policy in the First Quarter of 1931', p. 497.

industrial output varied from 25 to 40 per cent below its 1930 level. 'It is this great contraction in the industries producing the means of production which, together with the agricultural crisis, prevents any real development . . . in the light industries.'[11]

While drawing Varga's attention to the decisive relation between inventory accumulation, financial stability, and investment, the financial crisis also afforded his opponents a final opportunity to demonstrate their own zeal by sounding the alarm over the Hilferding deviation. If Varga had not been misled by *Finance Capital*, they charged, he would have seen that the greatest economic crisis of all time had inevitably to bring down the financial institutions. At a meeting of the Institute of World Economics and World Politics in December 1931 Varga confessed to his lack of foresight: 'For my own part, I was mistaken in my opinion, expressed at the end of 1929 (and repeated many times since), that in the present crisis there would not be, in general, a credit crisis. My error arose from underestimating the acuteness of the world economic crisis . . . and from overestimating the powers of monopolistic capital.'[12] When a more exhaustive self-criticism was demanded, Varga dug in his heels. Were every author of a mistaken forecast to be hounded into silence, he protested, all scientific work would become impossible. 'I must say that there are some fortunate people who are able to write of an event two years after it has occurred—and that is very convenient. But I find myself in a different position; I must make forecasts . . . and here there is certainly some risk. . . . I do not claim that I have the ability to foresee absolutely everything.'[13]

In Varga's opinion classical credit crises had been prepared by the speculative accumulation of inventories *prior* to the break in the conjuncture, during the period of rising prices. In the current cycle a different sequence had occurred: the credit crisis had developed *within* the industrial crisis as a result of monopolistic pricing.[14] When his critics insisted that the current crisis had also to be traced to an earlier phase of cyclical expansion, Varga adroitly sidestepped

[11] Varga, 'Economics and Economic Policy in the Second Quarter of 1931', p. 841.
[12] *Problemy Mirovovo Krizisa—Diskussiya*, p. 16.
[13] Ibid., p. 204.
[14] Varga, 'Economics and Economic Policy in the Third Quarter of 1931', p. 1092.

their protests. Stalin, he observed, had already told the Sixteenth Congress that there *was* no general economic expansion during the 1920s. The critics must surely be mistaken, 'for we all agree with the view developed by Comrade Stalin'.[15]

Sporadic grumblings continued to be heard throughout the spring of 1932. In May Amo Amatuni published an article in *Bol'shevik* entitled 'The Struggle for the Purity of the Marxist-Leninist Theory of Crises'. Quoting Stalin's address to a conference of agrarian Marxists in 1929, Amatuni complained that recent Soviet research into monetary and credit questions provided an excellent illustration of the thesis that economic theory was lagging behind practice: 'Comrade Stalin's reference to . . . the lag in theoretical work on the part of Communists . . . is fully applicable to the study and elucidation of the current world economic crisis.'[16] Varga's belief that finance capital could forestall industrial bankruptcies was 'a component part of the theory of "organized capitalism". . . . This theory has nothing in common with Marxism. Its sole purpose is to spread the "bourgeois fairy tale" concerning the abolition of crises . . . in the area of credit and the circulation of money.'[17] According to Amatuni, the present difficulties had existed in a 'veiled form' since 1929. To say otherwise was to deny capitalism's internal contradictions and to detach 'the credit-monetary crisis from the *entire cyclical* development of capitalism. . . . This is methodologically incorrect'.[18]

Amatuni's article was timed to coincide with a new discussion of monetary questions at the Institute. On this occasion the introductory report was given by I. Trakhtenberg, a clear indication that Varga was again under suspicion. Trakhtenberg attempted to make his own reputation at Varga's expense. Agreeing with Amatuni, he argued that the credit crisis originated with the stock-market crash, even though it had been 'hidden' for the following two and a half years.[19] Realizing the absurdity of this thesis, a number of other

[15] *Problemy Mirovovo Krizisa—Diskussiya*, p. 204.

[16] A. Amatuni, 'Bor'ba za Chistotu Marksistsko-Leninskoi Teorii Krizisov', *Bol'shevik*, no. 10 (31 May 1922), p. 80.

[17] Ibid., p. 83.

[18] Ibid.

[19] *Sovremennyi Kreditnyi Krizis—Diskussiya v Institute Mirovovo Khozyaistva i Mirovoi Politiki Komakademii*, Moscow 1932, p. 11.

participants offered their own widely divergent interpretations of how and where the credit crisis had begun. When the session ended, everyone realized it had been futile. In a foreword to the published proceedings, Varga and three of his critics expressed the editorial opinion that problems of monetary theory still required 'further critical discussion'.[20] Of all those in attendance at this meeting, Varga emerged most successfully. 'What is a *hidden* credit crisis?' he asked. 'And how . . . can there be a crisis that has the character of a *hidden* eruption? Apparently the comrades meant to say that the prerequisites of a credit crisis existed. . . . But if all of the prerequisites existed, there would have been an eruption.'[21] Unable to refute this simple logic, Varga's opponents became less vocal after the spring of 1932. Varga's pre-eminence among his colleagues would not again be brought seriously into question for the remainder of the decade.

2. From the Financial Crisis to Capitalist 'Planning'

More important than the origin of the financial crisis was the issue of where it might lead. For Social Democrats, state intervention represented a new initiative in economic planning that made revolution even less attractive as an instrument of change. At the Leipzig Congress of the Social Democratic Party of Germany in 1931 Tarnov had declared that Socialists had no interest in overthrowing the existing government, since it was a 'lesser evil' than the alternative offered by Hitler. 'We must become doctors', he pleaded, 'whose responsibility is to heal the patient.'[22] In its resolutions the congress called for 'strict control over monopoly capitalism, the reduction of tariff barriers, a policy of systematic influence over the conjuncture and employment of workers, planned regulation of orders by society, [and] a strengthening of social control over the banks in order to avoid improper investments'.[23] The Viennese *Arbeiter Zeitung* expressed identical senti-

[20] Ibid., p. 4.
[21] Ibid., p. 229.
[22] Quoted in P. Ditrikh, 'Nemetskaya Sotsial-Demokratiya i Ekonomicheskii Krizis', *Mirovoe Khozyaistvo i Mirovaya Politika*, no. 7–8 (July-August 1931), p. 46.
[23] Ibid., p. 47.

ments: 'Our entire economic system must be essentially reformed. The state must become the decisive force in the national economy. Occupation by the state of the "commanding heights of the economy" will be equivalent to . . . the appearance of a large sector of state-planned economy within the midst of capitalist anarchy.'[24] At the twelfth plenum of the ECCI in the summer of 1932 Manuilsky ridiculed these hopes and denied the possibility of another 'breathing space', of a fourth or a fifth 'period'. Foreign Communists were again warned against lagging behind 'the favourable objective conditions' and missing the opportunity to win over the masses from the Social Fascists, the 'party of capitalist stabilization'.[25] On 30 January 1933 the real fascists came to power, Adolf Hitler becoming chancellor of the German Reich.

In the official Soviet interpretation Hitler had been allowed to triumph in order to alleviate divisions within the ruling class over the distribution of surplus-value. Rationalization had bequeathed German industry a legacy of high fixed costs, and the Junker aristocracy was heavily mortgaged. The discrepancy between expenditures and revenues provoked conflict between agrarian and industrial capital. 'On this basis', wrote Varga, 'there has been a pronounced intensification . . . in the struggle between the individual sections of the ruling class for their share of the dwindling profit and with a view to shifting the loss incurred onto other shoulders.'[26] Unable to continue ruling 'in the old way', the finance capitalists had decided to end their fratricidal struggle by giving Hitler the opportunity to increase the rate of industrial exploitation. The Hitler government, Varga predicted in the spring of 1933, 'as the champion of the interests of monopolist capital, is bound in the near future to effect a further reduction of wages and salaries. . . . The Hitler movement has been financed, fostered, and placed in authority only in order that it may enhance the exploitation of the

[24] Quoted in I. Markov, 'Demogogicheskaya Boltovnya o Narodnokhozyaistvennom Planirovanii pri Kapitalizme', *Kommunisticheskii Internatsional* no. 92–93 (31 October 1931), pp. 64–5.

[25] D. Manuilsky, 'O Kontse Kapitalisticheskoi Stabilizatsii', *Mirovoe Khozyaistvo i Mirovaya Politika*, no. 9 (September 1932), pp. 4–5.

[26] Varga, 'Economics and Economic Policy in the Fourth Quarter of 1932', *International Press Correspondence*, XIII, no. 12 (16 March 1933), p. 291.

working class and attempt to get the better of the crisis at the expense of the proletariat.'[27]

Officially, the programme of the Nazi party catered to the interests of the petty bourgeoisie. It called, among other things, for abolition of unearned incomes, nationalization of trusts, the death penalty for usurers, and the elimination of department stores, whose space was to be leased to independent merchants. Varga believed the true extent of the crisis was revealed by the fact that 'the mobilization of the petty-bourgeois masses in defence of capitalism and for the terrorization of the working class has in part had to be effected with the aid of anti-capitalist slogans such as "destruction of interest slavery" and "opposition to predatory capital" '.[28] Hitler's survival would depend on his ability to manipulate the petty bourgeoisie as a reserve of counter-revolution. The nature of their mission would prevent the Nazis from increasing the petty-bourgeoisie's share of the existing national income. And an increase in the total national income could be ruled out in advance, because excess industrial capacity would stand in the way of new investments.

Embarrassed by his earlier predictions of financial stability, Varga seriously misjudged Hitler's prospects. Since *Capital*, Marxists had considered production the fundamental and 'real' determinant of economic activity, leaving virtually no scope for a positive monetary or fiscal policy. By rejoining the mainstream of Marxist thought, Varga missed the possibility that the capitalist state might re-activate idle money-capital by spending *future* tax revenues—in other words, by deficit financing. Preoccupied with the allocation of current surplus-value, he overlooked the ability of the state to re-employ 'real' factors of production and thereby to increase both the social product and state revenues in the long run. The majority of Soviet economists believed that a programme of deliberate reflation would cause a crisis similar to that which broke out during the imperialist war. But the problems of the 1930s differed from those of 1914–18. In the earlier period 'fictitious values' had proliferated because commodities were destroyed and

[27] Varga, 'Economy and Economic Policy', *International Press Correspondence*, XIII, no. 27 (21 June 1933), p. 587.
[28] Ibid., p. 585.

fixed capital depleted. During the 1930s there were no 'real' obstacles to a recovery of industrial output. Having no respect for any but 'real' economics, Hitler allowed Schacht to finance the state's spending requirements by any means necessary. All that mattered to the Nazis was to put men and equipment back to work. Schacht's technique in pursuing this objective was elementary: Germany would spend herself to recovery. Tax credit bonds and other government securities were used to purchase commodities first for work-creation projects and later for rearmament, the securities discountable at the Reichsbank. Domestic prices were kept under control by forced saving and direct regulations, which avoided the political consequences of overt inflation. All that the recovery programme required from the Nazi party was a stable political and institutional framework.

In May 1933, turning a deaf ear to pledges of co-operation from the Social Democratic trade unions, the new regime destroyed the trade-union movement. Collective bargaining was replaced by a system of 'labour trustees' responsible for the maintenance of 'labour peace'. For peasants, the Hereditary Farm Law was passed in September 1933, providing that farms of up to 125 hectares were not to be sold, divided, or mortgaged. As Walther Darré, head of the Reich Food Estate proclaimed, the peasantry was 'the life source of the Nordic race'. To guarantee the sanctity of Junker estates, small farmers were discouraged from competing with landed property in the production of grains. As compensation, prices for animal and dairy fats were raised, and Darré warned the peasants that any further increase in grain production would lead to acreage restrictions. Here Varga detected a parallel with the programme Roosevelt was introducing in America: 'in its efforts to secure high grain prices . . . German fascism is being driven . . . along the path which Roosevelt has had to take—compulsory restriction of output. The rottenness of the whole capitalist system is revealed here in its crassest form.'[29] The Nazi regime also appeared to resemble the New Deal in its industrial policy. To minimize concern about redundant capacity and price-cutting competition, Hitler embarked upon compulsory cartelization. 'German fascism', re-

[29] Varga, 'Economy and Economic Policy in the Third Quarter of 1933', *International Press Correspondence*, XIII, no. 53 (6 December 1933), p. 1198.

marked Varga, '. . . supports the big monopolies with all possible means. Roosevelt's laws to enforce "fair competition" also resolve themselves . . . into open support of the cartels.'[30] Both governments were said to be following a programme of 'crisis rationalization', lowering costs through the concentration of production. The implication of these comparisons was to interpret the New Deal as covert fascism.

The Hoover administration had come to the rescue of large firms even before Roosevelt was elected. Espousing the virtues of self-reliance—and the ennobling character of private charity—Hoover created the Reconstruction Finance Corporation to assist insurance companies, banks, mortgage companies, and other corporate borrowers. Accused by Roosevelt of coddling the banks and forgetting the 'people', Hoover retorted during the election campaign of 1932 that his sole interest was to protect farmers and preserve jobs. Varga scoffed at this sort of rhetoric: 'the unemployed receive nothing but charity, that is to say, no manner of government relief. United States democracy permits thousands of millions of Federal money to be distributed to bankrupt capitalist enterprises, but thinks it is incompatible with the dignity of the American worker to draw unemployment relief. He may die of starvation on the streets, but not draw a cent of government money.'[31] To Soviet observers, the election campaign of 1932 had but one purpose: to decide whether Hoover or Roosevelt was the better demagogue. V. Lan told Soviet readers: 'The real masters of contemporary America—the bankers and industrialists—looked upon the whole election clamour as a tournament to demonstrate which of the two contestants is the stronger, which of them is the best demagogue, which of them is better able to deceive the broad masses of labouring people in the USA.'[32]

Lapinsky's appraisal of American politics was no more generous: '. . . the single combat between Hoover and Roosevelt appears to us above all as *a "clash" between the policy of the most implacable,*

[30] Ibid., p. 1203.

[31] Varga, 'Economics and Economic Policy in the Fourth Quarter of 1931', *International Press Correspondence*, XII, no. 12 (10 March 1932), p. 252.

[32] V. Lan, 'Pobeda Ruzvel'ta', *Mirovoe Khozyaistvo i Mirovaya Politika*, no. 11–12 (November-December 1932), p. 18.

violently conservative bourgeoisie . . . and that of the more flexible, more "liberal" bourgeoisie, which is subject to pressure "from below".[33]

Whichever candidate proved successful, Varga thought the most urgent problem in America, as in Germany, was the decline in surplus-value. The net profits of more than 200 large corporations had fallen from $741 million during the first nine months of 1930 to $18 million during the same months of 1932.[34] The struggle between opposing elements of the ruling class over the apportioning of diminished profits had resulted in 'industrial buccaneers', or independent entrepreneurs, gaining the upper hand over honest businessmen, or the finance capitalists. One of the first items on Roosevelt's agenda was therefore the National Recovery Act. Erasing the anti-trust legislation of the past forty years, the NRA won immediate support from big business. In each branch of industry manufacturers were invited to draw up a code of 'fair competition' designed to guarantee a 'reasonable profit'. Prescribing either minimum prices or limitations of output, the codes used the force of law to create what were in effect compulsory cartels. Varga denounced the NRA as 'fascism disguised as "planned state capitalism" '.[35] The Act made provision for collective bargaining, but Soviet economists were not impressed. V. Lan wrote that 'the establishment of a close union between the leaders of the AFL, the entrepreneurs, and the government, such as this law foresees, means a step towards the fascization of the Federation [of Labour] and its control by the state along the lines of Italy or Germany. Green, head of the AFL, praises this law as the road to real co-operation and recommends that the workers have complete faith in the government and General Johnson [the NRA administrator].'[36]

The second major component of the New Deal, the Agricultural Adjustment Act, appeared analogous to Hitler's Hereditary Farm

[33] P. Lapinsky, *V Kotle Krizisa—Krizis, Vodka i Vybory*, Moscow 1932, p. 16.

[34] Varga, 'Economics and Economic Policy in the Fourth Quarter of 1932', pp. 296–7.

[35] Varga, 'Economy and Economic Policy in the Second Quarter of 1933', *International Press Correspondence*, XIII, no. 40 (11 September 1933), p. 876.

[36] Lan, 'Ruzvel't u Vlasti', *Mirovoe Khozyaistvo i Mirovaya Politika*, no. 8 (August 1933), p. 11.

Law. Farm mortgages were to be refinanced and a Farm Credit Administration created to consolidate debts and liquefy bank assets. The purchasing power of the 'farm dollar' was to be restored to the level of 1910–14, benefits being paid farmers who undertook to restrict acreage. The funds would come from a processing tax levied on firms working up agricultural products. Varga expected a rise in food prices to result in 'tremendous wage struggles'.[37] Roosevelt, like Hitler, was attempting to manoeuvre the petty bourgeoisie into supporting an attack on the working class. The AAA constituted further evidence of 'fascization of government methods in the United States'.[38]

3. The 'Military-Inflationary Boom' and Depression 'of a Special Kind'

Until the appearance of Roosevelt and Hitler, the prevailing Soviet consensus held that no recovery of economic activity in the West was possible. Varga believed that 'there can be no question of overcoming the crisis in the old way'. The most the bourgeoisie might hope for—as Engels had long ago suggested—was 'stagnation more or less at the present extremely low level of output, with small fluctuations up or down. There can be no question of a . . . "solution" in the old sense of the word'.[39] By July 1933 L. Mad'yar could write that 'every literate economist knows that the transition from a crisis to depression, and all the more to a new expansion, is unthinkable without new construction and the replacement of fixed capital'.[40] Seeing that state subsidies to the finance capitalists actually discouraged the destruction of existing capital and crippled the normal recovery process, Mad'yar claimed that recent signs of improvement in the capitalist world had to be part of a 'military-inflationary boom'.[41] Mad'yar's new concept

---

[37] Varga, 'Economy and Economic Policy', p. 595.
[38] Ibid.
[39] Varga, 'Economics and Economic Policy in the Third Quarter of 1932', *International Press Correspondence*, XII, no. 54 (3 December 1932), p. 1157.
[40] Mad'yar, 'SSSR i Kapitalisticheskie Strany na Ekonomicheskoi Konferentsii', *Kommunisticheskii Internatsional*, no. 19–20 (10 July 1933), p. 34.
[41] Ibid.

reflected concern during 1933 that the 'fascist' experiments being launched in America and Germany would create an 'artificial' basis for recovery. In October M. Ioel'son proposed to adopt the 'military-inflationary boom' as a general analytical category.[42] Although the affinity between the artificial 'boom' and 'organized capitalism' should have been manifest, at the end of 1933 Otto Kuusinen told the thirteenth plenum of the ECCI that 'the revival of industry . . . this year bears mainly a *military-inflationary charac-ter*'.[43] New sources of demand were being created through subsidies and state orders, 'but this demand is of a special character. Production increases, but not for consumer goods or even for producer goods, but only for unproductive, parasitic purposes'.[44]

To see Kuusinen endorsing the category of 'military-inflationary boom' was in itself probably sufficient to provoke Varga into asserting the exact opposite. 'Neither Marx, Lenin, nor the Comintern', he exclaimed, had ever denied the possibility of a capitalist recovery.[45] In fact, the only people who believed the spontaneous recovery mechanism had been paralysed were the Hitlerites, who attributed recent improvements to Nazi planning: 'These are the people who rally to the ideas of Comrade Preobrazhensky.'[46] Lest these comments be taken to mean that the recovery mechanism was really operative, however, Varga made this qualification: 'What is the basis of [bourgeois] optimism? Its basis is ignorance of the fact that this crisis is not a normal one but a crisis on the basis of the general crisis of capitalism . . . in other words, the internal mechanism which works in accordance with the laws of capitalism to overcome every cyclical crisis has not been put out of action in the present crisis . . . but these forces are not strong enough . . . owing to the pressure of the general crisis.'[47]

From the first successes of Roosevelt and Hitler, Varga found

[42] Ioel'son, 'The General Situation of the World Capitalist System', *International Press Correspondence*, XIII, no. 53 (6 December 1933), p. 1205.

[43] Kuusinen, 'Fascism, the Danger of War, and the Tasks of the Communist Parties', *International Press Correspondence*, XIV, no. 5 (30 January 1934), p. 100.

[44] Ibid., p. 102.

[45] Varga, 'Problemy Sovremennovo Etapa Mirovovo Krizisa', *Mirovoe Khozyaistvo i Mirovaya Politika*, no. 3 (March 1934), p. 7.

[46] Ibid., p. 8.

[47] Varga, 'Economy and Economic Policy in the Second Quarter of 1933', p. 879.

himself poised on a razor's edge, trying to balance two opposing views. To the extent that a recovery was beginning, it was the result of capitalism's internal laws, not of fascism and an artificially induced 'military-inflationary boom'. On the other hand, no real recovery could occur, because of the 'general crisis'. Every one of Varga's surveys emphasized that excess productive capacity constituted an insuperable obstacle to renewed investments. How then could the recovery mechanism conceivably function? According to Varga, it could not do so until the capitalists accomplished the impossible: they must first resolve 'the insoluble market problem'. Stalin had shown that 'the market problem is the chief problem of capitalism'.[48] Varga explained that contrary to what Marx and Lenin had written, investment depended on consumption: 'In other words, *the volume of consumer power . . . determines in the last resort* the productive consumption . . . which determines *the capacity of the market.*'[49] Expansion of the capitalist market was impossible because there were no new peasants to exploit. The conversion of 'third parties' into commodity producers was '*a process which can take place only once. . . .* In so far as this process is more or less ended in the highly developed capitalist countries . . . capitalism in these countries is approaching nearer and nearer to the stage of "pure" capitalism. . . . Therefore these countries show the chronic limitation of the market characteristics of the general crisis of capitalism.' This interpretation, Varga added, had 'nothing whatever to do with Luxemburgism'.[50]

Indirectly acknowledging that fixed-capital renewal was the 'material basis' of recoveries, Varga still did not understand the cyclical process of market creation that Marx had described in *Capital* and Lenin had explained to the Narodniks. Indeed, the latest evidence from Germany and America appeared to provide fresh support for 'Varga's Law'. From August 1932 to August 1933 the number of workers employed in German industry had risen by 7.5 per cent, the number of hours worked by 4 per cent, the index of industrial output by no less than 22.4 per cent.[51] The figures from

[48] Ibid., p. 865.
[49] Ibid., p. 866.
[50] Ibid., p. 867.
[51] Varga, 'Economy and Economic Policy in the Third Quarter of 1933', p. 1196.

America were even more amazing. From March to July 1933 the index of industrial production climbed by a phenomenal 80 per cent, compared to a 23 per cent increase in the employment index.[52] 'Crisis rationalization' had assumed astounding dimensions, leading Varga to predict that the number of employed Americans would never again reach the level of 1919.[53] Had Varga not been so explicit in his references to 'crisis rationalization', it would be difficult to believe that he failed to understand the real meaning of these data.

To keep an industrial plant in operation at any level of output required a minimum work force. Successive decreases in the scale of operations had lowered labour productivity; successive increases were raising it just as dramatically during the first phase of recovery. Far from proving that a recovery was impossible, the unemployment figures from Germany and America represented clear evidence that it was under way. When the American economy suffered a new setback late in 1933, Varga was jubilant. Roosevelt's measures had proven futile: they were accompanied by 'an increase of about the same volume as . . . in other countries (France, Sweden, Poland, Germany, Canada, etc.).' 'Artificial' state initiatives had merely ensured that 'the normal improvement, which would have taken place in any case on the basis of the inner laws of the development of capitalism . . . did not proceed more or less uniformly but in the form of a rapid leap upwards and a subsequent sudden relapse which . . . exhausted itself by December to make way for a further trend towards improvement'.[54]

In January 1934 Varga published *New Phenomena in the World Economic Crisis*. Appearing 'on the advice of Comrade Stalin', this was an 'official' work that other economists could not afford to ignore. The transition from crisis to depression, or the first phase of recovery, was now traced to July and August 1932. Admitting that the struggle over the allocation of surplus-value had caused 'a sudden strengthening of the role of the state',[55] Varga persisted in

[52] Varga, 'Economy and Economic Policy in the Fourth Quarter of 1933', *International Press Correspondence*, XIV, no. 22 (10 April 1934), p. 582.

[53] Varga, 'Problemy Rastushchei Khronicheskoi Besrabotitsy', *Kommunisticheskii Internatsional*, no. 24 (20 August 1933), p. 14.

[54] Varga, 'Economy and Economic Policy in the Fourth Quarter of 1933', p. 583.

[55] Varga, *Novye Yavleniya v Mirovom Ekonomicheskom Krizise*, 1934, p. 42.

his belief that it was wrong to attribute any success to state intervention: 'capitalism's immanent laws of movement' had caused production to resume once inventories of finished consumer goods had fallen below customary levels. In *The Decline of Capitalism* Preobrazhensky had maintained that the deterioration of fixed capital would set a 'natural limit' on contraction. Pointing out that the physical wear of equipment had exceeded replacements during the crisis, Varga now saw that the process of rebuilding inventories would require that the deficiency of fixed capital be made up. 'Hence there is an increased sale of iron and steel and, *although in very small measure*, a growth in the production of machines.'[56] But there was still no prospect of the current phase of depression giving way to a normal cyclical expansion. In that sense the depression was historically unique:

'*We are not talking of a normal depression, but of one that is unique. . . .* The main difference between the current depression and those of prewar times is to be found in the fact that the current depression does not represent a stable foundation for the transition to recovery and expansion. . . . *The retarding influence of the general crisis of capitalism—the chronic excess of fixed capital . . . the chronic agrarian crisis*, the enormous *chronic unemployment*, the resulting contraction of the domestic market, and so forth—*will appear much more forcefully in this cycle than before*, because the economic crisis has deepened the general crisis of the capitalist system. We are talking of a "depression" *in conditions of the end of capitalist stabilization*.'[57]

In Varga's triumph of inconsistency Stalin discovered unsuspected theoretical agility that at once attracted his approval. In January 1934 he reported to the Seventeenth Congress of the Communist Party, warning against overestimating the economic potential of the capitalist state: 'some people' were inclined to ascribe recovery entirely to the 'military-inflationary boom'. In certain countries this had played 'no small part'. Nevertheless, to omit other factors, in particular the rise in working-class exploitation, would be a 'gross mistake'.[58] Concerning the future outlook,

[56] Ibid., p. 64.
[57] Ibid., p. 71.
[58] Stalin, *Works*, XIII, p. 295.

Stalin defined the depression 'of a special kind' in the same manner as Varga: 'Evidently what we are witnessing is a transition from the lowest point of decline of industry, from the lowest point of the industrial crisis, to a depression—not an ordinary depression, but a depression of a special kind, which does not lead to a new upswing and flourishing of industry, but which, on the other hand, does not force industry back to the lowest point of decline.'[59]

At a session of the Institute in March 1934 Varga referred to 'Comrade Stalin's remark that the internal forces of capitalism continue to operate even in the course of the current crisis', saying it had 'enormous theoretical significance for our further work'.[60] It was wrong, he insisted, to maintain 'that there is not and will not be any restoration and renewal of capital'.[61] In *The Great Crisis and its Political Consequences*, completed in September 1934, Varga continued to prevaricate. Affirming once again that 'the inner forces of capitalism' continued to function, he repeated his belief that no spontaneous recovery was possible because the 'depeasantizing' process had ended.[62]

Probably the incident that revealed more strikingly than any other the theoretical dilemma Soviet economists faced by the mid-1930s was the publication of a volume of articles entitled *Lenin on Problems of Contemporary Imperialism*. In it A. Itkina reviewed 'The Leninist Legacy in the Theory of the Market and Crises'; she began with this remark: 'It is only in the works of Lenin and Stalin, the genius-like continuer of Lenin's great work . . . that the thread of revolutionary Marxism develops.'[63] After saluting the Leader, Itkina proceeded to demonstrate that 'realization of the entire social product . . . is fully possible within capitalist society, for [in Lenin's words] "the development of production creates a market" '.[64] For Lenin, a chronic realization crisis—and by implication a depression 'of a special kind'—was nonsense:

'The question of the external market, of expanding the sphere of

[59] Ibid., p. 297.

[60] Varga, 'Problemy Sovremennovo Etapa . . .', p. 8.

[61] Ibid., p. 10.

[62] Varga, *The Great Crisis and its Political Consequences*, London n.d., p. 76.

[63] Varga, Khmel'nitskaya, and Itkina (eds.), *Lenin i Problemy Sovremennovo Imperializma*, Moscow 1934, p. 281.

[64] Ibid., p. 295.

influence of capital to the noncapitalist environment, is a question not of the general theory of realization, but of capitalism's concrete development, that is, a question of a historical nature, as Lenin pointed out more than once in his polemic with the Narodniks . . . *disproportionality, the uneven development of separate branches and countries, and the search for a higher norm of profit and superprofits: these determine the tireless effort of capital to go beyond the limits of the internal market.* But all of these processes have nothing in common with the abstract theory of realization; they are not conditioned by the absolute impossibility of realizing surplus-value within the confines of capitalism.'[65]

The market-creating process would continue without interruption so long as the proper proportions were maintained. Demand was subordinate to production and the rate of investment.[66] Having allowed the genie to escape from the proverbial bottle, Itkina then hastened to conform to the current standard of duplicity. Citing the contradiction between 'the social character of production and individual appropriation',[67] she argued that under imperialism the income of the working class manifests a 'tendency towards *absolute* contraction'.[68] In short, a chronic realization problem was not inevitable, because Lenin said capitalism creates a market; but at the same time, it *was* inevitable, because Lenin's greatest pupil declared it to be so. From a theoretical viewpoint, Soviet economists had yet to escape from the ideological impasse created by the decline of cycle theory after 1929.

4. 'Artificial Stimuli'

Unable to achieve a breakthrough on the level of general theory, Soviet economists turned in the mid-1930s to partial problems that might more easily be understood in the light of empirical evidence. The differences between national policies in these years appeared to grow in relation to their presumed similarities. In Germany events could be conceptualized most readily by reference to the theory of

[65] Ibid., p. 307.
[66] Ibid., pp. 296–8.
[67] Ibid., p. 332.
[68] Ibid., p. 329.

'war economy' originally expounded by Bukharin in *The Economics of the Transition Period*. In the spring of 1934 Varga observed, 'Organizationally, the whole economic system is being prepared for war.'[69] Politically, a parallel reorganization was occurring in an effort to end rivalries over surplus-value: the various 'sections and groups' of the ruling class were being obliged by the new regime to submerge their differences. The Nazis were 'violently forcing unity upon them under the leadership of finance capital and by abolishing parliament'.[70] The barbarity of the Roehm purge in 1934 demonstrated that Hitler was following the directives of 'German monopolist capitalism' and ignoring petty-bourgeois demands for a 'second revolution' to implement the party's programme. When small shopkeepers called for the end of 'interest slavery', wrote one Soviet author, Schacht was quick to defend finance capital. His motto was 'Hands off bank capital! Find speculators and usurers wherever you can, Mr. Hitler, but not among us!'[71]

The objective basis of unity within the ruling class, Varga now realized, was the *expansion* of surplus-value—not simply its *redistribution*.[72] To account for the realization of a new stream of surplus-value, Varga began to reassess the significance of state expenditures. The Nazis had proven that the state could expand the market by bringing idle capital back into circulation even in the absence of 'third parties'. As if this argument were perfectly consistent with his previous emphasis on capitalism's internal and spontaneous forces, Varga now attributed much of Hitler's success to conscious policy decisions: 'It is very difficult to calculate how far the consumer power of society is increased as a result of increased war expenditure. The latter problem depends above all upon the manner in which the expenditure is financed. If this expenditure is financed chiefly from taxation, then there is no effect upon the consumer capacity of society because the population receives back

[69] Varga, 'Economy and Economic Policy in the First Quarter of 1934', *International Press Correspondence*, XIV, no. 35 (19 June 1934), p. 920.

[70] Varga, 'Economy and Economic Policy in the Second Quarter of 1934', *International Press Correspondence*, XIV, no. 49 (17 September 1934), p. 1280.

[71] Z. Atlas, 'Sotsial-Fashistskoe i Fashistskoe "Regulirovanie" Kapitalizma', *Pod Znamenem Marksizma*, no. 3 (May-June 1934), p. 61.

[72] Varga, 'Economy and Economic Policy in the Fourth Quarter of 1934', *International Press Correspondence*, XV, no. 11 (12 March 1935), pp. 315–16.

from war expenditures only that sum which was previously taken away from it in taxation. However, if war expenditures are financed by the floating of loans, that is to say, if idle loan-capital is brought into action, then the result is a temporary invigoration of industrial activity.'[73]

Recognizing that 'a very considerable part of [the] increased production in Germany' was due to 'artificial stimuli', Varga came within a hair's breadth of enunciating a theory of artificial market creation.[74] In *The Decline of Capitalism* Preobrazhensky had shown that a minor increment of private spending would have a multiple effect on social production and purchasing power. In the Luxemburg debate Dvolaitsky had held that by regulating public spending the state could control changes in the market. Before the end of the decade, Varga's own neo-Luxemburgism, however paradoxically, would lead to a similar position. In the meantime, he became more aware of the similarity between Hitler's Germany and Bukharin's description of the war economy of 1914–18.

In 1935 Varga began to write of 'state war-monopoly capitalism'.[75] The 'artificial stimuli' were not merely supplementing private spending, but were actually interfering with the renovation of fixed capital. Germany's industrial plant was being sacrificed to armaments production; the output of consumer goods was declining in spite of the growth in employment; the dialectical turning point of the 'war boom' was approaching. Soon 'real values' would once more be displaced by the 'fictitious values' of state securities.[76] The obsessive movement in the direction of a war economy would cause 'a severe dislocation of the whole capitalist economic system'[77]—or what Bukharin had described as negative expanded reproduction. At the end of 1936 Varga believed that the turning point was drawing near. After an initial outburst of expansion, the war economy was defeating its own purpose: 'This is clearly shown

---

[73] Varga, 'Economy and Economic Policy in the Second Quarter of 1934', p. 1281.
[74] Ibid.
[75] Varga, 'Economy and Economic Policy in the Fourth Quarter of 1934', p. 314.
[76] Varga, 'Economy and Economic Policy in the Fourth Quarter of 1935', *International Press Correspondence*, XVI, no. 13 (12 March 1936), p. 350.
[77] Ibid., p. 342.

by the fact that [the index of] industrial production in the typical democratic countries . . . is just as high or still higher than in Germany.'[78] In reaction to growing domestic problems, Hitler would soon seek an external diversion. As Bismark once commented, 'one can do many things with bayonets, but one cannot sit on them indefinitely'.[79]

The progress of Roosevelt's New Deal created greater conceptual difficulties than German fascism inasmuch as no similar historical precedent could be found. Not only had Roosevelt avoided the creation of a war economy, but the earlier political parallels between Germany and America were also becoming less convincing. The entire edifice of the New Deal was being placed in question by the bourgeoisie through its opposition to unbalanced budgets. A lack of 'confidence' within the ruling class paralysed the state and simultaneously discouraged private investments. The focus of bourgeois hostility had become the NRA provision that 'employees shall have the right to organize and bargain collectively through representatives of their own choosing'. Refusing to negotiate with any but company unions, employers had by the end of 1934 incited the greatest wave of strikes in more than a decade. The explosion of working-class unrest encouraged finance capital to hold the president personally responsible for provoking a virtual class war. For the capitalists the NRA seemed more trouble than it was worth. Small businessmen claimed that the codes of 'fair competition' had been devised by and favoured big capital. Clarence Darrow, the radical lawyer, published a study that condemned the government for promoting monopoly. General Johnson, speaking on behalf of the NRA, replied that Darrow had launched 'an open attack on our whole system in favour of the semi-barbarous violence of semi-civilized Russia'.[80]

Varga defined Roosevelt's failure in terms of his inability to emulate Hitler by imposing unity on the ruling class. The American experiment in 'state fascism' was being sabotaged by the very

[78] Varga, 'Economy and Economic Policy in the Second and Third Quarters of 1936', *International Press Correspondence*, XVI, no. 55 (10 December 1936), p. 1451.
[79] Varga, 'Economy and Economic Policy in the Fourth Quarter of 1935', p. 352.
[80] Quoted in Varga, 'Economy and Economic Policy in the Second Quarter of 1934', p. 1297.

groups it was designed to serve. 'The main reason [for the failure] is that in view of the strong antagonisms between the various sections and groups of the bourgeoisie, arising as a result of their struggle for the limited market, it is not possible to pursue a policy which would satisfy all these sections and groups at the same time.'[81] The great 'captains of industry', men like Henry Ford, were ideologically prejudiced against state interference. Other monopolists had lowered their unit costs of production by increasing output and no longer needed the codes. From their viewpoint there was no reason for 'coming to any sort of terms with their opponents'. The 'international bankers' believed Roosevelt's policy of devaluing the dollar would threaten New York's position as a world banking centre and give the competitive edge to London. Although every element of the ruling class had come to oppose the New Deal, Varga remained confident that 'despite this opposition . . . the "New Deal" favours monopoly capital'.[82] Having in mind the potentially positive effects of 'artificial stimuli', Varga had decided that Roosevelt knew better than the bankers and industrialists what was in the interests of capitalism.

In May 1935 Soviet economists were shocked to learn that the Supreme Court had ruled the NRA unconstitutional. P. Shubin facetiously described the about-turn by saying God had changed sides: 'In April, "God, who protects our America" [Roosevelt's words in a radio address] stood firmly on the positions of the . . . NRA, but by May He had already turned up in the camp of its gravediggers. "God is always on the side of the strongest battalions", asserted Napoleon. And the American God deserted the "new order", which was being defeated, to side with victorious extreme reaction.'[83]

At this point the analogy between fascism and the New Deal finally disintegrated. That Aaron Schechter, a poultry merchant, could use litigation to frustrate the American president seemed nothing less than incredible. The only conceivable explanation was

[81] Varga, 'Economy and Economic Policy in the Third Quarter of 1934', *International Press Correspondence*, XIV, no. 61 (5 December 1934), p. 1634.
[82] Ibid.
[83] P. Shubin, 'Bankrotstvo NIRA i Obostrenie Protivorechii Amerikanskovo Kapitalizma', *Kommunisticheskii Internatsional*, no. 20–21 (20 July 1935), p. 114.

that the Court had ratified a decision already taken by the National Association of Manufacturers, the Chamber of Commerce, and the Association of Bankers—a decision to launch a counter-offensive against the concessions awarded the working class by the NRA.[84] Writing under the *nom de plume* M. Tanin, Soviet Commissar of Foreign Affairs Maxim Litvinov declared that the Court had performed its 'traditional role as an instrument in the hands of the most reactionary and militant circles of finance capital'. The 'paper codes' of 'economic democracy' had not stood up against the 'iron codes of the class struggle'.[85] 'The collapse of the complex, bulky system of "planning" in the USA', Litvinov wrote, 'took place in queer forms, obscuring the moving forces of this truly enormous event. "Aaron Schechter vs. the United States of America"—that is the official designation of the legal case that produced the decision . . . [and] dealt a crushing blow to the "new era" so widely acclaimed throughout the whole world. On the one side the plaintiff—a poultry merchant, on the other . . .—the state, and above them the unbiased, impartial arbiter, the Areopagus of the priests of justice—that is the grotesque context in which . . . the destruction of the Roosevelt system was staged.'[86]

After losing the support of business circles, Roosevelt undertook what Soviet economists described as a 'left' manoeuvre to save his opponents from their own narrow-mindedness. The banks and industry had attacked relief and public works expenditures. Roosevelt secured passage of a Wealth Tax Act, with steeply graduated income taxes. Measures were also introduced to provide unemployment and old-age insurance and to extend the rights of trade unions under the Wagner Act. Litvinov described the reaction of the American bourgeoisie to the new 'unbearable' taxes. In one American journal he had read that Roosevelt was embracing a doctrine that 'originated in the criminal minds of the leaders of the Paris Commune and was consecrated in the mind of the eastern fanatic Lenin'.[87]

[84] Ibid., pp. 120–21.

[85] M.T., 'Amerikanskaya Burzhuaznaya Literatura o Planirovanii', *Bol'shevik*, no. 8 (1 May 1935), p. 83.

[86] M. Tanin, 'Na Razvalinakh "Planirovaniya" v SShA', *Mirovoe Khozyaistvo i Mirovaya Politika*, no. 7 (July 1935), p. 3.

[87] Ibid., p. 19.

In his effort to impose interpretive order on American politics, Varga found himself temporarily at a loss. In July 1935 he wrote that Roosevelt had changed direction when he discovered that 'there is only a limited opportunity in the United States for the operation of those internal forces of capitalism which might overcome the existing depression of a special kind'.[88] Three months later, Varga was saying the very opposite: abolition of the codes had 'normalized' American economic policy, and 'the internal forces of capitalism, which are working to overcome the cyclical crisis, [have] made themselves vigorously felt. . . . All the prophecies which have been made during the past few months are without exception unusually optimistic.'[89] Output of means of production had risen by 30 per cent since 1934. 'For the most part, it is the result of the fact that during the past five years the purchase of production goods was so small as not even to make good the results of ordinary wear and tear.'[90] A 'tremendous' expansion of industrial production was under way by the third quarter of 1935.

Roosevelt's greatest success during the period of uncertainty had been in manipulating the petty bourgeoisie. The position of farmers, especially the well-to-do, had been improved by 'heavily burdening urban consumers, and above all the workers'.[91] Restricting agricultural output, the state had prevented radicalization of rural groups and proven 'the whole absurdity of capitalist society'. When the Supreme Court threatened to invalidate the agricultural programme of the New Deal, Roosevelt by-passed the new obstacle by paying farmers to 'conserve' their soil rather than restrict acreage. According to R. Levina, Roosevelt outmanoeuvred the Court because the main beneficiaries of government premiums were the insurance companies, banks, and multiple landlords who had acquired enormous properties by foreclosing on mortgages.[92] S. Dalin concurred in this assessment, seeing a need to maintain the

[88] Varga, 'Economy and Economic Policy in the First Half Year of 1935', *International Press Correspondence*, XV, no. 38 (22 August 1935), p. 988.
[89] Varga, 'Economy and Economic Policy in the Third Quarter of 1935', *International Press Correspondence*, XV, no. 72 (31 December 1935), p. 1773.
[90] Ibid.
[91] Ibid., p. 1775.
[92] R. Levina, 'Perevybory Prezidenta i Amerikanskii Fermer', *Mirovoe Khozyaistvo i Mirovaya Politika*, no. 12 (December 1936), pp. 52–3.

upper strata of farmers as 'a reserve of finance capital in the struggle against the revolutionary masses'.[93]

In *The Economic Policy of Roosevelt* (1936), Dalin summarized the new role of the state in American capitalism. However much the finance capitalists criticized Roosevelt for excessive 'liberalism', he had understood that concessions were temporarily required because of 'the intensification of the class struggle and considerations of social manoeuvring'.[94] When the final results were tallied, it would be apparent that the most significant income transfer achieved under the New Deal was from the masses to the monopolies.[95] Roosevelt's methods differed from Hitler's, but their purpose was the same—to enlarge the flow of surplus-value. State intervention entailed political stress in a democracy because it 'cannot equally satisfy the interests of groups of the bourgeoisie who are struggling among themselves'.[96] Notwithstanding the chequered history of the New Deal, the need for state intervention would continue to grow; 'artificial stimuli' would be used to compensate for disruption of the spontaneous recovery mechanism of classical capitalism. 'The downfall of capitalist "planning" . . .', Dalin wrote, 'will not bring an end of state intervention in economic life. Capitalism finds itself at such a stage of decay that the action of its internal spontaneous forces has become impaired and no longer leads either to a speedy overcoming of economic crises or to a new flourishing of the capitalist economy. The so-called automatic nature of the capitalist economy has been disrupted . . . Hence an attempt to reinforce the action of capitalism's internal forces with artificial state measures . . . intervention in general cannot be halted.'[97]

The conclusion that capitalism's internal forces might have to be reactivated by 'artificial stimuli' during the 'general crisis' had practical consequences for Soviet foreign policy. In France Stalin undertook to apply the new insight. A mutual security pact had been negotiated between France and the USSR for the purpose of deterring Nazi aggression. In the summer of 1934 the French

[93] S. Dalin, *Ekonomicheskaya Politika Ruzvel'ta*, Moscow 1936, p. 128.
[94] Ibid., p. 208.
[95] Ibid., p. 229.
[96] Ibid., p. xv.
[97] Ibid., p. 231.

Communist Party entered an electoral alliance with Leon Blum and the Socialists, intending to forestall a repetition of the attempted fascist coup that had occurred the previous February. The new relationship with the Socialists required a revision of 'official' attitudes towards the 'united front', hitherto condemned as a Trotskyist deviation from Leninism. Kuusinen had taken the first step in 1933, denying that the Comintern had ever opposed a united front against fascism. 'There is no such principle in Bolshevik tactics', he told the thirteenth plenum of the ECCI.[98] In 1935 Manuilsky announced that 'bourgeois democracy' was no longer a reactionary slogan—at least not by comparison to fascism. By raising this new banner it would be possible to attract 'broader strata than under the slogan of a direct struggle for proletarian dictatorship'.[99] The united front would prepare the way for 'national front' governments, which in turn would lead the struggle against war and fascism.

France had been Russia's ally against Germany in the First World War. To revive that tie in the mid-1930s seemed especially attractive: in addition to its system of alliances in Eastern Europe, France possessed substantial gold reserves that could be used to acquire *matériel* in the event of a new war. In the early years of the crisis France had been an island of stability in a sea of turmoil. Currency stabilization had come later than in other countries, and the renewal of fixed capital, delayed until the late 1920s, imparted a buoyant momentum during the early 1930s. But Stalin's courtship of Paris came at the very moment that the French economy began to crumble after several years of deflation in defence of the gold standard. Communist participation in the Popular Front gave Blum a parliamentary majority in 1936. With Moscow's anxious support and advice, the new government set about relaunching industry with the aid of the newly discovered 'artificial stimuli'.

Hoping to solve the 'problem of markets', Blum pressured employers to raise wages. By the autumn of 1936 the wage index had risen by nearly 20 per cent. French capitalists responded to the rise in production costs by transferring funds into safer currencies in

[98] Kuusinen, 'Fascism, the Danger of War . . .', p. 113.
[99] Manuilsky, 'Itogi VII Kongressa Kommunisticheskovo Internatsionala', *Bol'shevik*, no. 18 (30 September 1935), p. 13.

anticipation of a devaluation of the franc. Varga warned of a calculated bourgeois plot to sabotage the franc and weaken France's defence capabilities.[100] Arguing that devaluation would bring inflation and erosion of working-class incomes, he insisted that the finance capitalists were endeavouring to turn the masses against the government and create a favourable environment for fascism. In the interest of French military security the outflow of gold must be stopped at once.[101] Following this advice, Communist deputies strenuously objected to devaluation, saying it would reward the speculators. When the value of the franc was lowered in the autumn of 1936, Varga feared the worst. In an effort to defend real incomes the working class had no recourse but to strike. A defensive struggle would then assume the 'outward character of attacks on capital, a situation shown by experience to be very favourable to the bourgeoisie and giving the opportunity for a great campaign of [fascist] demagogy'.[102] After denouncing the Social Democrats as 'social fascists', the Communist Party had now become the party of 'labour peace' and 'class harmony'. The resulting dilemma had been sketched by Varga as early as 1930: 'Speaking in an "abstract-theoretical" way, it is possible to avoid a crisis . . . with the help of a strong rise in the consuming power of society, that is, with a rise in wages in the first place. . . . This is the road the Social Democrats propose. . . . But it is perfectly obvious to every Marxist that the capitalist class will never agree voluntarily to surrender to the working class a portion of the surplus-value in order to permit it to sell more commodities to the working class.'[103]

Hitler and Roosevelt had given the answer to this contradiction: national income must *increase* at the same time as it is redistributed. With this end in view, Blum inaugurated a programme of public works and provoked a surge of bourgeois protests against excessive taxation. The failure of the public works programme was related to the currency problems in that the outflow of capital undermined the

---

[100] Varga, 'Zagovor Vragov Naroda protiv Franka', *Kommunisticheskii Internatsional*, no. 11–12 (25 June 1936), p. 108.

[101] Ibid., p. 110.

[102] Varga, 'Economy and Economic Policy in the Second and Third Quarter of 1936', p. 1459.

[103] Varga, *Konets Amerikanskovo Protsvetaniya*, p. 59.

government's fiscal policies. When the Popular Front began to disintegrate, Varga saw ominous similarities between France and America. Ignorant of their own needs, the finance capitalists in both countries thwarted government measures by waging their own strike, or refusing to invest.[104] Like Roosevelt's opponents, the French bourgeoisie complained of declining labour discipline, 'government by the masses', and a 'parallel government' on the part of trade unions.[105] By the time of Blum's resignation in June 1937, the French economy had sunk into stagnation. Stalin's intended ally, for whom he had amended the whole of received Comintern doctrine, turned out to be the one country that confirmed the theory of the 'general crisis' and the depression 'of a special kind'. When Daladier signed the Munich Agreement with Hitler in 1938, it was understandable that Stalin should rush to reach his own compromise with the Nazis before it was too late. Not only was French capital too short-sighted, degenerate, and weak to resist Germany, but Stalin was probably also possessed by a sense of betrayal. His concern at this point was to let the French reap the reward of their own treachery.

5. Expansion 'of a Special Kind'

From Varga's standpoint the failure of Blum's attempt to replicate the New Deal resulted from the tense political conditions that prevailed in France. On the level of general theory, Hitler and Roosevelt had shown that it was possible to initiate an economic recovery through state intervention. In March 1937 Varga drew the appropriate conclusion: 'If one begins . . . with the fact that the boundary between revival and prosperity is the high point of the preceding cycle, it follows that now, at the beginning of 1937, *the position of the capitalist world economy as a whole can be characterized as a transition from recovery to the phase of expansion.*'[106] The whole

---

[104] Varga, 'Frantsiya', *Mirovoe Khozyaistvo i Mirovaya Politika*, no. 3 (March 1937), p. 101.
[105] Varga, 'Frantsiya', *Mirovoe Khozyaistvo i Mirovaya Politika*, no. 8 (August 1937), p. 114.
[106] Varga, '1936 god: Itogi i Perspektivy', *Mirovoe Khozyaistvo i Mirovaya Politika*, no. 3 (March 1937), p. 12.

theory of capitalism's 'general crisis' was now becoming suspect: the 'throttling narrowness of the market' had not prevented the resumption of capital construction.

At the very moment that Varga began to contemplate this conclusion, however, something unusual occurred. Although American orders for new machinery were nearly twice as high as in 1929, the surge of demand was 'mainly restricted to the renewal of equipment in *existing enterprises*; the expansion of fixed capital by means of new construction is still just beginning'.[107] When the expected wave of construction failed to materialize, Varga began to speak of an expansion 'of a special kind'.[108] In place of the traditional phase of building new enterprises, the recovery of investments in this cycle had been halted by the existing redundance of fixed capital, 'which is characteristic of the general crisis of capitalism'.[109] By the end of 1937, production indicators were tumbling in America and another crisis appeared to be at hand. Varga immediately predicted that the new crisis in 1938 would become 'just as deep as that of 1929'.[110] The theory of the 'general crisis' had finally been vindicated: the depression 'of a special kind' could not grow over into a new phase of cyclical prosperity.[111] All the troublesome questions had been answered at one stroke. The collapse of capitalism was back on schedule. And with renewed enthusiasm, Varga was willing to explain why.

In *Capitalism and Socialism After Twenty Years* (1937) Varga resurrected the theory of the 'general crisis' in neo-Luxemburgist terms. 'Crisis rationalization' during the 1930s had intensified labour without broadening the market. The theory that capitalism created its own internal market was nonsense, for '*in the most highly-developed countries a tendency can be observed towards an absolute decline in the number of productive workers*'.[112] 'Varga's Law' had

[107] Varga, 'K Ekonomicheskomu Polozheniyu v SShA', *Kommunisticheskii Internatsional*, no. 5 (May 1937), p. 44.
[108] Varga, 'Kapitalisticheskoe Khozyaistvo v Pervoi Polovine 1937g', *Mirovoe Khozyaistvo i Mirovaya Politika*, no. 8 (August 1937), p. 57.
[109] Varga, 'Soedinennye Shtaty Ameriki', *Mirovoe Khozyaistvo i Mirovaya Politika*, no. 9 (September 1937), p. 113.
[110] Varga, 'Nachalo Novovo Ekonomicheskovo Krizisa v Stranakh Kapitala', *Bol'shevik*, no. 23–4 (15 December 1937), p. 61.
[111] Ibid., pp. 47–8.
[112] Varga, *Kapitalizm i Sotsializm za 20 Let*, Moscow 1938, p. 65.

triumphed over capitalist planning efforts. Chronic unemployment and a chronic crisis were inevitable because the 'depeasantizing' process had ended.[113] A recovery in heavy industry was impossible because of society's limited 'consuming power'.[114] In *The Capitalist World on the Eve of a New Crisis* (1937) Varga took an identical position. The one novelty to appear in both these works was the new importance attached to one particular form of capital expenditure, investments in transportation. In previous decades railway construction was said to have played a unique role in alleviating the 'problem of markets'. Railways differed from other forms of production in Department I in one critical respect: 'they are intended only for the shipment of commodities, not for their production. This means that they do not increase the mass of commodities being produced, unlike means of production in the narrow sense of the word. For this reason they are not a source of overproduction.'[115] Once Varga made this discovery, the game was up.

From here no other course remained open but to concede that *any* form of investment that created employment in Department I without simultaneously creating a new stream of traditional commodities would alleviate the 'problem of markets'. Luxemburg had made a similar discovery in *The Accumulation of Capital*, commenting that military production was 'a pre-eminent means for the realization of surplus-value; it is in itself a province of accumulation'.[116] The question that now emerged was: what would happen if the democracies accelerated rearmament without incurring Hitler's excesses and without creating a genuine 'war economy'? The answer was not long in coming, first in Britain and then in America.

The British economy had already made a mockery of Stalinist theory throughout the 1930s. From being a model of stagnation in the 1920s, Britain had led the way in recovery—and without recourse to 'artificial stimuli'. In 1935 Varga had written that 'in England more than anywhere else, the depression displays the characteristic features of a "normal" depression . . . and even a

[113] Ibid., p. 81.
[114] Ibid., p. 80.
[115] Varga, *Kapitalisticheskii Mir na Poroge Novovo Krizisa*, 1938, pp. 19–20.
[116] Luxemburg, *The Accumulation of Capital*, p. 454.

certain transition from depression to recovery'.[117] In spite of 'Varga's Law', the number of employed workers had reached record levels in 1935.[118] In April 1936 Varga spoke of a 'relatively normal development of the industrial cycle'.[119] Six months later a 'boom' was said to be in progress.[120] Since a 'normal' cycle implied the inevitability of an ensuing crisis, Varga insisted that the British economy would have to contract by 1937 or 1938. The level of activity in Britain did decline during 1938, but armaments production cushioned the effects on the iron and steel industry. In America, where the recent downturn had been much more severe, Varga saw 'certain signs of improvement' by the summer of 1938. The conclusion was obvious: 'In rich countries, such as the United States and Great Britain, where there is a surplus of capital . . . armament expenditures [can be financed] chiefly by floating loans . . . [They] represent an extension of the capitalist market and as a result encourage economic recovery and diminish the unfavourable effects of the economic crisis.'[121] In terms of the theory of realization and markets, armaments expenditures could play the same role as railways in an earlier phase of capitalist development, broadening the market without contributing to overproduction.

At the Eighteenth Congress of the Soviet Communist Party early in 1939 Stalin continued to refer to a 'serious economic crisis' in America, Britain, and France.[122] Varga knew better. American production had been steadily rising: 'the purchasing power of the working masses' had been 'reinforced by great government expenditures on public works, unemployment support, and so on'.[123]

[117] Varga, 'Ekonomicheskoe Polozhenie Anglii i Dal'neishie Perspektivy', *Mirovoe Khozyaistvo i Mirovaya Politika*, no. 4 (April 1935), p. 8.

[118] Varga, 'Economy and Economic Policy in the Third Quarter of 1935', p. 1772.

[119] Varga, 'Economy and Economic Policy in the First Quarter of 1936', *International Press Correspondence*, XVI, no. 26 (4 June 1936), p. 703.

[120] Varga, 'Economy and Economic Policy in the Second and Third Quarters of 1936', p. 1454.

[121] Varga, 'Economy and Economic Policy in the Second Quarter of 1938', *World News and Views* [formerly International Press Correspondence], XVIII, no. 43 (9 September 1938), pp. 988–9.

[122] Stalin, 'Report on Activity of the CC of the CPSU', *World News and Views*, XIX, no. 16 (29 March 1939), p. 314.

[123] Varga, 'Economy and Economic Policy in the Second Half-Year 1938', *World News and Views*, XIX, no. 13 (23 March 1939), p. 254.

In other words, the American state had consciously created the prerequisites for a new expansion. Unable to concede that the capitalists had found a solution to the problem of the business cycle, Varga saw no alternative but to move in that direction. The Americans had demonstrated that 'government expenditures . . . for armaments and public works influence and modify the cyclical development of reproduction which is based upon the internal laws of capitalist society'.[124] In 1935 Varga had speculated that armaments might indeed provide the key to capitalist prosperity: 'The thesis that the more money is expended on armaments the better is the situation of the capitalist economy . . . would mean no more and no less than that the key to permanent prosperity had been found: all the capitalist governments would have to do when a crisis loomed up would be to increase their expenditures on armaments and the solution would be achieved.'[125]

Having ridiculed this 'solution' four years earlier, Varga admitted by October 1939 that the 'internal cyclical movement' in Britain had been relegated to an altogether secondary role: 'With Great Britain's abundance of capital . . . and labour-power', armaments expenditures were having 'a stimulating effect upon . . . all branches of industry without exception.'[126] The continuing increase in production was 'almost entirely due to the enormous armaments'.[127]

6. Conclusion

Varga's reassessment of the economic role of the capitalist state, although still somewhat tentative, had potentially far-reaching consequences. It demonstrated that neo-Luxemburgism had run its theoretical course, culminating in a new variant of 'organized capitalism'. Logically, Varga's reasoning ran parallel to that of John Maynard Keynes in *The General Theory of Employment, Interest and Money*, published in 1936. Criticizing the traditional attitudes

---

[124] Ibid., pp. 263–4.
[125] Varga, 'Economy and Economic Policy in the Fourth Quarter of 1935', p. 342.
[126] Varga, 'Economy and Economic Policy in the First Half of 1939', *World News and Views*, XIX, no. 48 (7 October 1939), p. 1019.
[127] Ibid., p. 1018.

of British political leaders, Keynes had urged a programme of 'loan expenditure', or public investment financed by borrowing, with which to stimulate both private investment and consumption. According to Keynes, what mattered was not the pattern but the volume of public expenditure: 'Pyramid-building, earthquakes, even wars may serve to increase wealth, if the education of our statesmen on the principles of classical economics stands in the way of anything better.[128] The Great Depression had created the rudiments of a theoretical truce between Soviet economists and their Western counterparts.

In the years following 1945 the change of theoretical perspective raised hopes of political co-existence. In 1946 Varga published *Changes in the Economics of Capitalism as a Result of the Second World War*. Postwar prospects were shown to depend on the success or failure of the capitalist state in controlling crises through deliberate policies of 'employment creation'. By re-activating idle capital the state would acquire a 'limited' opportunity to 'alleviate the threat of chronic mass unemployment'.[129] Moreover, by spending these funds on 'non-productive purposes, for instance the construction of schools, hospitals, housing, care for the aged and so forth'—rather than armaments—the threat of new imperialist wars could be reduced.[130] The origin of Khrushchev's claim (in the mid-1950s) that wars were no longer 'fatalistically inevitable' could be found in Varga's acknowledgement that modern capitalism required a measure of economic planning in one form or another. The same was true of Khrushchev's assertion that peaceful co-existence might result in a peaceful transition to socialism. Varga explained that the workers had been politically activated by the war; the question of 'a greater or lesser participation in the management of government' was therefore destined to become 'the main content of the political struggle between . . . the bourgeoisie and the proletariat' in coming years.[131] Recalling the Popular Front strategy of

[128] J.M. Keynes, *The General Theory of Employment, Interest and Money*, London 1961, p. 129.

[129] Varga, *Izmeneniya v Ekonomike Kapitalizma v Itoge Vtoroi Mirovoi Voiny*, 1946, pp. 299–300.

[130] Ibid., p. 300.

[131] Ibid., p. 318.

the 1930s, Varga expected the working class to ally with 'progressive parties' in pursuit of democratic nationalization and the peaceful competition of rival social systems.

In 1946 Varga's new ideas were still embryonic. In the spring of 1947 the Cold War was approaching and Stalin resolved to halt the drift into 'revisionism' before it proceeded any further. Varga was again subjected to public denunciation, and Stalin delivered his last authoritative pronouncement on the 'problem of markets'. In *Economic Problems of Socialism in the USSR* (1952) Stalin argued that capitalism's 'general crisis' was deepening because of the rise of People's Democracies in Eastern Europe and the victory of the Chinese revolution. The geographic contraction of markets meant that 'the sphere of exploitation of the world's resources by the major capitalist countries . . . will not expand but contract; that their opportunities for sales in the world market will deteriorate, and that their industries will be operating more and more below capacity. That . . . is what is meant by the deepening of the general crisis.'[132]

The death of the dictator in 1953 brought with it a renewal of theoretical inquiry and accorded Varga the last word in the debate. In 1963 he published *Politico-Economic Problems of Capitalism*, summarizing the issues that had been in contention. In a chapter entitled 'The Question of the Bourgeois State' he recalled the denunciations of 1947 and took his adversaries, including Stalin, to task. Although it was self-evident 'that under capitalism there can be no planned economy in the Marxist sense of the word', he insisted that 'this does not imply that under capitalism there can be no "planning" of any sort'. [133] During the Second World War 'a substantial share of production' had been planned; emergent bourgeois states such as India were achieving 'a certain effect' with five-year plans; and the industrialized countries of the Common Market had 'planned' their economic policy for a period of twelve years in advance. These facts proved that the alternative posed by Stalinists—'complete anarchy of production or complete planned economy'—was 'impractical, untrue and hence anti-Marxist'.[134]

In comparison to Stalin's 'dogmatism' Varga's final position was

---

[132] Stalin, *Economic Problems of Socialism in the USSR*, New York 1952, p. 27.
[133] Varga, *Politico-Economic Problems of Capitalism*, Moscow 1968, p. 48.
[134] Ibid., p. 50.

undoubtedly one of enlightenment and restraint. But was it Marxist? In 1929 Varga had eliminated disproportionalities as the cause of economic crises. In 1939 the 'problem of markets' likewise disappeared. A Marxist might well inquire, therefore, not whether elements of a planned economy were possible, but whether Varga's views any longer entailed the *necessity* of economic crises. Did they not, in fact, suggest—as Bukharin had maintained many years before—that the capitalist state might preserve a moving economic 'equilibrium'? To this question Varga continued to reply in the negative. In *Politico-Economic Problems* he promised a new generation of Soviet readers that crises must inevitably result from 'the contradiction between the social character of production and the private capitalist appropriation of the fruits of labour'.[135] For Lenin, private appropriation had implied private and unco-ordinated investments along with inevitable disproportionalities— e.g., the production of automobiles for which there might be insufficient fuel, or appliances for which there might be inadequate supplies of electrical energy. The socialization of production and the rise of partial planning coincided with and contributed to overall economic instability. For Lenin, the contradiction between socialized production and private appropriation inevitably led to Marx's call to expropriate the expropriators. For Varga, the same contradiction had become a magic formula and a substitute for any serious attempt to interpret contemporary issues in terms of the classical summons to proletarian revolution. In that respect it might be said of Varga that he led the way not only in repudiating Stalinism, but also in making Soviet Marxism all but indis-tinguishable from Social Democratic 'revisionism' or even Keynesian liberalism.

[135] Ibid., p. 166.

Appendix

In an article entitled 'The Theory of the Long Cycle: Kondrat'ev, Trotsky, Mandel', I have used graphs provided by Trotsky and Kondrat'ev to distinguish their respective approaches.[1] Trotsky's graph appeared in his article 'On the Curve of Capitalist Development', published in June 1923. Although Trotsky described the graph as a 'schematic drawing', in fact it was based on the data for English foreign trade that he originally found in *The Times* and then used to illustrate the stages of capitalist development in his address to the Comintern in 1921. The drawing is reproduced overleaf (Diagram 1).

Besides showing the relation between the cyclical and the basic 'curve', Trotsky's drawing also indicated how the latter, which depicts the trend of capitalist development, was occasionally interrupted. While the cyclical curve was governed by the *internal* mechanism of the capitalist market, the slope of the underlying trend was determined by changes in *external conditions* and by the relative autonomy of superstructural phenomena. The fact that external conditions did not change with the same regularity as internal market forces implied that long cycles possessed no 'strict rhythm'. The turning-points of development were unpredictable by nature, and no automatic periodicity of long cycles could be expected.

Kondrat'ev's approach can also be illustrated in Diagram 1, by imposing a single curve on Trotsky's original drawing (the dotted

[1] Richard B. Day, 'The Theory of the Long Cycle: Kondrat'ev, Trotsky, Mandel', *New Left Review*, no. 99 (September–October 1976), pp. 67–82.

DIAGRAM 1
The Curve of Capitalist Development

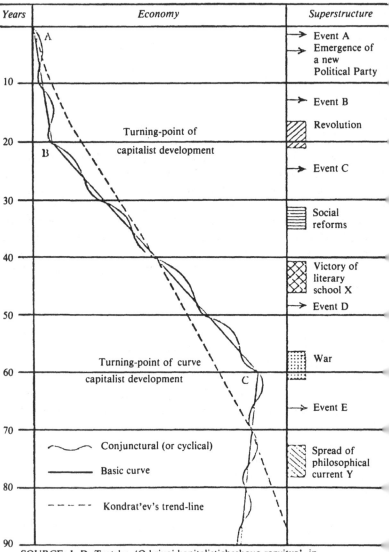

SOURCE: L.D. Trotsky, 'O krivoi kapitalisticheskovo razvitya', in
Vestnik Sotsialisticheskoi Akademii, No. 4, April-July 1923.

DIAGRAM 2
English Foreign Trade Turnover
(Per 1,000 population in 1,000's of Pounds Sterling)

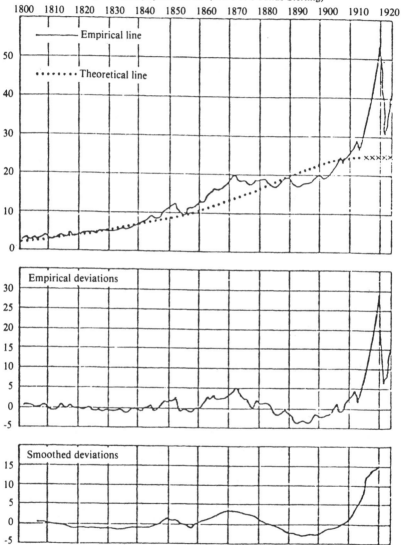

Source: N.D. Kondrat'ev and D.I. Oparin, Bol'shie tsikly kon'yunktury. Moscow 1928, p. 27.

line designated as Kondrat'ev's trend-line). By deriving a single trend-line, or a smooth curve with a single equation, Kondrat'ev made explicit his assumption of a continuous 'moving equilibrium' and thereby challenged the Marxist case for uneven development in the history of capitalism. This implication emerged more clearly when Kondrat'ev produced his own graphs in 1926.

Using both real and monetary data, Kondrat'ev explained that he had determined his trend-line by applying the least-squares technique to each series of empirical data. The deviations of the empirical data from the trend-line were then measured and plotted horizontally. Short-term (or cyclical) influences were removed through the use of a nine-year moving average, producing a third graph, which portrayed the movement of the long cycle about the trend-line. Kondrat'ev's results for English foreign-trade data are given in Diagram 2.

According to Kondrat'ev, the graph of smoothed deviations charted the waves of the long cycle in the following sequence:

1790 to 1810–17 rising wave	first long cycle
1810–17 to 1844–51 falling wave	
1844–51 to 1870–5 rising wave	second long cycle
1870–5 to 1890–6 falling wave	
1890–6 to 1914–20 rising wave	

This brief comparison of the two approaches explains why Kondrat'ev had to internalize Trotsky's external conditions. For Kondrat'ev, technological change, wars, revolutions, changes in the money supply, and so forth could be no more than passive manifestations and 'regularities' of the long cycle. To extend even relative autonomy to external conditions and 'superstructural' forces was implicitly to forego the 'strict rhythm' of the long cycle. To internalize the external conditions, in contrast, was to assert that the development of capitalism depended on a single internal regulator (the reproduction of fixed capital in its most durable forms) and that the postwar crisis would inevitably give way to a restored equilibrium.

Selected Bibliography

1. *Journals and Newspapers*
Bol'shevik
Byulleten' Instituta Mirovovo Khozyaistva i Mirovoi Politiki
Ekonomicheskaya Zhizn'
Ekonomicheskoe Obozrenie
International Press Correspondence (World News and Views)
Kommunisticheskaya Revolyutsiya
Kommunisticheskii Internatsional
Kon'yunktura Mirovovo Khozyaistva
Kon'yunktura Mirovovo Khozyaistva—Byulleten'
Krasnaya Nov'
Kredit i Khozyaistvo
Mezhdunarodnaya Letopis' Politiki
Mirovoe Khozyaistvo i Mirovaya Politika
Na Agrarnom Fronte
Narodnoe Khozyaistvo
Planovoe Khozyaistvo
Pod Znamenem Marksizma
Pravda
Problemy Ekonomiki
Problemy Marksizma
Sotsialisticheskoe Khozyaistvo
Sputnik Kommunista
Torgovo-Promyshlennaya Gazeta (Za Industrializatsiyu)
Vestnik Sotsialisticheskoi Akademii (Vestnik Kommunisticheskoi Akademii)
Vneshnyaya Torgovlya

2. Books and Articles

Bogolepov, M. I., *Evropa Posle Voiny*, Petrograd: Izdatel'stvo 'Pravo', 1921.

——, *Evropa vo Vlasti Krizisa 1920–1922*, Petersburg: Izdatel'stvo 'Pravo', 1922.

——, *Valyutnyi Khaos—k Sovremennomu Polozheniyu Evropy*, Petersburg and Moscow: 'Kooperativnoe Izdatel'stvo', 1922.

Bonch-Osmolovsky, A. and Tyrtov, S., *Angliya i Soedinennye Shtaty v Bor'be za Mirovuyu Gegemoniyu*, Moscow and Leningrad: Gosudarstvennoe Izdatel'stvo, 1930.

Bukharin, N. I., *Imperialism and World Economy*, London: Merlin, 1972.

——, 'K. Teorii Imperialisticheskovo Gosudarstva', *Revolyutsiya Prava: Sbornik Pervyi*, Moscow, 1925, 5–32.

——, *Ekonomika Perekhodnovo Perioda*, Moscow: Gosudarstvennoe Izdatel'stvo, 1920.

——, *Historical Materialism*, Ann Arbor: University of Michigan Press, 1929.

——, *Kapitalisticheskaya Stabilizatsiya i Proletarskaya Revolyutsiya*, Moscow and Leningrad: Gosudarstvennoe Izdatel'stvo, 1927.

——, *Imperialism i Nakoplenie Kapitala*, 3rd ed., Moscow and Leningrad: Gosudarstvennoe Izdatel'stvo, 1928.

Bukhartsev, Dm. *Garantiinyi Dogovor*, Moscow and Leningrad: Izdatel'stvo 'Planovoe Khozyaistvo', 1926.

Dalin, S., *Ekonomicheskaya Politika Ruzvel'ta*, Moscow: Gosudarstvennoe Sotsial'no-Ekonomicheskoe Izdatel'stvo, 1936.

Day, R. B., *Leon Trotsky and the Politics of Economic Isolation*, London: Cambridge University Press, 1973.

——, 'Dialectical Method in the Political Writings of Lenin and Bukharin', *Canadian Journal of Political Science*, IX, no. 2 (June 1976), 244–60.

——, 'The Theory of the Long Cycle: Kondrat'ev, Trotsky, Mandel', *New Left Review*, no. 99 (September–October, 1976), 67–82.

——, 'Trotsky and Preobrazhensky', *Studies in Comparative Communism*, X, no. 1–2 (spring-summer 1977), 69–86.

——, 'Rosa Luxemburg and the Accumulation of Capital', *Critique.*

Dityakin, V., *Mirovaya Torgovlya v Epokhu Velikovo Ekonomicheskovo Krizisa 1917–1921gg*, Kazan: Gosudarstvennoe Izdatel'stvo, 1921.

Dvolaitsky, S. and Rubin, I., eds., *Osnovnye Problemy Politicheskoi Ekonomii*, Gosudarstvennoe Izdatel'stvo, 1922.

Engels, F., *Herr Eugen Dühring's Revolution in Science [Anti-Dühring]*, translated by Emile Burns and ed. by C. P. Dutt, London: Martin Lawrence, n.d.

Eventov, L. Y., Fel'dman, G. A., and Mendel'son, L. A., eds., *Mirovoe Khozyaistvo na Rubezhe 1929g*, Moscow: Izdatel'stvo 'Planovoe Khozyaistvo', 1929.

——, and Mendel'son, L. A., eds., *Krizis v Severo-Amerikanskikh Soedinennykh Shtatakh*, Moscow: 'Moskovskii Rabochii', 1930.

——, and Mendel'son, L. A., eds., *Problemy Mirovovo Khozyaistva*, Moscow: Gosudarstvennoe Planovo-Khozyaistvennoe Izdatel'stvo, 1930.

Fal'kner, S. A., *Proizkhozhdenie Zheleznovo Zakona Zarabotnoi Platy*, Moscow: Vysshii Sovet Narodnovo Khozyaistva, 1920.

——, *Stroenie i Kon'yunktura Mirovovo Khozyaistva*, Moscow: Vysshii Sovet Narodnovo Khozyaistva, 1920.

——, 'Teoreticheskaya Ekonomika Sotsial'noi Revolyutsii', *Nauchnye Izvestiya: Sbornik Pervyi*, Moscow, 1922, 223–247.

——, *Perelom v Razvitii Mirovovo Promyshlennovo Krizisa*, Moscow: Vysshii Sovet Narodnovo Khozyaistva, 1922.

——, *Problemy Teorii i Praktiki Emissionnovo Khozyaistva*, Moscow: Izdatel'stvo 'Ekonomicheskaya Zhizn', 1924.

Gertsbakh, M., *Mezhdunarodnye Monopolii*, Moscow: Izdatel'stvo Kommunisticheskoi Akademii, 1930.

Gertsenshtein, A., *Teoriya Kapitalisticheskovo Rynka*, Moscow: Izdatel'stvo Kommunisticheskoi Akademii, 1928.

——, *Sushchestvuyut li Bol'shie Tsikly Kon'yunktury?*, Moscow: Izdatel'stvo Kommunisticheskoi Akademii, 1929.

Gol'man, M., *Vseobshchii Krizis Kapitalizma v Svete Vzglyadov Marksa-Engel'sa i Lenina*, Moscow: Izdatel'stvo Kommunisticheskoi Akademii, 1929.

Gorfinkel', E.S., *SSSR v Sisteme Mirovovo Khozyaistva*, Moscow: Izdatel'stvo Kommunisticheskoi Akademii, 1929.

Guberman, S., *K Teorii Kapitalisticheskovo Rynka*, Moscow: Izdatel'stvo Kommunisticheskoi Akademii, 1929.

Hilferding, R., *Das Finanzkapital*. Frankfurt am Main: Europäische Verlagsanstalt, 1968.

Ioffe, A.A., *Ot Genui do Gaagi—Sbornik Stat'ei*, Moscow and Petrograd: Gosudarstvennoe Izdatel'stvo, 1925.

Jasny, N., *Soviet Economists of the Twenties—Names to be Remembered*, London: Cambridge University Press, 1972.

Kasharsky, L., ed., *Burzhuaznye Ekonomisty o Mirovom Krizise*, Moscow and Leningrad: Gosudarstvennoe Sotsial'no-Ekonomicheskoe Izdatel'stvo, 1931.

——, and Serebryakov, V., eds., *Mirovoi Krizis 1929–1931*, Moscow and Leningrad: Gosudarstvennoe Sotsial'no-Ekonomicheskoe Izdatel'stvo, 1931.

Keynes, J.M., *The Economic Consequences of the Peace*, New York: Harper and Row, 1971.

Khmel'nitskaya, E., Gurvich, E., and Ioel'son, M., eds., *Bankovskii Krakh i Inflyatsiya v SASSh—Diskussiya v Institute Mirovovo Khozyaistva i Mirovoi Politiki Komakademii*, Moscow: Partiinoe Izdatel'stvo, 1933.

Kondrat'ev, N.D., *Mirovoe Khozyaistvo i evo Kon'yunktury vo Vremya i Posle Voiny*, Vologda: Gosudarstvennoe Izdatel'stvo, 1922.

——, ed., *Voprosy Kon'yunktury*, Moscow: Finansovoe Izdatel'stvo NKF SSSR, 1925.

——, and Oparin, D.I., *Bol'shie Tsikly Kon'yunktury*, Moscow, 1928.

Lapinsky, P., *Garantiinyi Dogovor i Mezhdunarodnoe Polozhenie*, Moscow: Izdatel'stvo 'Pravda' i 'Bednota', 1925.

——, *Novaya Faza Imperializma i ee Ekonomicheskie Istochniki*, Moscow: Izdatel'stvo Gosplana SSSR, 1925.

——, *Krizis Kapitalizma i Sotsial-Fashizm*, Moscow and Leningrad: Gosudarstvennoe Izdatel'stvo, 1930.

——, *V Kotle Krizisa—Krizis, Vodka i Vybory*, Moscow: Partizdat, 1932.

Lenin, V.I., *Collected Works* (45 vols.), Moscow: Progress, 1972–1974.

——, *Selected Works* (3 vols.), Moscow: Foreign Languages Publishing House, 1960–1961.

Lewis, W.A., *Economic Survey, 1919–1939*, London: Allen and Unwin, 1949.

Livshits, B., ed., *Problema Rynka i Krizisov*, Moscow: Izdatel'stvo 'Planovoe Khozyaistvo', 1926.

Lozovsky, A., *Mirovoe Nastuplenie Kapitala i Edinyi Proletarskii Front*, Moscow: Izdanie Profinterna, 1922.

Luxemburg, R., *The Accumulation of Capital*, translated by Agnes Schwarzschild, London: Routledge and Kegan Paul, 1963.

——, and Bukharin, N., *Imperialism and the Accumulation of Capital*, translated by Rudolf Wichmann, ed. by Kenneth J. Tarbuck, London: Allen Lane the Penguin Press, 1972.

Maisky, I., *Sovetskaya Rossiya i Kapitalisticheskii Mir (Gaagskaya Konferentsiya)*, Moscow: Izdatel'stvo 'Krasnaya Nov', 1922.

Maksakovsky, P.V., *Kapitalisticheskii Tsikl—Ocherk Marksistskoi Teorii Tsikla*, Moscow: Izdatel'stvo Kommunisticheskoi Akademii, 1929.

Marx, K., *Capital* Volume 1 and Volume 2, Harmondsworth: Penguin in association with New Left Review, 1977 and 1978; Volume 3, Moscow, Foreign Languages Publishing House, 1962.

——, *The Poverty of Philosophy*, New York: International Publishers, n.d.

——, *Theories of Surplus-Value*, translated by G.A. Bonner and Emile Burns, ed. by Karl Kautsky, London: Lawrence and Wishart, 1954.

——, and Engels, F., *Selected Works* (2 vols.), Moscow: Foreign Languages Publishing House, 1962.

Mendel'son, L. and Khmel'nitskaya, E., eds., *Krizis i Zagnivanie Kapitalisticheskoi Promyshlennosti*, Moscow: Partiinoe Izdatel'stvo, 1934.

Mezhdunarodnye Problemy—Stat'i o Politike i Ekonomiki Sovremennoi Evropy, Moscow, 1922.

[Milyutin, V.P. et al.], *Kondrat'evshchina—Sbornik*, Moscow: Izdatel'stvo Kommunisticheskoi Akademii, 1930.

Oparin, D.I., *Kon'yunktura i Rynki*, Moscow: Izdatel'stvo 'Tekhnika Upravleniya', 1928.

Osinsky, N., *Mirovoi Krizis Sel'skovo Khozyaistva*, Moscow: 'Novaya Derevnya', 1924.

——, *Mirovoe Khozyaistvo i Krizisy*, Moscow: Izdatel'stvo Kommunisticheskoi Akademii, 1925.

294

——, *Moi Lzheucheniya o Soedinennykh Shtatakh Severnoi Ameriki*, Moscow: Izdatel'stvo 'Pravda' i 'Bednota', 1926.

——, Spektator, M., Smit, M., and Politikus, *Istoricheskii Krizis Angliiskovo Kapitalizma*, Moscow and Leningrad: Gosudarstvennoe Izdatel'stvo, 1926.

——, *Ugrozhaet li Amerike Ekonomicheskii Krizis?*, Moscow and Leningrad: Gosudarstvennoe Izdatel'stvo, 1928.

Pashukanis, E.B., *Imperializm i Kolonial'naya Politika*, Izdatel'stvo Kommunisticheskoi Akademii, 1928.

Pervushin, S.A., *Khozyaistvennaya Kon'yunktura*, Moscow: Izdatel'stvo 'Ekonomicheskaya Zhizn', 1925.

Poslevoennyi Kapitalizm v Osveshchenii Kominterna: Sbornik Dokumentov i Resolyutsii Kongressov i Ispolkoma Kominterna, Moscow: Partiinoe Izdatel'stvo, 1932.

Preobrazhensky, E., *Itogi Genuezskoi Konferentsii i Khozyaistvennye Perspektivy Evropy*, Moscow: Gosudarstvennoe Izdatel'stvo, 1922.

——, *Zakat Kapitalizma*, Gosudarstvennoe Sotsial'no-Ekonomicheskoe Izdatel'stvo, 1931.

Radek, K., *Vneshnyaya Politika Sovetskoi Rossii*, Moscow and Petrograd: Gosudarstvennoe Izdatel'stvo, 1923.

——, *Chto Takoe Era Demokraticheskovo Patsifizma?*, Moscow and Leningrad: Gosudarstvennoe Izdatel'stvo, 1925.

Roginsky, G., ed., *Zakat Kapitalizma v Trotskistskom Zerkale*, Partiinoe Izdatel'stvo, 1932.

Rubinshtein, M., *Sovremennyi Kapitalizm i Organizatsiya Truda*, 2nd. ed., Moscow: Moskovskii Rabochii, 1923.

——, *Kapitalisticheskaya Ratsionalizatsiya*, Moscow: Izdanie Profinterna, 1929.

——, *Protivorechiya Amerikanskovo Kapitalizma*, Moscow and Leningrad: Moskovskii Rabochii, 1929.

——, *Mirovoi Ekonomicheskii Krizis 1930 goda*, Moscow and Leningrad: Gosudarstvennoe Izdatel'stvo, 1930.

——, *Mirovoi Ekonomicheskii Krizis Kapitalizma*, Moscow and Leningrad: Moskovskii Rabochii, 1931.

Sandomirsky, G.B., ed., *Materialy Genuezskoi Konferentsii*, Moscow, 1922.

Segal, Y.E., *Mirovoi Krizis i Protivorechiya Kapitalizma*, Moscow: Partizdat, 1932.

Serebryakov, V. and Karsharsky, L., *Protiv Trotskistskoi Kontseptsii Imperializma*, Moscow and Leningrad: Partiinoe Izdatel'stvo, 1932.

Shtein, B.E., *Gaagskaya Konferentsiya*, Moscow: Gosudarstvennoe Izdatel'stvo, 1922.

——, *Torgovaya Politika i Torgovye Dogovory Sovetskoi Rossii, 1917–1922gg*, Moscow and Petrograd: Gosudarstvennoe Izdatel'stvo, 1923.

——, *Vneshnyaya Torgovaya Politika SSSR*, Moscow and Leningrad: VSNKh, 1925.

Slutskina, S.D., *Osnovnye Zakonomernosti Razvitiya Imperializma—Zakon Neravnomernovo Razvitiya i Zagnivanie Kapitalizma*, Moscow and Leningrad: Gosudarstvennoe Sotsial'no-Ekonomicheskoe Izdatel'stvo, 1931.

Smit, M., *Klassovaya Bor'ba v Sovremennoi Anglii*, Moscow: Izdanie Profinterna, 1922.

——, *Dinamika Krizisov i Polozhenie Proletariata*, Moscow: Izdatel'stvo Kommunisticheskoi Akademii, 1927.

Sokol'nikov, G.Y., ed., *Problemy Mirovovo Denezhnovo Obrashcheniya—Sbornik Stat'ei*, Moscow: Finansovoe Izdatel'stvo NKF SSSR, 1927.

Spektator, M. [Nakhimson], *Mirovoe Khozyaistvo do i posle Voiny* (2 vols.), Moscow and Leningrad: Tsentral'noe Upravlenie Pechati i Prompropagandy (T.U.P.) V.S.N.K., 1924–1926.

——, *K Voprosu o Stabilizatsii Kapitalizma*, Moscow: Izdatel'stvo 'Planovoe Khozyaistvo', 1926.

——, *Vvedenie v Izuchenie Mirovovo Khozyaistva—Opyt Postroeniya Teorii Mirovovo Khozyaistva*, Moscow and Leningrad: Gosudarstvennoe Izdatel'stvo, 1928.

——, *Teoriya Agrarnykh Krizisov*, Moscow: Izdatel'stvo 'Mezhdunarodnyi Agrarnyi Institut', 1929.

——, *Bor'ba za Rynki posle Mirovoi Voiny*, Sotsekgiz, 1934.

Stalin, J.V., *Works* (13 vols.), Moscow: Foreign Languages Publishing House, 1953–1955.

——, *Economic Problems of Socialism in the USSR*, New York: International Publishers, 1952.

——, *Problems of Leninism*, Moscow: Foreign Languages Publishing House, 1954.

[Trakhtenberg, I. et al.], *Sovremennyi Kreditnyi Krizis—Diskussiya v Institute Mirovovo Khozyaistva i Mirovoi Politiki Komakademii*, Moscow: Partiinoe Izdatel'stvo, 1932.

Trotsky, L., *The First Five Years of the Communist International* (2 vols.), (Vol. 1) New York: Pioneer, 1945, (Vol 2) London: New Park, 1953.

——, *Europe and America*, translated by John G. Wright, Colombo, Ceylon: Lanka Samasamaja, n.d.

Varga, E., *Krizis Mirovovo Kapitalizma*, Moscow: Vysshii Sovet Narodnovo Khozyaistva, 1921.

——, and Lozovsky, A., *Mirovoi Krizis. Zadachi i Taktika Profsoyuzov*, Moscow: Otdel Pechati Krasnovo Internatsionala Profsoyuzov, 1921.

——, *Le Déclin du Capitalisme*, Hamburg, Editions de l'Internationale Communiste, 1922.

——, *Plan Dauesa i Mirovoi Krizis 1924 Goda*, Moscow: Moskovskii Rabochii, 1925.

——, *Mirovoe Khozyaistvo i Khozyaistvennaya Politika v 1925 Godu*, Moscow and Leningrad: Moskovskii Rabochii, 1926.

——, *Les Partis Social-Démocrates*, Paris: Bureau d'Editions, de Diffusion et de Publicité, n.d.

——, *The Decline of Capitalism*, London, 1928.

——, *Problemy Mirovovo Khozyaistva i Mirovoi Politiki*, Moscow: Izdatel'stvo Kommunisticheskoi Akademii, 1929.

[—— et al.], '*Organizovannyi Kapitalizm*'—*Diskussiya v Komakademii*, 2nd ed., Izdatel'stvo Kommunisticheskoi Akademii, 1930.

——, *Konets Amerikanskovo Protsvetaniya*, Moscow and Leningrad: Gosudarstvennoe Izdatel'stvo, 1930.

[—— et al.], *Mirovoi Ekonomicheskii Krizis* (*Kollektivnaya Rabota Instituta Mirovovo Khozyaistva i Mirovoi Politiki*), Moscow: Izdatel'stvo Kommunisticheskoi Akademii, 1930.

——, Motylev, V. and Mendel'son, L., *Problemy Mirovovo Krizisa Kapitalizma*, Moscow and Leningrad: Gosudarstvennoe Sotsial'no-Ekonomicheskoe Izdatel'stvo, 1931.

[——, et al.], *Problemy Mirovovo Krizisa—Diskussiya v Institute Mirovovo Khozyaistva i Mirovoi Politiki Komakademii*, Moscow: Partiinoe Izdatel'stvo, 1932.

[——— et al.], SSSR *na Mirovoi Ekonomicheskoi Konferentsii*, Moscow, 1932.

———, *Novye Yavleniya v Mirovom Ekonomicheskom Krizise*, Partizdat, 1934.

———, *The Great Crisis and its Political Consequences—Economics and Politics 1928–1934*, London: Modern Books, n.d.

———, Khmel'nitskaya, Itkina, eds., *Lenin i Problemy Sovremennovo Imperializma*, Moscow: Partiinoe Izdatel'stvo, 1934.

———, *Proizvoditel'nye Sily Buntuyut protiv Kapitalizma* and *Planovoe Khozyaistvo u Nas—'Planovyi' Obman u Nikh*, Partizdat, 1935.

———, ed., *Mirovye Ekonomicheskie Krizisy 1848–1935*, 3 vols. Moscow, 1937–1939.

———, *Kapitalizm i Sotsializm za 20 Let*, Partizdat, 1938.

———, and Mendel'son, L., eds., *New Data for V.I. Lenin's 'Imperialism, The Highest Stage of Capitalism'*, New York: International Publishers, n.d.

———, *Kapitalisticheskii Mir na Poroge Novovo Krizisa*, Gosudarstvennoe Izdatel'stvo Politicheskoi Literatury, 1938.

———, ed., *Mirovoe Khozyaistvo, Ezhegodnik 1937–1938*, Moscow: Gosudarstvennoe Sotsial'no-Ekonomicheskoe Izdatel'stvo, 1938.

———, *The USSR as a World Economic Power*, Moscow: Foreign Languages Publishing House, 1939.

———, *Izmeneniya v Ekonomike Kapitalizma v Itogi Vtoroi Mirovoi Voiny*, Gosudarstvennoe Izdatel'stvo Politicheskoi Literatury, 1946.

———, *Politico-Economic Problems of Capitalism*, Moscow: Progress, 1968.

Index

Printed in the United States
by Baker & Taylor Publisher Services